# INCOME INEQUALITY IN CAPITALIST DEMOCRACIES

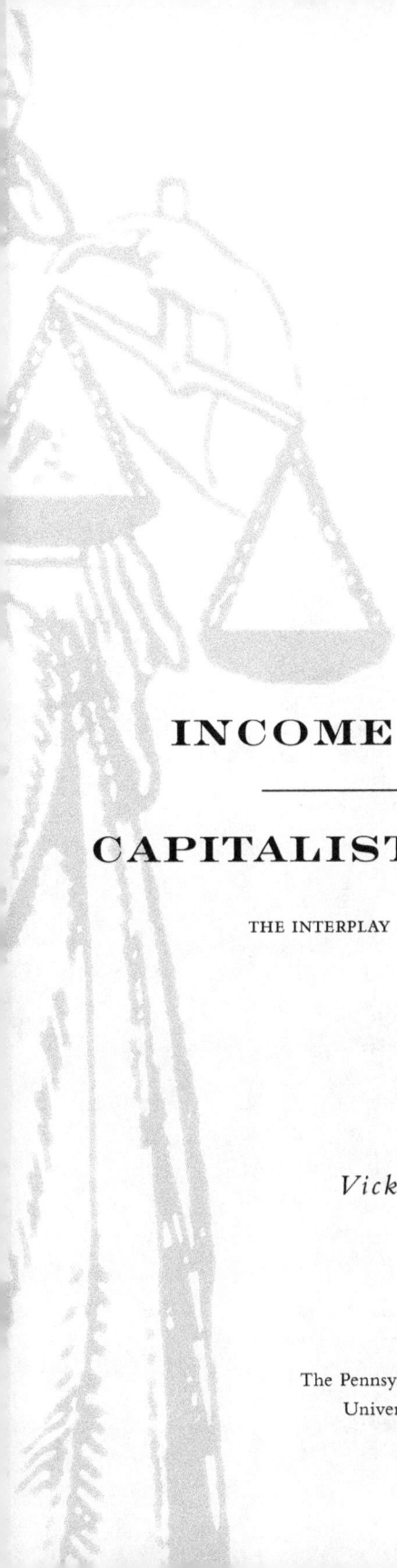

# INCOME INEQUALITY
## ——IN——
# CAPITALIST DEMOCRACIES

THE INTERPLAY OF VALUES AND INSTITUTIONS

*Vicki L. Birchfield*

The Pennsylvania State University Press
University Park, Pennsylvania

Library of Congress Cataloging-in-Publication Data

Birchfield, Vicki L., 1965–
Income inequality in capitalist democracies : the interplay of values and institutions /
Vicki L. Birchfield.
p.      cm.
Includes bibliographical references and index.
Summary: "Examines patterns of income inequality among 16 advanced
democracies from the mid-1970s to the early 2000s and explains why some
societies have a large and growing divide between the rich and the poor while
others, facing similar global economic pressures, maintain more egalitarian
income distributions"—Provided by publisher.
ISBN 978-0-271-03440-9 (cloth : alk. paper)
ISBN 978-0-271-03441-6 (pbk : alk. paper)
1. Income distribution—Developed countries.
2. Capitalism—Developed countries.
3. Equality—Developed countries.
4. Democracy—Economic aspects.
5. Political culture—Developed countries.
I. Title.

HC79.I5B56 2009
339.2—dc22
2008030446

The Pennsylvania State University Press is a member of
the Association of American University Presses.

It is the policy of The Pennsylvania State University
Press to use acid-free paper. Publications on uncoated
stock satisfy the minimum requirements of American
National Standard for Information Sciences—
Permanence of Paper for Printed Library
Material, ANSI Z39.48–1992.

# CONTENTS

# FIGURES AND TABLES

# PREFACE AND ACKNOWLEDGMENTS

Complex ideas, multiple motivations, and challenging circumstances shaped the evolution of this book, which had its origins in early 2000. The complexity of the ideas stems primarily from the nature of the subject itself. Income inequality and how it varies among societies are age-old dilemmas that have preoccupied minds from Aristotle to Adam Smith and continue to be objects of inquiry for almost all the social sciences as well as a problem that elicits commentary from both politicians and philosophers. Although income inequality is treated here with the tools and language of a political scientist, my intellectual curiosities are rarely, if ever, bound by my disciplinary training, which may explain why hard-nosed positivists will dislike my work but also why (I hope) the book may appeal to a broader community of scholars. Indeed, of the many motivations for writing this book, chief among them is the desire to move the problem of income inequality beyond technically sophisticated audiences of econometricians and to reposition it as a fundamentally political issue. As the rather prosaic title suggests, I am interested in examining the roles that both institutions and values play in understanding income inequality and how it varies across the world of capitalist democracies. In essence, this book is about the need to rearticulate income inequality as a sociopolitical issue that is a function of both structural and ideological forces. By studying it in comparative analytical context, my goal is to persuade social scientists that we can and should consider the possibility that ideas and values have causal weight in explaining broadscale economic outcomes and that political institutions facilitate the direction and impact of this significant causal mechanism. More importantly, I will demonstrate that increasing income inequality is not a given across capitalist societies and therefore certainly not an inexorable consequence of globalization. To ensure that this remains the case, the overarching message of this book is that citizens can and should reclaim the economic sphere as a legitimate and necessary realm of democratic deliberation to preserve choices about the kind of society they wish to inhabit.

When I first started this project in the late 1990s, very few political scientists were concerned with the issue of income inequality. Since then it has become a key organizing theme at the annual meetings of both the American Political Science Association and the International Studies Association as well as in a litany of important publications by prominent scholars that have appeared in recent years. I hope this book will serve to continue these debates and will make distribution problems a more central focus of comparative political economy as well as democratic theory. When I say the book emerged from multiple motivations, I mean that I also wanted to speak to several different normative and epistemological concerns. On the one hand, I wanted to address the political nature of income inequality and clearly assert it as a matter of social justice. But on the other hand, I wished to insert the problem of income inequality into the ongoing debates among political scientists—especially comparativists—about the contending roles of culture and institutions and their respective pride of place in our analytical and methodological toolkit. Taking a real-world phenomenon that interests me deeply and exploring it with a goal of assessing some of the most important theoretical concepts and analytical frameworks of my field was only a secondary motivation, but this assessment receives considerable attention in this book. So although the book is an empirical study of cross-national variation in income inequality, it is equally a theoretical exploration of how we can move beyond the culture-versus-institutions or ideational-versus-structural approaches to social scientific inquiry. With an eye to this preoccupation, I hope the book may enjoy a wider readership.

Thus far in my life, speed has never been a key attribute of my major accomplishments. Like my completion of the Paris marathon and the delivery of my daughter, this book took a while to finish. It had a long gestation period with significant bouts of inattention and complete neglect due to the challenging but rewarding circumstances of having assumed my first tenure-track job and, along with it, the role as director of a study abroad program. These new positions allowed me to introduce more than two hundred (mostly American) students to a world beyond adversarial, winner-take-all-politics and into one of the most fascinating experiments in modern political history. I am speaking of the European Union (EU) and the seven years I have devoted to studying and making the EU a more comprehensible and awe-inspiring project to my students as well as to many disillusioned European leftists whom I count among my closest friends—although some are still not entirely persuaded by my insistence that the EU is not a neoliberal ploy. Despite this considerable time commitment and no summers for research and writing, I maintained a relatively modest belief that what I had to say about the consequences of market ideology and about income inequality and how it is studied by contemporary social science was significant. I owe this confidence almost entirely to two very inspiring and accomplished women whom I am honored to have as mentors and close friends, Molly Cochran and Patricia Goff. Their models of scholarship and humanity are truly remarkable, and by virtue of my lucky association with them both—not to mention their unwavering support for me—I have survived some of the most perilous hazards of our profession. Michelle Dion is perhaps singularly responsible for forcing me to write, revise, and stay on task. She generously gave of her valuable time and energy reading drafts, imposing deadlines, and going way beyond the call of duty in her extensive handholding as I dealt with the review process and tackled a complete reworking of the statistical analysis in Chapter 5. If it were not for her persistence and support, I may very well have thrown in the towel. She bears no responsibility whatsoever for any shortcoming in the quantitative analysis, but she deserves tremendous credit for the extent to which readers find Chapter 5 a compelling and sophisticated attempt to assess quantitatively a very complex set of relationships. I would also like to thank Eddie Keene, Katja Weber, and Sylvia Maier for their moral support over the years and for making Georgia Tech an interesting and supportive work environment. Wanda Moore and Marilu Suarez were always there for me when I needed help getting the manuscript in proper format and getting things done more expeditiously than I ever could have alone.

I would be remiss if I did not thank my dissertation committee for the role they played in seeing me through the Ph.D. and helping me to launch my academic career. Christopher Allen, William Chittick, Markus Crepaz, Robert Grafstein, Stephanie Lindquist, and, in the early stages, Joya Misra were all significant influences in my intellectual development, and I hope they will be pleased with the evolution of my thinking demonstrated in my first book. Special thanks also to Chris and Markus for the support they have provided beyond the Ph.D.

A very sincere and special debt of gratitude is owed to my editor, Sanford Thatcher, who read every word and several drafts of my manuscript and who believed in the merit of the project from the very beginning, which came at a crucial time in my career when I was succumbing to the plague of self-doubt. Although Sandy and I had never met in person and had only spoken on the phone once during the two-year period of our working relationship, I feel certain that without his guidance and support, my career could very well have taken a decisive downturn. Instead, his generosity of spirit, expert judgment, keen insight, and vast knowledge helped steer this manuscript toward a better-crafted argument and book. Thank you, Sandy. I would also like to acknowledge the important and valuable contributions made by the external reviewers of my manuscript whose expertise and careful critique of my work served to strengthen my central argument and improve the overall quality of the book.

Finally, I dedicate my first book to my loving and most lovely daughter, Nicole, and to her dad, Steve, my soul mate and my rock. You two have been with me every step of the way, and you have kept me sane and whole through what at times was the most wrenchingly fragmented and overcommitted period of my life. We did it!

# INTRODUCTION

An imbalance between rich and poor is the oldest and most fatal ailment of
all republics.

—PLUTARCH

Capitalist democracies have demonstrated a remarkable capacity for producing
wealth, and social scientists understand quite well the processes whereby profit
and economic growth are generated. The mechanisms by which economic
prosperity is distributed throughout society, however, are more elusive; why
prosperity is more evenly distributed in some countries than others remains
a persistent puzzle. This book examines patterns of income inequality among
sixteen advanced capitalist democracies and aims to deepen our understanding of why some societies are more—or less—egalitarian than others. Recent
studies have provided evidence that income inequality is growing in many
of the world's most affluent democratic countries (Atkinson, Rainwater, and
Smeeding 1995; Gottschalk and Smeeding 1997; Birchfield and Crepaz 1998;
Smeeding and Higgins 2000; Moene and Wallerstein 2001, 2003; Bradley et al.
2003; Mahler 2004; Kenworthy and Pontusson 2005; Iversen and Soskice 2006).
The cross-national data on income distribution reveal substantial variation in
the degree of income inequality within and among capitalist democracies, however.[1] For instance, the quintile measure of income inequality shows Sweden
and Finland to be the most egalitarian societies, with approximately 31 percent

---

1. The most comprehensive study presenting the first truly comparable and authoritative data
was the report by Atkinson, Rainwater, and Smeeding (1995) titled *Income Distribution in OECD Countries*. Prior to this publication, Mahler (1989) had offered an important critique of the earlier studies of cross-national income inequality highlighting the theoretical and practical problems arising
from measurement flaws and inconsistencies in the reporting of the data.

of total income accruing to the top 20 percent of their populations; by comparison, the top 20 percent in the United States and Australia receive roughly 47 percent of total income, ranking these two countries as the least egalitarian in this group of capitalist democracies. Kenworthy and Pontusson (2005) present data from the 1980s and 1990s illustrating the trend of rising income inequality across the members of Organization for Economic Development and Cooperation (OECD) finding that earnings inequalities increased in nine out of fifteen of these countries, whereas levels of inequality were reduced slightly or held steady by the six others. Employment patterns and compensatory redistributive spending were shown to be key factors explaining differences among the countries. Comparing trends over the past decade for working-age households and distinguishing between inequalities in market income (before taxes and benefits) and in postdistribution disposable income, Esping-Andersen (2005) also finds that worsening inequalities in market incomes is the predominant trend among these wealthy nations, with the interesting exceptions being France and the Netherlands.

This general pattern of income dispersion within the developed countries is likewise revealed when we examine the Gini coefficients, a standard measure of income inequality that plots the share of households in a given country against the cumulative share of income. Gini coefficients range from 0 to 100 where 0 means complete equality and 100 represents a single household possessing all the income. Thus, the higher the coefficient, the greater the inequality. As displayed in Table 1, the most unequal societies as measured by income distribution are the United States, Australia, and Switzerland, with Gini coefficients ranging roughly from 41 to 34, whereas the most egalitarian societies—such as Finland, Sweden, Belgium, and Denmark—have Gini coefficients in the 24 to 28 range. These figures clearly demonstrate that despite the purported trend toward growing income inequality across these capitalist democracies, there is indeed a considerable degree of variation that warrants systematic investigation and comparative assessment.

Such variation provides one of the core justifications for comparative political economic analysis, yet until very recently, research in this area has been relatively scant. As noted by Iris Marion Young, "Political theorizing about social and economic inequality across national boundaries remains underdeveloped" (1998, 484). Addressing this deficiency in the literature, this study seeks to contribute to our theoretical and empirical understanding of cross-national differences in income inequality. With a goal of advancing new

**Table 1** Values, Institutions, and Income Inequality

| | | POLITICAL INSTITUTIONS | | |
|---|---|---|---|---|
| | | Majoritarian | Mixed/Ambiguous | Consensual |
| **SOCIETAL VALUES** — MARKET JUSTICE | High | U.S. (41.4)★ Australia (37.5) | | Switzerland (34.3) |
| | Medium | New Zealand (32.6) Canada (30.3) | Norway (31.7) | |
| | Low | | | Sweden (24.3) |
| POLITICAL JUSTICE | High | | Ireland (36.2) | Italy (34.1) |
| | Medium | France (30.8) U.K. (30.9) | | |
| | Low | | Germany (29.3) | Netherlands (28.7) Denmark (27.2) Finland (28.0) Belgium (28.0) |

★Gini coefficient in parentheses

theoretical generalizations, this study examines the institutional and ideational factors that shape distributive outcomes in sixteen countries over a three-decade period from roughly the mid-1970s to the early 2000s. A much broader frame of analysis distinguishes this line of inquiry from the spate of recent works treating the subject and seeks to identify how different levels of income inequality vary according to the specific political-institutional and value contexts within which distributive and redistributive mechanisms operate. Other scholars have taken a more narrowly focused approach and emphasize, for example, how different social strata get what share of income (Bradley et al. 2003), the relationship between wage inequality and social spending (Moene and Wallerstein 2001, 2003), the impact of unemployment and labor market dynamics on income inequality (Pontusson 2005), and the influence of electoral institutions on redistributive policies (Iversen and Soskice 2006). Although this burgeoning literature underscores the significance of income inequality as a growing area of research for students of comparative political economy, the knowledge being produced is of a more limited scope than it should be.

Two purposes of this study are to widen the debate beyond the contending theories of the welfare state and to inject more democratic and normative theorizing into the discussion of a subject that is often treated with greater technical precision than philosophical concern. With the exceptions of Iversen and Soskice (2006) and Kenworthy and Pontusson (2005), very little attention has been paid to the way in which popular preferences might influence income inequality. For the most part, these four scholars incorporate preferences via the median voter theory, whereas my objective is to identify (via survey data) societal values and attitudes about market-versus-government allocations of income and then to examine the linkages between those values, political institutions, and actual distributive outcomes. Thus, my concern lies less in developing a positivist, monocausal explanation than in presenting a multidimensional, systematic account of cross-national patterns of income inequality and persuading readers that the ideational and value element has both normative and empirical implications not only for matters of distributive justice but also for the quality of democracy.

Table 1 provides information on the variation in the dependent variable, income inequality, as measured by the Gini coefficient and averaged over the thirty-year period. The countries in this study are classified according to variance on the two core independent or explanatory variables—political institutions and societal values about distributive justice, which will be explained in detail in a subsequent section of this introduction. What is significant to underscore for now is the variation across all of the core variables. For the dependent variable, the cases are broken into high, medium, and low levels of income inequality. The Gini coefficients are provided in parentheses beside each country in the table. Across the top of the table, the type of political institutional system that characterizes each country is identified using Lijphart's (1999) well-known and commonly used measures for consensus and majoritarian democracies. The countries are also situated according to their predominant value orientation as drawn from survey data and labeled here as either political or market justice societies. This dichotomy is explained below, but it is sufficient to note here that a value orientation of political justice means that citizens generally support state intervention in the economy and redistributive policies, whereas market justice societies find market allocations of income fair or legitimate and typically do not show broad support for government redistribution. For example, we see here that France can be described as a political justice society characterized by more majoritarian political institutions and a moderately high level of income inequality. Switzerland and the United States exhibit high levels of income inequality and are market justice societies but have contrasting types of political institutions. Four countries cluster in the lower right hand quadrant; the Netherlands, Belgium, Denmark, and Finland are all consensus systems with political justice value orientations and low levels of income inequality.

Overall, the table displays some broad patterns indicating that majoritarian systems tend toward market justice and higher levels of income inequality and consensus systems are more inclined toward political justice and lower levels of inequality. This study is primarily devoted to explaining why these patterns or associations exist and how they shape distributive outcomes like income inequality. There are important exceptions, however, such as Canada, which more or less conforms to the institutional and value classification but has lower income inequality than most of the other majoritarian systems, and the United Kingdom, which has a level of income inequality only slightly higher than that of Canada but is identified as a political justice society in its value orientation. Also interesting to highlight is fact that only two of the consensus systems, Switzerland and Sweden, appear to have market justice value orientations, but whereas Switzerland has a high level of income inequality, Sweden is one of the most egalitarian countries in the sample. How can we explain both these general patterns as well as the some of the key exceptions?

Income distribution is a complex phenomenon that is determined by a vast array of structural, technological, and macroeconomic factors as well as the myriad influences of history, politics, and culture. Consequently, cross-national trends in income inequality should not be analyzed strictly as a policy outcome but rather should be understood within a much broader conceptual framework. Although globalization, the skills bias, and technological change have all been posited as key causal agents driving increasing income disparity, the evidence is contradictory and inconclusive and, until quite recently, was often limited to single-country studies (typically the United States) and microlevel analyses. The analytical approach developed here is one that puts the phenomenon in comparative political context, explores the nexus of societal values and political institutions, and shows how the interaction and variance of these two social forces can better inform our understanding of why income inequality is wider in some countries than in others. Because "the roots of political science are in the study of institutions" (Peters 1999, 1), it is not surprising that political institutions figure quite prominently in the story I offer here about why levels of income inequality differ so dramatically among this set of democratic societies. What is unique about this institutional perspective is an insistence on "bringing culture in," not as a straw man or a competing explanatory variable but as an integral part of the basic logic that drives this line of analysis. The key argument is that the impact of political institutions on socioeconomic outcomes such as income inequality is powerful and even determinative, but it is also conditioned by the societal values and contingent upon the types of political economy within which they operate. Values and norms that characterize collective views on state-market relations or that determine what role governments should play in the economy may in fact impinge on the degree to which political institutions function to inhibit or facilitate certain types of redistributive policies. These values are both embedded in and reflective of the type of democracy and the nature of the political economy in a given society. Unraveling how these forces interrelate and coalesce to explain a large-scale phenomenon such as cross-national variation in the gap between the rich and poor may not give pride of place to the goal of parsimony. Instead, this study aims to yield a deeper analysis and produce a more compelling generalization about the interplay of institutions, values, and income inequality in affluent democracies.

The ever-accelerating processes of globalization lend greater urgency to our quest to understand the causes and consequences of socioeconomic change and thus necessitate a much more encompassing explanatory strategy. In an era of widespread speculation about increasing political and economic homogenization or convergence toward one particular model of political economy, it is more important than ever to analyze and explain the differences that exist among nations, particularly democratic countries where citizens presumably have a voice in shaping the kind of society in which they live. The need is more pressing as many countries face important decisions about which institutions to adopt as they transition to political democracy and market economies. For that matter, even some well-established polities have recently engaged in institutional reform with explicit political-economic goals in mind, such as the recent electoral changes in New Zealand and Italy.[2] What I develop in this study is not a prescriptive or formulaic model that advocates one set of political institutions over another but a more complex institutional analysis that takes the role of values seriously and, perhaps more ambitiously, demonstrates that ideational factors can play a causal role in shaping broadscale societal outcomes.

The book is structured around the central premise that neither institutions nor values in isolation can adequately explain cross-national patterns of income inequality. Consequently, in addressing the core research puzzle of why income inequality is greater in some democracies than in others, the three broad questions probed in the book are distinctly framed and inherently connected in the following manner: (1) Why and how do societal values matter when attempting to explain cross-national patterns in income inequality? (2) Do political institutions shape income distribution and do particular types of institutions engender certain types of social norms and values that in turn set the parameters of institutional capacity? (3) How do specific constellations of institutions and values interact to affect outcomes such as income inequality? The theory developed and tested here posits that the fundamental causes of income inequality stem from the interaction of political and cultural values about the legitimacy of government-versus-market action and the political institutional milieu within which such preferences operate. In spite of the diversity of this group of countries, broad and meaningful generalizations are nevertheless possible to achieve through an approach that embeds the institutional and ideational analysis in a holistic perspective on political economy with democratic theory as its starting point. Although most of the recent literature

2. Rogowski and Kayser (2002), for example, have shown how the dynamics of majoritarian electoral institutions result in lower prices and privilege consumer over producer interests in society.

has been primarily concerned with explaining how tax and transfer policies and specific labor-market institutions alter market inequalities (Moene and Wallerstein 2001, 2003; Bradley et al. 2003; Kenworthy and Pontusson 2005; Iversen and Soskice 2006), I take one step back from what I see as intervening variables (i.e., specific redistributive policies and institutions such as centralized wage bargaining). Instead, my central preoccupation is with first-order questions. Do citizens perceive market distributions of income as fair or consider pure market allocations as inevitably unfair and inegalitarian? Is income inequality viewed as a problem that can b e legitimately redressed by governments? If so, how do political institutions serve to transform those values (varying degrees of tolerance or intolerance for inequality) into more equitable distributive outcomes? Whereas welfare state scholars tend to focus on the specific mechanisms of redistribution, such as social spending programs, corporatist institutions, and wage bargaining, my goal is to in vestigate the broader institutional and value context within which those policies and practices emerge.

The conceptual framework of the book is organized into four interrelated components representing distinct stages in the theoretical and causal schema developed to address the three questions above. The first part derives from the need to reconcile the major concerns of political economy and democratic theory; both bring critical insight to bear on the issue of income distribution, although rarely are these two traditions of thought united in contemporary scholarship. The second component flows from this foundational claim and the applied democratic theoretical perspective developed in response to it, which impels a focus on societal values and preferences about the proper scope of action for both go vernments and markets. Once we have established that values *should* matter, we must examine how such intangible forces shape the causal mechanisms underlying socioeconomic outcomes such as income inequality. Thus, the third component addresses the role that political institutions play in shaping d istributional outcomes and what, if any, relationship exists between certain types of political institutions and the specific values that we find most germane to understanding cross-societal variation in income inequality. The last component entails putting the various pieces of this puzzle together so we can empirically test these complex relations and examine their separate as well as combined impact on income inequality in this set of sixteen capitalist democracies. In this final part, we move from the abstract and conceptual level to more rigorous empirical ground to examine the interaction of institutions, values, and income inequality. The empirical analysis proceeds in two stages—first, in a quantitative, multivariate model, and then, through the lens of qualitative analysis and comparative-historical case studies. The next section describes each of these components and related issues of operationalization and methodology in greater detail.

## Political Economy as Applied Democratic Theory

Eschewing economistic strategies, I examine the socioeconomic problem of income inequality and its cross-national variance from a more general level of comparative political analysis, beginning by asking if theories of political economy can h elp to id entify the critical explanatory factors underlying cross-national patterns of income inequality in capitalist democracies. I argue affirmatively by developing a p erspective defined as "political economy as applied democratic theory." If political economy is essentially about the interplay of politics and markets, and democratic theory is concerned with matters of justice and with what governments can and should do, then both lines of inquiry must be brought to bear on the problem of in come inequality. This study conceptualizes political institutions as the common link between political economy and democratic theory. Income distribution is not a purely economic phenomenon that can be studied in isolation from larger questions of political power and distributive justice. Instead, a more comprehensive understanding of income inequality in capitalist democracies must begin with a holistic institutional framework that conjoins normative democratic theory and empirical analysis with an explicit integration of societal values as a mediating force.

Now that the Soviet-style command economies have disappeared and most former communist countries have been transformed or continue the transition toward market economies, facile comparison between these two economic systems gives way to the more pertinent analysis of the myriad variation among capitalist democracies.[3] And despite the purported homogenizing trends

3. This study of in come inequality as an o utcome variable across capitalist democracies falls squarely within the burgeoning literature on comparative capitalism or what has become the "varieties of capitalism" (VOC) research program. In addition to Hall and Soskice 2001, see Schmidt 2002, Pontusson 1995, and Chilcote 1994, especially chapter 9. We, of course, owe a debt to Sh onfield (1965) and Schumpeter (1942), who served as progenitors of such schools of thought. For a sophisticated practitioner's perspective on this theme, see Michel Albert's *Capitalism vs. Capitalism* (1993).

of economic globalization, more reasoned assessments and empirical investigations (Berger and Dore 1996; Boyer and Hollingsworth 1997; Garrett 1998;
Hall and Soskice 2001; Hirst and Thompson 1996; Swank 2002; Wade 1996)
have shown that it is precisely this extensive variation in models of political
economy that challenges the globalization thesis, thus rendering comparative
analysis of advanced industrialized countries all the more meaningful. Although
many have asserted that income inequality is a consequence of increasing
globalization, few have offered specific empirical analyses to substantiate the
claim. The present study of variation in income inequality among this set of
capitalist democracies contributes directly to the debates on globalization by
examining the problem of income distribution through the prism of comparative political economy with an emphasis on both the cultural and institutional capacity to resist or redirect the pressures of international economic
change. Whereas the varieties of capitalism (Hall and Soskice 2001) approach
has certainly advanced our knowledge about the comparative advantages and
differentiating role that institutions play, very little attention has been directed
to the impact of values. Vivien Schmidt's (2002) work on distinctive models
of European capitalism is an important exception in that she incorporates
ideas and discourse into her explanatory framework as she debunks the convergence thesis. In a sense, this study follows her lead but peels the onion back
one layer more by looking directly at values among the mass citizenry as
opposed to how such values and attitudes are invoked by political elites.

## Bringing Culture In

Unlike the most common research strategy in the social sciences, which tends
to pit culture and institutions against one another as rivals for greater explanatory power, both forces are critical to our causal stories.[4] By invoking
culture here, I am limiting its definition somewhat and intend to convey the
complex of values, ideas, and general attitudes held by citizens of a particular society. This view of culture is the predominant one used by political

4. This dichotomy has long been a central intellectual battleground among philosophers of
science as well as social scientists. In one form or another, most of our work takes an implicit stand
on the great "mind over matter" debate. My position in these perpetual debates and my approach
to understanding causal processes have been largely influenced by the work of Antonio Gramsci,
who enjoins us to "uncover the relations between structure and superstructure" to find the forces
active in any given historical moment (1971).

scientists, yet it extends slightly beyond the political cultural connotation imparted through the classic study of Almond and Verba (1963) in that here the use of values or norms taps into what anthropologists and sociologists call "total ways of life." Obviously, the scope of the typology is much less elaborate than ethnographers would ever accept because I am only concerned with the notion of ways of life as it relates to specific political-economic phenomena. Nonetheless, the approach to culture in this study is distinctive in two ways. First, the ideational typology set forth here is grounded in the theoretical argument about the relevance of values and democratic theory to matters of political economy. Second, rather than emphasizing culture to validate uniqueness or particularity among developed nations, I intentionally reduce political culture strictly in terms of societal convictions about the proper roles of states versus markets. Moreover, the conceptualization of political justice versus market justice as the salient cultural or ideational agent shaping distributive outcomes acknowledges that more often than not these opposing value orientations coexist within each society, albeit in varying proportions. In this vein, this approach has an affinity with the cultural theory of Thompson, Ellis, and Wildavsky who argue that the "viability of different ways of life [depends] on mutually supportive relationships between a particular cultural bias and a particular pattern of social relations" (1990, 2).[5] In an age of global capitalism and growing marketization, government regulation and market forces might be construed as the two predominant and viable modes of organizing social life in capitalist democracies. What these theorists refer to as cultural biases that shape and constrain the viability of various ways of life, I simply call preferences and values. My fundamental aims are to give equal theoretical weight to these ideational (values) as well as the material (institutional) forces that I believe are at work in shaping income distribution and to measure empirically both the separate and combined effects of each on income inequality in a comparative context.

An important starting assumption of this study is that the level of income inequality extant in contemporary advanced capitalist democracies is a direct result of the way in which the polity and economy are organized and linked to one another both conceptually and practically. "Conceptually" refers to the ways in which citizens in these societies conceive the respective roles of markets and politics in shaping distributional outcomes. Because all of the cases

---

5. I will comment more extensively on their work in Chapter 2 when the parallels between our approaches to understanding the role of culture will become more apparent.

in this study are long-established democracies with market economies, it is reasonable to assume that individuals in these societies have values and preferences about whether income distribution should be left solely to market forces or whether some type of intervening or redistributive governmental action should attempt to ameliorate inequitable market outcomes. The word "values" in the title of this book reflects this concern and reveals the approach I take toward integrating cultural or ideational variables. It is possible to speak in broad terms about political culture and the role of ideas in shaping outcomes by isolating the specific values, attitudes, and beliefs that are directly relevant to the outcome variables we are studying. In particular, I am interested in defining specific values about political economy and social justice. Robert E. Lane's "Market Justice, Political Justice" (1986) was an effort to explain why the American public displays an apparent preference for market justice over political justice when comparing the way governments and markets serve different purposes, satisfy wants and needs, and distribute valued goods in society.

Inspired by Lane's insights, I incorporate this sociocultural element into my analytical framework. Lane's emphasis on the idea that the American public tends to make justice-based defenses of the functioning of markets and governments is directly relevant to how individuals formulate opinions about distribution and redistribution of income. Given that market economies will inevitably produce income inequities, it is important to identify to what extent individuals in these countries accept market distributions as just or, conversely, prefer that market allocations be altered through some form of "political justice." In identifying such patterns of opinion, we are able to elucidate a salient cultural factor that is critical to our understanding of at least one aspect of why income inequality varies among these countries.

In countries where there is an acceptance of market justice, one would expect a higher degree of income inequality as this prevailing societal judgment tends to preclude or preempt a political solution or discourage attempts to alter an outcome that is deemed to be fair and legitimate in the first place. Conversely, a cultural predisposition that favors political justice creates a more policy permissive environment that tends toward legitimizing governmental action (cum welfare state policies) intended to offset or supplement market allocations of income that are considered inequitable. Ideally, this intervention would in turn produce a more egalitarian income distribution. Such a specification of cultural norms or societal preferences is a useful way to think about the relationship between political culture and outcomes. "Political justice verses market justice" captures an important distinction that serves to map out public conceptions or cultural attitudes about the roles of markets and politics in distributing material resources such as income. Given even the most basic assumptions of democratic theory, one would expect these prevailing patterns of citizen opinion to have some bearing on policy outcomes. However, these data merely reflect attitudes and values; we must also address how such ideational influences are channeled through formal political processes and institutions. This brings in the practical side of the equation and is a direct reference to "institutions" in the book's title.

## The Role of Political Institutions

The practical side of the equation comes into play when we consider how certain institutional arrangements influence and coordinate the nature and function of markets and politics and how this relationship operates in response to public opinion and societal values to produce different collective outcomes such as relatively egalitarian or inegalitarian income distributions. The reemergence of institutional analysis in political science during the past two decades has produced convincing analytical argumentation and empirical evidence that "institutions matter" (Knight 1992; Koelbe 1995; Ostrom 1995). As I investigate the impact of political institutions on distributional outcomes such as income inequality, I am particularly motivated by the need to employ an encompassing and general institutional framework that can capture the distinction between individual political institutions, such as the type of legislature or the party system, while also representing a broader notion of a system of governance that is better suited for explaining macrosocial outcomes. Again, a major difference between my approach and that of welfare state scholars is my focus on institutions as representing different types of democracy rather than as specific mechanisms of welfare and redistribution.

Lijphart's (1984) approach to institutional analysis is particularly appealing for this cross-national study of income inequality because he has provided an encompassing empirical typology of advanced industrial democracies. It is the precision with which Lijphart classified and combined various dimensions of political institutional settings, such as executive-legislative relations, federal-unitary dispersal of power, electoral rules, and party systems, that has made his approach so analytically useful. In bringing all of these features together and creating an empirical index by which to classify democracies along a majoritarian-consensus continuum, Lijphart's institutional framework provides a compelling and elegant way of thinking about two distinct approaches to democratic governance. In fact, an entire research program has coalesced around investigations of the dimensions of Lijphart's two models of democracies constituting what Grofman (2000) suggests is a separate and distinctive variant of the "new institutionalism."

Indeed, much of the literature has employed the consensus-majoritarian typology to examine how these two contrasting amalgams of political institutions influence a wide range of different policy outcomes (Crepaz 1996a, 1996b; Crepaz, Koelbe, and Wilsford 2000); exhibit differing propensities to provide for accountability, stability, and accommodative decision making (Powell 1982; Baylis 1989; Linz 1993); and produce different levels of congruence between citizens and policymakers (Huber and Powell 1994), as well as how the degree of satisfaction with democracies varies across the two system types (Anderson and Guillory 1997). This study builds upon this research and assesses the differentiating impact that consensual and majoritarian political institutions have on income inequality.

Just as I specify two broad and distinctive patterns of opinion along a market versus politics basis, Lijphart's models of democracies also fall into two general categories, consensual and majoritarian. Conceptualizing and then empirically substantiating such generalizations is a chief goal of comparative analysis; here Lijphart's institutional model is retained while coupling it with a political cultural typology. While relying on Lijphart's approach to institutions, I seek to bring into focus the interplay between these two broad types of institutions and political cultures as specified through these two contrasting conceptions of justice. To reiterate, a more realistic explanation of income inequality must address how the economy and polity are organized and linked both conceptually and practically. Rather than seeing culture and institutions as competing forces, I explore how the two combine to produce variations in income inequality across the sixteen countries studied. Table 2 provides an initial overview of how these countries are aligned in terms of the measures for the two core explanatory factors discussed here. The countries are listed in descending order (from highest to lowest) in relation to the strength of political justice as its prevailing value orientation and the strength of its consensus political institutions. For example, France is the country with the strongest sense of political justice, whereas Switzerland is the most inclined toward market justice. On the institutions side, Switzerland is the strongest consensus democracy and the United Kingdom is the weakest or the most majoritarian political system.

## Research Strategy

The complexity and significance of an outcome variable such as income distribution and the political, cultural, and historical richness of each of these sixteen countries provide a gold mine for comparative analysis and present an important opportunity to refine and advance our theories of democracy and comparative political economy. The methodological strategy I pursue to tackle such a task draws upon the insights of Brady and Collier (2004) whose edited volume makes the case that our effort to make valid causal inferences should be achieved by exploiting the full potential of both statistical and case-based methods. Bolstering this approach is the following view articulated by

**Table 2** Rank Ordering of Ideational and Institutional Factors Theoretically Conducive to Lower Income Inequality

| Values | Institutions |
| --- | --- |
| *Strength of Political Justice* | *Strength of Consensual Democracy* |
| France | Switzerland |
| Ireland | Finland |
| Italy | Denmark |
| Belgium | Belgium |
| Netherlands | Netherlands |
| United Kingdom | Italy |
| Germany | Sweden |
| Denmark | Norway |
| Finland | Germany |
| Norway | Ireland |
| Sweden | United States |
| New Zealand | Australia |
| Canada | France |
| Australia | Canada |
| United States | New Zealand |
| Switzerland | United Kingdom |

Tarrow in his critique of King, Keohane, and Verba (1994), whose seminal volume sought to harmonize qualitative and quantitative methodologies through a singular and shared logic of inference essentially imported from physics.

> My argument, rather, is that a singl e-minded adherence to eith er quantitative or qualitative approaches straightjackets scientific progress. Whenever possible, we should use qualitative data to interpret quantitative findings, to get insid e the processes underlying decision outcomes, and to investigate the reasons for tipping points in the historical time-series. We should also try to use different kinds of evidence together and in sequence and look for ways of triangulating different measures on the same research problem. (1995, 474)

Accordingly, I construct a variable-oriented research design that employs multivariate regression analysis combined with two critical comparative case studies. Lockhart's work (1989, 2001) was instructive in settling an important epistemological issue I had grappled with for some time because I have been drawn to critical, interpretative, and empirical approaches to social scientific research. In his comparative analysis of social p olicy and pensions schemes, Lockhart offered a compelling account of how culture and values play a key explanatory role in understanding cross-national variation in providing care for the elderly. In addition to his rigorous and solid scholarship on such a vitally important topic of social p olicy, what particularly resonated with me was the author's conviction that "political life involves activity that is p urposeful in deeper, more significant than ways institutional analyses frequently suggest" (2001, ix). Like Lockhart, my focus on societal values and concern with citizens' conceptions of distributive justice offers a less mechanistic way of thinking about causation while still employing a methodology in which hypotheses are derived and empirically tested. Understanding the causal agents behind an o utcome as complex as income inequality presents a d aunting research task but certainly not a novel one. Many economists and sociologists have devoted their entire research careers to the study of income inequality, yet the subject has much less frequently been treated by political scientists.[6]

6. Treatment of th is topic by political scientists becomes even more compelling if one recalls Duesenberry's famous caricature that whereas the world of e conomists provides us with nothing but choices, in the world of the sociologists, there are no choices at all. In this light, it is incumbent upon the student of politics to dispel the myth of these two extremes by underscoring with normative conviction and empirical rigor that politics really is "the art of the possible."

Given Harold Lasswell's (1936) classic definition of politics as "who gets what, when and how," one would think the question would have long been a central preoccupation of political scientists; instead, David Bradley and co-authors note: "Given that the degree to which governments redistribute income is arguably one of the most consequential outcomes of the political process for citizens' living conditions, it is surprising that there have been so few studies attempting to explain variation across advanced industrial societies in distributive outcomes and the redistribution process" (2003, 195).

This lacuna in part can be explained by the simple lack of comparable data, which the fortunate availability of the Luxembourg Income Study (LIS) data archive has now rectified. Using this data, the countries examined in this study are Australia, Belgium, Canada, Denmark, Finland, France, Germany, Ireland, Italy, the Netherlands, New Zealand, Norway, Sweden, Switzerland, the United Kingdom, and the United States. Because this is a study of the variation in income inequality among advanced industrial democracies, the sample is nearly exhaustive, with the exception of only a handful of otherwise eligible countries.[7] Again, the underlying premise of this study is that cross-national variation in income inequality is a function of the diverse political economies that are themselves products of specific cultural and institutional environments.

Using survey data to identify societal values, I explore the conceptual dimension and will refer to it broadly as the values or ideational influence on income inequality, whereas the practical or structural element investigates the impact of formal political institutions. I measure these preferences for political or market justice through survey data that register individual attitudes about the boundaries of legitimate governmental action with regard to income redistribution. Both the Eurobarometers and the international module of the General Social Surveys have administered "Role of Government" surveys that ask individuals whether government action is appropriate to address inegalitarian income distributions. I use these data to connect individual attitudes to the broader societal level of analysis and thereby ascertain whether coherent cultural patterns exist regarding public conceptions of distributive justice.

The statistical analysis is supplemented with comparative historical case studies of Switzerland and the United Kingdom. Interestingly, both countries proved to be critical cases in this study. Switzerland is a prototype of Lijphart's

---

7. Certainly many other countries would qualify to be among this group, such as Japan and Austria, for example, but to address the research question in the manner I have formulated, I am constrained in my number of cases by the lack of reliable and truly comparable data.

consensus democracies, yet the survey data show it to b e a m arket justice society and show it to ha ve a high degree of income inequality. Without a more nuanced understanding of the role of culture and societal values, I show that Lijphart's framework cannot accurately predict or explain this exception to what might be considered as the rule of consensus democracy and what Lijphart (1999) claims is their tendency toward "kinder and gentler" policies. Likewise, the United Kingdom is the exemplar of the majoritarian model, yet on the values front, it was one of the more political justice-oriented societies and it falls among the countries with a h igh degree of income inequality. Such paradoxical combinations of institutional and ideational data provide for a much richer comparative analysis of th e relative and combined weight of the two core independent variables, values and political institutions. Combined quantitative and qualitative analyses generally corroborate my theory and substantiate the claims that income inequality is a function of more than the mechanical capability of institutions to shape outcomes, that individuals whose collective opinions aggregate to a general political culture and value system also determine the parameters and impact of political action versus acquiescence to market forces, and that we get more explanatory mileage when we assess the impact of both. Having now spelled out the motivation and logic of the argument driving my study, the remainder of this introduction provides an overview of the book.

## Structure of the Book

Chapter 1, "Theoretical Foundations: Political Economy as Applied Democratic Theory," presents the theoretical and conceptual foundation of the study and provides an analytical synthesis of the literature. In considering a dependent variable like income inequality, I emphasize how cross-national variation in income inequality reveals a g reat deal about the differences in soci etal organization and the scope of democratic politics in each of these countries. I show how these forces undergird the dynamics of labor markets and the specific policies of welfare institutions that actually produce varying degrees of income inequality. I argue that contemporary political science has overcompartmentalized socioeconomic problems and that this trend, combined with the encroachment of economic theories, has pushed democratic theorizing and indeed "the political" to the margins of the discipline. Political economy as applied democratic theory requires a focus on what norms and values prevail in a society that, at least partially, defines the scope, the limits, and the responsibilities of state action. What do citizens want governments to do regarding the economy and market forces? How does the public define social justice? These are the kinds of questions that should be of interest as we explore the cross-national context of income inequality.

Furthermore, I argue that democratic theory is intellectually inseparable from the concerns of political economy, and the issue of income inequality brings the argument into sharp focus because it necessarily entails a clarification of distributive justice. I connect this theoretical abstraction to the concrete phenomenon of the equality-efficiency trade-off. This trade-off serves as the starting point for most classical and neoliberal economists who try to explain distributional outcomes.[8] I offer a critique of this trade-off by first elucidating the normative roots of such an interpretation and then by showing that the trade-off is actually illusory in light of recent empirical evidence (Kenworthy 1995, 2004). I also integrate the contributions that contemporary research on social democracy and the welfare state have made toward further refuting the trade-off thesis.[9]

After examining the major findings of previous research on income inequality, I then conclude with a comment on the recent, though burgeoning, literature on globalization. This detour serves three distinct purposes. First, increasing economic internationalization has been a popular culprit invoked by politicians, journalists, and academicians for growing income inequality and welfare retrenchment. Because one dimension of this study is attuned to popular opinion and attitudes about economic outcomes, the discourse factor is of critical significance. Second, in arguing against the globalization thesis with a nondeterministic, "primacy of the political" version of political economy, I can further define and explicate what I mean by applied democratic theory and the need to examine citizens' values. And third, I use this discussion as an opportunity to distinguish my approach from the broader welfare state literature and the contributions from leading scholars in the field

8. The classic articulation of the trade-off thesis is Arthur Okun's *Equality and Efficiency: The Big Trade-off* (1975). Others include Arrow 1951; Friedman and Friedman 1980; and Hayek 1960. Some of those who have challenged the thesis are Kuttner 1984; Thurow 1980; and Freeman 1989.

9. Some of the most important studies that have contributed to this line of research include Castles and Dorwick 1990; Esping-Andersen 1985, 1990; Friedland and Sanders, 1985; Garrett and Lange, 1986; Hicks 1988; Hicks and Swank 1984; Korpi 1985, 1989, and Korpi and Palme 1997; and, more recently, Kenworthy 2004.

who have only very recently turned their attention to this understudied issue area. Political economy as applied democratic theory generates a broader frame of analysis and compels a research strategy of bridging the institutional and ideational explanations of macrolevel phenomena and multicausal outcomes such as income inequality.

Chapter 2, titled "Political Justice Versus Market Justice: Why Values Matter," develops more fully what applied democratic theory entails. I offer a critique of the various iterations of the seminal debates generated by Rawls and Nozick and suggest that there is a substantial disconnect between theoretical and popular conceptions of distributive justice. I propose that the ideas of Robert Lane may lead the way out of what is essentially an ideological impasse in the justice debates by bridging normative and applied approaches to democratic theory. Both normative and empirical approaches to democracy should be concerned with the values, beliefs, and preferences of actual citizens. Popular conceptions of justice probably exercise a greater explanatory role on outcomes of distributive justice than three decades of unresolved theoretical debate. In contrast, Lane's aim was not to clarify philosophical justice but to elucidate concepts of the legitimacy of markets and politics to understand the forces of social change. Next, I ask if Lane's theory, developed specifically for analyzing the American public, is portable to other democracies. I show how the debates revolving around the notion of the European "social model" and its quest for preservation in the face of growing pressures to reform in the direction of the Anglo-American or neoliberal model capture precisely the salience of this conceptualization of ideology and values among the mass publics. Moreover, I argue that in an age of market triumphalism, it is important to investigate public opinion and attitudinal data to distinguish between the dominant discourse (elite rhetoric) and popular beliefs. Focusing on the problem of income inequality, we can operationalize the pertinent cultural norms or values through survey instruments that gauge the degree to which citizens support government redistribution to alter market allocations of income. I examine survey data on beliefs in government and social inequality for a set of sixteen capitalist democracies. Analysis of this opinion data produces a useful portrait of the prevailing ethos or values orientation in each individual society from which I then construct a political justice/market justice continuum along which each country is arrayed.

Chapter 3, "The Power and the Limitations of Political Institutions: Retooling the Consensus/Majoritarian Framework to 'Bring Culture In,'" turns our attention to the impact of institutions. As Bo Rothstein argues, "political institutions are both empirical and normative orders" (1998, 216). Sharing this view, I articulate how the values I have pinpointed and the justice continuum I present relate to the political institutions within which they operate. As I made clear above, the approach that I find most conducive to bringing values in is that of Lijphart's widely used typology of democracy, yet I find the model itself to be empirically over specified (too many variables) and normatively underspecified (no real theory). Juxtaposing Lijphart's model with other variants of neo-institutionalism, I nonetheless conclude that this ideal-type approach to institutions and democratic governance is most appropriate for analyzing differences in broadscale outcomes such as income inequality.[10] Incorporating insights from critics such as Barry and Lustick, I reject certain elements of Lijphart's framework and reconstruct the empirical model adding an explicit ideational dimension. By offering this positive critique and bringing in an explicit political cultural dimension, I conclude that Lijphart's institutional framework has a much more realistic connection to both historical conditions that gave rise to distinct constitutional structures and to the contemporary sociopolitical ethos that sustains them. The modified typology addresses the following questions: What are the core institutions in contemporary democracies that tell us the most about the nature of political life and governance in a given society? What is the relationship between those institutions and the structure of the political economy? Finally, what is the relationship between these two distinct approaches to democratic governance and the values and norms of the actual societies in which they exist, and how does this relationship affect outcomes such as income inequality? In essence, do winner-take-all politics necessarily produce winner-take-all economics?

Chapter 4, "The Interaction of Institutions, Values, and Income Inequality: A Quantitative Analysis," brings the theoretical insights of Chapters 2 and 3 together and puts them to an empirical test. Employing multivariate regression analysis, I investigate the joint effect of values and institutions on income inequality in sixteen capitalist democracies. The empirical analysis demonstrates that we cannot take values and norms for granted as we assess the impact of institutions on socioeconomic outcomes. If Lijphart is right that consensus democracies tend to pursue "kinder, gentler policies," then we would expect

10. The fact that leading comparative political economists, such as Iversen (2005) and Gourevitch and Shin (2005), have recently employed Lijphart's typology further confirms its validity as a powerful measure of political institutions.

more egalitarian income distribution in consensual polities. However, as my critique of Lijphart emphasizes, there is no reason to hypothesize about societal values when we can find meaningful and reliable indicators to convey this information. Once we integrate such variables into our causal analysis, the relative and contingent weight of both institutional and ideational forces is more adequately understood. The chapter also explores alternative theories by constructing a model of welfare transfers to more directly demonstrate the complex relations between institutions, values, and the welfare state and to elucidate the complex causal paths through which income is distributed in capitalist democracies.

The next chapter, "The Exceptions Prove the Rule: Case Studies in Income Inequality in Switzerland and the United Kingdom," offers a more in-depth, structured case study of two countries in the sample. Paradoxically, as I noted above, the two prototypes of consensus and majoritarian democracies, Switzerland and the United Kingdom, respectively, are characterized by a prevailing ethos and a level of income inequality that are contrary to the expectations and norms for the other countries in their institutional classification. Such combinations allow for a more inductive analysis of the relative strengths of values vis-à-vis institutions and how they reciprocally shape income inequality. The comparative case studies provide historical insights about the cultural and institutional roots of income inequality in both countries and reinforce the more general findings from the preceding chapter. My formulation shows that the exception in fact proves the rule—the rule in this case being that institutions do not operate in ideational and normative vacuums. Where market justice prevails in a consensual political environment, we find higher levels of income inequality, whereas in a majoritarian setting where political justice is predominant, there is still a high degree of inequality. The winner-take-all system, particularly if it produces a leader such as Prime Minister Margaret Thatcher, insulates policymakers from the negative consequences of going against the prevailing ethos of the public and its preference for a particular approach to distributive justice. This does not mean that majoritarian systems are necessarily inegalitarian. We cannot project that institutions in and of themselves—whether majoritarian or consensual—will systematically produce certain types of outcomes. But we can and should be attentive to what capacity such institutional environments have for adequately reflecting public preferences and our explanatory models should be attuned to what those preferences are.

Consensual polities do prove superior in more faithfully translating the preferences of its citizens into policy outcomes; thus, when a market justice value orientation prevails as in the case of the Swiss public, we can expect higher income inequality. A singular institutional logic would not have predicted this outcome, but bringing values in allows the exception to prove the rule.

The Conclusion restates the thrust of the argument and summarizes the overall implications of the study. Although labor market institutions, centralized wage bargaining, and the welfare state explain a g reat deal about the degree of economic egalitarianism in society, my study pursues a more general level of analysis that seeks to identify the broader structures of power—both ideational and institutional—within which such redistributive mechanisms operate. In so doing, I hope to have produced a more meaningful portrait of the determinants of socioeconomic differences among democratic capitalist societies. Although my study breaks important theoretical ground, perhaps the most significant implication is of a m ore practical nature. Institutional design and reform is a pressing issue for areas as diverse as the former Communist countries, war-torn areas in the Balkans and Afghanistan, other developing countries, and even for the highly developed but ever-changing European Union. As decisions are made about the best types of institutions to adopt, it is appropriate to recognize that institutions are merely mechanisms that serve to channel the norms and values of a society. The more inclusive the political institutions, the greater the likelihood that policies will reflect widely held norms and values, whereas winner-take-all institutions are capable of greater divergence between popular values and policy outcomes. To return to the problem of income inequality, the hope for a more egalitarian world hinges upon a preference for political justice over market justice and the development of more consensual, inclusive polities.

In the broadest sense, I hope to have contributed to our understanding about the causes of income inequality that the degree of inequality in a society is more than the result of an amalgam of fluctuating economic factors. Rather the cultural and institutional environment, or the political forces more generally, may in fact play the most decisive role in shaping whether a given country has relatively high or low levels of income inequality. In other words, the values and preferences of citizens and the capacity of political institutions to deliver outcomes reflecting such values provide us with a much more complete understanding of income distribution than has hitherto been offered.

One of the leading economists in the United States appears to concur with this general assertion. Paul Krugman observes:

> If calling America a middle-class nation means anything, it means we are a society in which most people live more or less the same kind of life. In 1970 we were that kind of society. Today we are not, and we become less like one with each passing year. . . . In 1970, according to the [Census] bureau, the bottom 20 percent of U.S. families received only 5.4 percent of the income, while the top 5 percent received 15.6 percent. By 1994, the bottom fifth had only 4.2 percent, while the top 5 percent had increased its share to 20.1 percent. That means in 1994, the average income among the top 5 percent of families was more than 19 times that of the bottom 20 percent of families. . . . These are not abstract numbers. They are the statistical signature of a seismic shift in the character of our society. . . . In 1970 the CEO of a typical Fortune 500 corporation earned about 35 times as much as the average manufacturing employee. It would have been unthinkable to pay him 150 times the average, as is now common, and downright outrageous to do so wh ile announcing mass layoffs and cutting the real earnings of m any of the company's workers, especially those who were paid less to st art with. So how did the unthinkable become first the thinkable, then doable, and finally if we believe the CEOs—unavoidable? The answer is that *values changed* [emphasis added]—not the middle-class values politicians keep talking about, but the kind of values that helped to sustain the middle-class society we have lost. (1996, 44–47)

Thus, the phenomenon of g rowing inequality in th e United States is attributed by this prominent economist to a shift in values, not the forces of globalization or the popular technological or "skills bias" explanation suggested by many economists. Krugman's assessment is pertinent to this study because it g ives an imp ressionistic explanation for what I ha ve attempted to conceptualize and empir ically identify as a potent ial source of inc ome inequality. If Krugman's discernment is taken at face value, and if values are changing more globally toward market justice, the world may expect increased disparities between the rich and the poor. If, however, as Robert Lane hoped in 1986, political justice is r estored to favor, then there is a g reater likelihood that this trend may be curtailed. But as I argue in the following pages, the institutional setting within which these values are fostered plays a predominant role as well. Thus it would seem that our task as social scientists and, indeed, a fundamental motivation of this study is to better understand the interrelationship between ideas and institutions so we may more adequately address some of the most pressing problems and challenges of today's increasingly global society.

# — 1 —

## THEORETICAL FOUNDATIONS: POLITICAL ECONOMY AS
## APPLIED DEMOCRATIC THEORY

> As soon as democracy is seen as a kind of society, not merely a mechanism of choosing and authorizing governments, the egalitarian principle inherent in democracy requires not only one man, one vote but also "one man, one equal effective right to live as fully humanly as he may wish."
>
> —C. B. MACPHERSON, *Democratic Theory*

Why is it that some democratic societies have a more egalitarian income distribution than others? To what extent can we answer this question by exploring the functioning of the market economy and the scope of democratic politics or, more pertinently, the interaction of these two spheres of social activity? Income distribution is an extremely complex phenomenon that is shaped by an array of macroeconomic factors, political institutions, and historical and cultural traditions. Cross-national variance in income inequality can be explained in an encompassing and systematic manner by showing that the level of income inequality in a given society is shaped by the interaction between political institutions and prevailing social values about distributive justice and the legitimacy of politics and markets.

In an era of increasing globalization and market triumphalism, it is perhaps more important than ever to figure out just what the market delivers and how it does so across different political environments with varying institutional and cultural traditions.[1] Such an endeavor becomes even more pressing

---

1. I refer here to the popularization of Fukuyama's "end of history" thesis (1989) and the widespread notion that liberal democracy and market-oriented capitalism are now unrivaled models for countries in transition. This view is dangerously misleading in that it belies the complex reality of contending models of capitalist democracy and the implications of such diversity for attempting to

given the pace at which various "convergence" hypotheses abound in the scholarly literature and popular discourse.[2] An important starting point in dealing with an outcome that is conventionally construed in economic terms (the distribution of material resources) is to recognize that markets do not operate in cultural or political vacuums; thus, we can never fully attribute economic outcomes such as income distributions solely to the workings of the market—no matter how free or encumbered it is deemed to be. Likewise, institutions, despite the much-heralded claims of the "new institutionalists" about how much they matter, do not function in isolation of deeper structural and cultural forces. Therefore, the explanatory strategy I pursue extends institutional analysis to include a political cultural dimension, which must first be derived from a conceptualization of political economy as applied democratic theory. This chapter lays the theoretical foundation for this study and articulates why such a reconceptualization of political economy is necessary—particularly for cross-national analyses of macroeconomic phenomena.

The theoretical underpinnings of this study are inspired by a reading of Robert Lane's "Market Justice, Political Justice" (1986) and guided by an effort to operationalize Lane's thesis through the key methodological insight of Antonio Gramsci: to "uncover the relations between structure and superstructure" to find the forces active in any given historical moment (1971, 177). What are the forces active in this historical epoch that are creating a widening of disparities between the rich and the poor in some of the world's most highly developed capitalist democracies, but that are contracting or at least maintaining income differentials in other similarly situated countries? Gramsci's injunction—which has often eluded many scholars who appropriate his ideas—is to carefully study and analyze the relations between the realm of ideas and culture and the concrete structures and institutions of social and political life.[3] As we shall see later in Chapters 2 and 3, applying Gramsci and

---

link the processes of democratization with marketization unproblematically. An excellent counterpoint to Fukuyama, although unfortunately not as widely read, is Michel Albert's *Capitalism vs. Capitalism* (1993). The more recent scholarly corollary of such debates is the burgeoning literature on "varieties of capitalism," which I will discuss in Chapter 3.

2. The "convergence" hypothesis suggests that the increasingly globalized economy will exert downward pressures on interventionist and redistributive policies and will generally restrict the macroeconomic policy options of governments, thereby forcing economic policies of advanced industrial states to converge around laissez-faire strategies. For empirical evidence against these claims, see Berger and Dore 1996; Boyer and Drache 1996; Garrett 1997; and Rodrik 1997.

3. Examples may be traced to the work of Louis Althusser (1971) as well as Perry Anderson (1977), both of whom wrongly (and narrowly) render Gramsci a cultural determinist. David Laitin's

conjoining Lane's conceptual constructs to Arend Lijphart's typology of democratic governance achieves two important aims. First, it adds depth to Lijphart's useful but undertheorized empirical model of democratic governance. Second, it facilitates a more encompassing and effective research strategy for explaining cross-national variation in income inequality within the context of the complex interplay of ideas (societal values, broadly speaking), political institutions, and economic structure—all of which must be considered in our examination of income inequality.

Chapter 2 will offer a full exposition of Robert Lane's argument, but it is necessary to say a few words in this chapter to show how it helped to shape the overarching theoretical structure as well as the key thesis of this book. Robert Lane is concerned with relating popular perceptions of justice to ideas about the legitimate roles of markets and politics. Though Lane does argue that perceptions may be structurally induced, ultimately his position is consistent with Gramsci's method because he assumes that perceptions and values we encounter and their institutional and material bases have reciprocal influences. These ideas significantly shape my approach to understanding causal processes and social change—particularly in terms of thinking about a complex macrosocial issue such as income inequality. To locate my position in the context of recent scholarly debates, I seek to move beyond the "culture versus structure" debates and show that such binary thinking leaves at least half of our causal stories untold.[4] I am interested in finding out how prevalent political cultural norms and values that characterize a given society interact with particular configurations of political institutions to shape outcomes, such as relatively egalitarian or inegalitarian income distributions, and whether this interaction gives us greater explanatory leverage than would a singular focus on institutional or cultural/ideational factors.

---

*Hegemony and Culture* (1986) is another example that, in an otherwise fascinating study of the impact of culture on power configurations in Nigeria, nevertheless employs such a thin read of Gramsci's concept of hegemony that it misses Gramsci's fundamental contribution to a Marxist/post-Marxist theory of consciousness. Laitin therefore uses Gramsci's concept in a manner radically inconsistent with Gramsci's intentions.

4. One of the latest and most significant entries in this grand debate emerged from the general disputation over the continuing relevance of area studies and the growing influence of rational choice approaches. For an overview of these debates, see the *Newsletter of the APSA Organized Section in Comparative Politics* 8, no. 2 (1997): 5–18, and the related articles by Ian Shapiro in *PS: Political Science and Politics* 30, no. 1 (1997): 40–42, and those by Robert Bates, Chalmers Johnson, and Ian Lustick in *PS: Political Science and Politics* 30, no. 2 (1997): 166–75.

I begin by examining the origins and the evolution of political economy with a special focus on illustrating how contending approaches have addressed the issue of income inequality, and I summarize the theoretical and empirical limitations of previous research. Next, I integrate perspectives from democratic theory and argue that the key issues dividing the various schools of thought in political economy are parallel to the central tensions in democratic theory. This section also engages the current globalization debates to illustrate the value of a more holistic approach to research problems that are increasingly the object of analysis of both comparative and international political economy, such as income inequality. Ultimately, the point of this exercise is to demonstrate the normative imperative of treating problems of political economy as "applied democratic theory."

## Income Distribution and the Evolution of Political Economy

To determine the laws which regulate this distribution is the principal problem in Political Economy.
—DAVID RICARDO, *On the Principles of Political Economy and Taxation*

It is impossible to discuss income distribution without relying on some conceptualization of political economy. In fact, as the above statement by one of the founders of classical political economy reveals, the modern origins of political economy (that of the eighteenth and nineteenth centuries) is tied to the effort to understand how income gets distributed. As the meaning of political economy may have as many definitions as there are individuals who invoke the term or purport to conduct analyses and research under this mode of inquiry, it is necessary at the outset to narrow the scope of this overview to its most salient elements for the present study.[5] The core ideas fall generally into four key schools of political economy—classical, Marxian, neoclassical, Keynesian/post-Keynesian—as they apply specifically to the question of distribution.

### The Classical Approach

Both Adam Smith and David Ricardo were concerned with explaining what portion of a nation's total wealth accrued to land, labor, and capital and what

---

5. The work by Caporaso and Levine (1992) pares down this voluminous literature and was valuable for distilling the essence of each major approach and drawing out their implications for research on income inequality.

mechanisms or processes determined this distribution. In Book I of *The Wealth of Nations,* Smith wrote:

> The whole annual produce of the land and labor of every country . . . naturally divides itself . . . into three parts: the rent of land, the wages of labor, and the profits of stock; and constitutes a revenue to three different orders of people; to those who live by rent, to those who live by wages, and to those who live by profit. These are the great, original and constituent orders of every civilized society, from whose revenue that of every other order is ultimately derived. (1937, 248)

So Adam Smith, in seeking to understand the causes of wealth, would establish the distribution of income as the key object of inquiry, and his method would guide the development of political economy for at least the next one hundred years.

The original and enduring paradox of political economy is that despite the fact that the term "political" appears first, it in no way means it is given primacy; in fact, it is quite the contrary with both the founders and many contemporary political economists steadily defining away any substantial role for politics in the determination of economic and social life. For the classical writers, this demotion of politics is due to their supposed elucidation of the "self-regulating" market, which in turn shaped the belief that private profit and public welfare would be reconciled through the forces of self-interest and pure competition. Smith, arguing against mercantilism and advocating a commercial policy that would later be dubbed "laissez-faire," formulated the following view of the appropriate functions of the state:

> According to the system of natural liberty, the sovereign has only three duties to attend to; three duties of great importance, indeed, but plain and intelligible to common understanding; first, the duty of protecting the society from the violence and invasion of other independent societies; secondly, the duty of protecting, as far as possible, every member of society from the injustice or oppression of every other member of it, or the duty of establishing an exact administration of justice; and thirdly, the duty of erecting and maintaining certain public works and certain public institutions, which it can never be for the interest of any individual, or small number of

individuals, to erect and maintain; because the profit could never repay the expense to any individual or small number of individuals, though it may frequently do much more than repay it to a g reat society. (1937, 651)

Thus, government (or the state) in Smith's depiction is quite lean; ultimately, his identification of the public good is entirely with the national product. He believes the larger the national product's size and growth, the more it would benefit both individuals and society as a whole. Despite the fact that Smith is essentially a microtheorist because his entire argument is presented in terms of the individual, his approach to distributional issues is primarily a functional theory from a macroeconomic perspective. Smith attempts to explain the sources of revenue accruing to each of his three "orders in society" by understanding each in terms of the various prices of factors of production. As Kaelble and Thomas summarize it, for Smith "the aggregate forces of supply and demand determined the division of the product between wages and profits (the supply of capital is especially crucial, given that it is the chief mechanism by which labor productivity, and therefore wages can rise), while Smith's notion of what set rents was considerably more vague. When Ricardo came to develop the main lines of the classical theory of distribution, he accepted Smith's blueprint" (Brenner, Kaelble, and Thomas 1991, 4).

Ricardo would extend Smith by embedding his model of factor prices in the production structure and developing a theory of value (prices, he believed, reflected the relative quantity of labor necessary to the production of commodities) that derived from the relationship between the division of labor and commodity exchange. He would echo Smith in that he endorsed only the most limited role for government and labored to show how an open economy would result in growth for both profits and wages (Ricardo 1903). Both John Stuart Mill and Karl Marx were the intellectual heirs to the classical approach and retained many of the concepts and theories elaborated by Ricardo and Smith. An important difference between these thinkers, however, was an interest in questions of equality by the former that were of little or no concern to the latter.

John Stuart Mill wrote an important synthesis of the works of political economy titled *Principles of Political Economy* (1848) and is widely considered to be one of the most significant, if not the preeminent, of the classical liberal political philosophers. So much is Mill recognized as a political philosopher that his thinking on matters of political economy are often underappreciated. Mill's thoughts about distributional issues are an illustrative case in point. Mill believed that as production had reached an appropriate level by 1879, society's focus should shift to equalizing distribution (Gagnier 1997, 436). Furthermore, Mill's more obscure and unfinished work, *Chapters on Socialism*, published posthumously in 1879, explicitly reveals his concern with fundamental issues of inequality arising from the social and economic arrangements of his Victorian England. As expert commentators have noted, we know from Mill's writings for example that

> while [he] found the ideal of socialism infinitely more attractive than the often unjust and selfish reality of capitalism, he believed that the actual practical and moral difficulties of socialism in the present stage of social and moral development meant that a greatly improved capitalism held out the more realistic hopes for human betterment in the short term. . . . [Nevertheless] he was willing to see the state take a somewhat more active part in the nation's social and economic life than was altogether acceptable to the dominant laissez-faire prejudices of the day, but in general he was skeptical of the state's efficiency, suspicious of its power, and worried about the consequent loss of self-reliance among its citizens. (Collini 1989, xxii–xxiii)

Thus, although Mill took note of certain inequities produced by capitalist production, he was not willing to abandon the important assumptions and premises laid down by Adam Smith and championed by those who saw in capitalism a method by which social order could be achieved and individual liberty preserved without a great deal of involvement from the state. Such assumptions would be radically reconsidered and contested by Karl Marx.

## The Marxist Approach

If the founders of classical political economy left as a fundamental legacy the notion of "separability and the primacy of the economic sphere" (Caporaso and Levine 1992, 34), then Karl Marx—the last major thinker immediately shaped by this tradition[6]—would start from this very premise but would reach

---

6. Caporaso and Levine (1992) suggest that Marx is widely considered the last of the important classical political economists. See their discussion on page 33.

dramatically different conclusions about its consequences. Those conclusions have a specific bearing on what a Marxian theory has to say about income distribution. Marx would adopt and extend many of Ricardo's ideas: the labor theory of value, the assumption of a declining rate of profit, and the notion of a subsistence wage. However, one of the most critical distinctions between Marx and Ricardo is Marx's theory of a two-class society, capitalist and proletariat, rather than the classical breakdown among landowner, capitalist, and laborer. Identification of the class struggle and its historical role in societal change would give political content to Marx's otherwise purely economic theorization. Yet, the materialist conception of history (outlined and explicated in *The German Ideology*) would lead Marx to posit that the realm of politics and public decision making were mere epiphenomena and subordinate to the economic sphere. For Marx, change would only occur through a major restructuring of the base of society.[7] As this relates to theories of distribution flowing from the Marxist approach to political economy, Anthony Giddens usefully summarizes:

> Class must not be identified with either source of income or functional position in the division of labor.... Marx's emphasis that classes are not income groups is a particular aspect of his general premise, stated in *Capital* that distribution of economic goods is not a sphere separate to and independent of production, but it is determined by the mode of production. Marx rejects as "absurd" the contention made by John Stuart Mill, and many of the political economists, that while production is governed by definite laws, distribution is controlled by (malleable) human institutions [Marx 1974, 717]. Such a view underlies the assumption that classes are merely inequalities in the distribution of income, and therefore that class conflict can be alleviated or even eliminated altogether by the introduction of measures which minimize discrepancies between incomes. (1971, 37)

A multitude of Marxist and neo-Marxist literature exists that grapples with the fundamental issues raised by the fact that Marx did not see the state as

---

7. Antonio Gramsci would depart from this view (while remaining true to the larger Marxist intellectual enterprise of theorizing radical economic and social change) by emphasizing that ideological domination and change at the superstructural level could produce systemic change. See especially "The Study of Philosophy" in *Prison Notebooks* (1971).

potentially autonomous from the ruling capitalist-class interest. From this element alone, different theories of the state (Anderson 1974; Miliband 1969; Block 1977; Offe 1984; Poulantzas 1969, to name but a few) emerged that relate directly to questions bound up with the conflict Marx had with the notion of social d emocratic reforms. Habermas (1973) recharacterized this problem as the "legitimation crisis" and added an important dimension to the debates by reformulating the contradictions of capitalism in terms of the new role the state had taken on to avert the crises endemic to capitalist production, which in turn created a new "administrative crisis" resulting from the dubious necessity of propping up a system that was assumed to be "natural" in the first place.

Understanding how income inequality has been treated—generally speaking—in Marxist approaches suggests that scholars either theorize strategies for fundamental change in the mode of production as the only means by which to attack the problem of rising income inequality—that is, the work of scholars such as Jon Elster (1989) and John Roemer (1996)—or they tend to embrace social democracy as an adequate palliative to the inevitable ills of capitalism. In this latter category are scholars such as Przeworski, who describes this position in the following terms: "True, the values of political democracy and of social justice continue to guide social democrats such as myself, but social democracy is a program to mitigate the effects of private ownership and market allocation, not an alternative project of society" (1991, 7). Regardless of the myriad differences among Marxist political economists and social democrats, the lasting (and perhaps unifying) influence of Marx's writings and critique of capitalism is the emphasis on the social relations embedded in the mode of production. This is extremely significant for a Marxian understanding of income inequality, as it posits the necessary linkage between production and distribution.

The clearest expression of Marx's vision for dissolving the link between production and distribution as it exists in bourgeois society is to el iminate the enslaving and alienating division of labor and replace it through a collective regulation of production so that man would no longer be confined to one exclusive sphere of activity.[8] Only then would distribution be just in the sense that this type of society, as Marx puts it, would have inscribed on its banners:

8. This idea is articulated in *The German Ideology*, in which Marx argues that in a c ommunist society, it is possible for one "to hunt in the morning, fish in the afternoon, rear cattle in the evening, criticize after dinner . . . without ever becoming hunter, fisherman, shepherd or critic" (quoted in Tucker 1978, 160).

"from each according to his ability, to each according to his needs" (e.g., 1968, 14). Although Marx would part company with the classical thinkers in obvious and important ways, his views here show a striking similarity to Smith in that both thought a spontaneous and harmonious order would arise from the economic organization of society. For Smith, this order flowed from the market system, whereas for Marx, it would arise in the wake of a communist revolution and communal ownership of property. The neoclassical political economists would mark a fundamental shift from such thinking and would offer a dramatically different theory and method for considering the relations among individuals, the state, and society.

### The Neoclassical Approach

The so-called marginal revolution of the 1870s, led primarily by Walras, marked the emergence of neoclassical economics. Neoclassical economics was revolutionary in that it completely departed from the classical agenda of growth, distribution, and the labor theory of value and instead advanced a conception of economic life consistent with the broader thrust of utilitarian philosophy. Such a conception represented a departure from class categories and a move toward a view of individuals as self-seeking utility maximizers. As two economic historians claim, this development

> completely undermined the classical theory of distribution, both in terms of its structure and intent. Political economy was transformed from a search for a theory of value to a theory of the allocation of scarce resources between competing uses. The concepts of opportunity cost, of marginal utility and productivity, and of the production function provided new building blocks for a new theory, in which the relative scarcity of goods (whether inputs, or outputs) determined their price. (Brenner, Kaelble, and Thomas 1991, 5)

The world depicted by neoclassical thinking is one in which scarcity is presupposed and individuals are motivated to seek their highest level of want satisfaction and do so through a ranking of options or "preference ordering." Once rational choices are made by individuals reflecting their preferences, maximization of individual satisfaction and group welfare are simultaneously achieved. Caporaso and Levine refer to the neoclassical development of subjective utility theory and the notion of "marginal product": "With these new ideas gathering momentum as they spread during the last quarter of the nine-teenth century, the economy came to be thought of less in terms of material production and reproduction and more as a logic of human action" (1992, 79). In this regard we can see how the gradual dominance of rational choice theories in political science has come to eclipse or marginalize political theories of human behavior.

The implications of understanding income distribution were enormous. In the neoclassical framework, distribution relates to the supply and demand of factors of production, and it is assumed that the volume of output, its distribution, and real wages are determined simultaneously with such variables as consumers' tastes, the availability of factors of production, and the level of technological efficiency assumed as "given." Neoclassical economics explains prices in terms of relative scarcity and the willingness of people to pay—in other words, demand determines supply. As Y. S. Brenner notes, "It is not concerned with class conflict and exogenous influences on income distribution but with what for all inte nts and purposes is a clo sed, almost perfectly competitive, equilibrium—seeking harmonious economic system in which the distribution of income is determined by the Law of Diminishing Returns and 'marginal productivity'" (1966, 14). In other words, as more contemporary neoclassical economists such as Milton Friedman have articulated it, income distribution is best determined through the market with the price of labor (wages) set by supply and demand, which reflects individual choices, free exchange, and, hence, achieves both efficiency and optimum social welfare (Friedman 1962).

In addition to the significant impact of this new way of thinking about economics for understanding distributional issues, the larger influence and continued relevance of the neoclassical school of thought lay in the wider application of its concepts and theories to all facets of life. Caporaso and Levine note: "In this sense we can interpret nearly all of l ife as the application of economic calculation, as economizing behavior. This result works against any effort, based on the neoclassical approach, to identify a distinctively economic subset of our lives and our social relations. It erases the distinction between the economy and the other spheres of social interaction" (1992, 81). In other words, there is only one form of human behavior and that is economizing, and it applies in both the market and in the world of politics. From this perspective, the state exists solely to provide the framework for property rights and contracts and is thus even further circumscribed than it had been in the world of the classical economists. As the history of political economy evolved, the trend was definitely toward emptying the body politic from any independent and authoritative substance in matters relating to social and economic decisions.

Ironically, the neoclassical framework sketched out here extends to one of the dominant approaches to political science, rational choice. One of its founders, William Riker, stated: "I visualize the growth in political science of a body of theory somewhat similar to . . . the neoclassical theory of value in economics."[9] Riker's vision has indeed come to fruition with choice theoretic approaches to political inquiry gaining a stronger and more unified presence in the discipline than any other single approach, despite the controversy sparked by the publication of Green and Shapiro's *Pathologies of Rational Choice Theory* (1994). From a pure theoretical standpoint, the rational choice paradigm has offered one of the most successful attempts at a universal theory of political behavior, even though it lacks a solid body of empirical verification of its sophisticated models and has other problems specific to its claim to universality (Huber and Dion 2002). The irony of this approach to political economy in its privileging of economic theories of human behavior is that it in effect subordinates the very object of our inquiry—the human being as a political animal and not merely *homo economicus.*

Gary J. Miller makes the following observation: "It is not an exaggeration to say that economics transformed the discipline of political science by proposing to explain fundamental political acts—voting, joining, rebelling, contributing—as the acts of self-interested, rational actors" (1997, 1181). The author adds—and in some ways sums up what a entire volume and round of debates required (e.g., Green and Shapiro 1994)—that "while much of the attraction for economic modeling in political science comes from the ability to explain both market and political phenomena from a single, parsimonious set of assumptions, economic imperialism carries its own dangers: persistent anomalies in the realm of politics threaten the validity of economic theory overall" (1997, 1181). Paradoxically, it was an economist, John Maynard Keynes, who chronologically preceded most neoclassical writers and whose ideas most trumped the fallacious neoclassical assumptions. Despite corrections by economists, these ideas remain intact in much of the rational choice theory of political scientists.

---

9. This was quoted in a recent article published in *The New Republic* by Jonathan Cohn and titled "'Irrational Exuberance' (When Did Political Science Forget About Politics?)," 25 October 1999, 27.

*Keynesian/Post-Keynesian Approaches*

Several assumptions made by the neoclassical economists should be reviewed briefly to provide context for Keynes's critique and subsequent contributions to the evolution of political economy. First, the neoclassical model is one in which the level of output is determined by technological efficiency and distribution by a neutral mechanism based on the concepts of utility and scarcity. Second, in this model, labor and capital are homogeneous and the demand for labor varies inversely and the supply of labor positively with the movement of real wages. Firms were described as maximizing profit constantly by varying the employment of labor and capital according to price variations, which led to the final assumption that the entire economic system would naturally gravitate toward full employment equilibrium.

Writing against the backdrop of the Depression of the 1930s undoubtedly influenced Keynes's thinking as he elaborated a model of unemployment that showed the belief in the self-correcting mechanism of the market economy to be dubious if not completely flawed. Keynes rejected the idea that the self-regulating market was capable of fully exploiting society's productive potential and instead advanced an argument that focuses on the instability of the reproduction process and growth cycles in a capitalist economy. Arguing against the notion of equilibrium, Keynes observes:

> In particular, it is an outstanding characteristic of the economic system in which we live that, whilst it is subject to severe fluctuations in respect of output and employment, it is not violently unstable. Indeed it seems capable of remaining in a chronic condition of sub-normal activity for a considerable period without any marked tendency either towards recovery or towards complete collapse. Moreover, the evidence indicates that full, or even approximately full, employment is of rare and short-lived occurrence. (1936, 249–50)

Keynesian economics would thus highlight the necessity of government intervention in the economy to ensure that resources were appropriately exploited and adequate levels of employment achieved. Caporaso and Levine claim that it is possible to "trace the peculiarities of the Keynesian approach, when contrasted with the neoclassical, to the premise that expectations of demand rather than costs of production drive investment" (1992, 114) and that this premise had implications for the wage contract and savings. Keynes's analysis of the labor market led him to conclude that there was a general failure of demand side of the economy in that the situation of unemployment provoked a scenario where those who depend on a wage contract could no longer purchase the goods for their livelihood, and firms were thus deprived of profits. Thus, it was in the interest of both employers and employees to stabilize things in such a manner that, as Caporaso and Levine put it, "at the microlevel, changes in the terms of the wage contract can lend stability to labor markets benefiting both employer and employee. At the macrolevel, demand management by the state can maintain levels of demand and employment by countering the instability born of the unregulated and uncoordinated decision of private agents" (1992, 116).

The authors also note that Keynes's analysis of savings would develop in a similar direction that would tend toward conflict between the rationality of individuals and that of the system as a whole. As Keynes explored the social ramifications of his ideas elaborated in *The General Theory,* he would note in his final chapter that the arguments he advanced could potentially undermine "one of the most fundamental and long-standing justifications for the inequalities of income and wealth we associate with [the] capitalist economy, especially under a regime of laissez-faire" (Caporaso and Levine 1992, 117). Keynes concludes accordingly: "Thus our argument leads towards the conclusion that in contemporary conditions the growth of wealth, so far from being dependent on the abstinence of the rich, as is commonly supposed, is more likely to be impeded by it. One of the chief social justifications of great inequality of wealth is therefore, removed" (Keynes 1936, 373).

The development of post-Keynesianism would continue to challenge the orthodox justification of income inequality in terms of productivity differences and argue against the idea that a certain degree of inequality is necessary to provide incentives for higher rates of growth. The post-Keynesian approach claims, in fact, that the "incomes earned in society can be explained independently of any direct relation to individual or class productivity and income differences are neither natural nor economic facts, but the result of social and political customs and decisions as well as market power" (Kregel 1979, 58). Post-Keynesianists' point of departure is Keynes's view that "given the psychology of the public, the level of output and employment as a whole depends on the amount of investment" (Kregel 1979, 46), and they extend this by arguing that investment is not only the determinant of the level of output but also the distribution between income from work and from property. One variant of post-Keynesianism, the French regulation school, offers a very rigorous and precise method (or analytical framework called "regimes of accumulation") for understanding capitalist development in the context of a dynamic and integrated model that considers the economic, social, and institutional dimensions.[10] The regulation framework defines each regime of accumulation as "a mode of distribution and systematic reallocation of the social product, realizing over a long period, a certain correspondence between the transformation of the conditions of production (volume of capital engaged, distribution between branches, and production norms) and the transformation in the conditions of final consumption (consumption norms of wage-earners and of other social classes, collective expenditures, etc." (Noel 1987, 311). Along these lines, Robert Boyer, a leading French political economist, urged economists not to confuse the ideology of the free market with the "actual and real, but limited capabilities of really existing market mechanisms, which are embedded within a complex mix of alternative and largely complementary governance modes" (1990, 31). The recognition that markets are social constructions and not law-like, infallible operating procedures is the appeal of this framework and the one most consistent with a vision of political economy as applied democratic theory.

What is most significant about the contributions of the regulation school is its clear distinction from the dominant, neoclassical paradigm where, as Noel summarizes,

> economic laws are the additive results of individual choice, and their formation is quite independent from structural factors, such as rules and institutions, which are considered constant and exogenous factors. According to the regulation approach, in contrast, laws are changing historical products that impose varying constraints on the individuals, who exist and choose within evolving institutional frameworks. This stress on changes in economic laws also distinguishes the approach from classical Marxism. (1987, 313)

10. See Brenner and Glick 1991 for an extensive review. Noel 1987 provides an excellent discussion of the regulation approach in relation to American political economy, and Jessop 1990 surveys the contributions of the French school of political economy and highlights the tensions and differences among some of its leading theorists.

Highlighting the differences between these broad schools of thought reveals that d espite the strong scientific basis and rigorous methodologies employed by the various contending approaches to political economy, what underlies the major divisions are fundamentally normative questions, not technical or empirical ones. Caporaso and Levine (1992) also draw attention to this element of normativity in the concluding remarks of their work:

> The foregoing considerations point up the need for political economy to deal with the categorical distinction between politics and economics, and to take that distinction seriously. The distinction clearly has a normative grounding and normative implications. It corresponds to the classification of wants into qualitatively different groups, and to a distinction between private and public more complex than usually employed. Developing the classification of wants (and needs), the normative grounding for a theory identifying the tasks appropriate to different institutions, and a more complex and meaningful distinction between public and private should be made an important part of the agenda of political economy. (225)

## Income Distribution and Democratic Theory

Income distribution and, more specifically, income inequality make the normative implications quite obvious. Even the term *income inequality* conveys a social judgment and requires a meticulous clarification of what one means by inequality and how the evaluation and measurement of inequality of incomes are handled. For example, as two scholars of income distribution put it, "the size distribution is primarily a descriptive device for rank ordering individuals in society, whereas the construction of a measure of income inequality makes relative judgments about individuals within the distribution. It is bound up with notions of social and distributive justice" (Brenner, Kaelble, and Thomas 1991, 15). Furthermore, if we take seriously the diverse capacities of individuals, one must admit at least a modicum of relativity. To be explicit, in addressing income inequality as a social problem that is dealt with more successfully by some societies than by others, I am certainly not advocating absolute equality of incomes as a desirable outcome. The problem I am examining is instead why stable, generally prosperous nations are experiencing a trend toward increasing inequality, what may be the roots of this shift toward more disparity between the rich and the poor, and why this varies significantly among these countries under investigation that are customarily perceived as having relatively similar political and socioeconomic structures. But even these foci do not entirely evade the underlying normative issues, and this is precisely why it is necessary to reconceptualize political economy as applied democratic theory. The term *applied democratic theory* is used here to convey the idea that, although income distribution is both the founding problem and an object of inquiry of continuing import to political economy, no adequate treatment of the subject can evade the notion that evaluations of income inequality (whether examining its causes or effects) are inextricably bound up with questions of democratic theory and practice and with discussions of social justice.

Income distribution is undeniably a function of both the structure of the economy and the organization of the polity and the various processes that connect these arenas of social life. However, as one surveys the leading approaches to political economy, it is evident that the issues dividing the multitude of scholars who work in this general tradition are precisely the conceptual difficulties arising from (or reflective of) underlying normative questions such as (1) how should one conceive the distinction between public and private spheres, (2) what is the relationship between the individual and society, and (3) what is the proper and legitimate role of government? Such questions, of course, lead us to the central concerns of democratic theory. A brief survey of the recent literature on income inequality underscores this point.

Mainstream economists who study income distribution have tended to do so strictly within the framework of the trade-off between growth and equity and, incidentally, have been predominantly concerned with only one case: the U.S. economy. This trade-off is originally rooted in the famous Kuznets curve, an inverted U-curve that implies that income inequality increases during the early phases of industrialization and economic development, reaches a peak, and then declines in the later stages of development (Kuznets 1955).[11] The modern version of this stems from Arthur Okun's *Equality and Efficiency: The Big Trade-off* (1975) wherein efforts to achieve more equal income

11. Much of the sociological literature is based on the Kuznets thesis and tends to focus on developing societies or more global analyses that examine the relationship between democratization and economic development. For a recent volume that provides both historical and new research in these areas, see Midlarsky 1997.

distribution and greater economic equality in society are seen as a hindrance to the goal of e fficiency. Although Okun professed an "ethical preference" for greater equality in income distribution, he believed this to be infeasible and thus traded off for efficiency, which he believed more conducive to over-all economic health.

A whole host of economists would be influenced by this classic trade-off and would continue to depict income distribution and any attempts at redis-tribution as detrimental to economic prosperity (Hayek 1960; Friedman and Friedman 1980). For example, Arrow (1951) would conclude that equal ity crowds out investment and diminishes the work incentive. More importantly, many would characterize any governmental interference and efforts to re-distribute income as an unjust infringement on the freedom of property own-ership (Nozick 1974; Friedman and Friedman 1980). In part, this literature was also a response to Rawls and his monumental influence with the pub-lication of *A Theory of Justice* (1971) in which he advanced a conception of "justice as fairness" and sparked an intense and venerable debate about exactly what the state can and should do.

In contrast to Nozick (1974), others would respond that the notion of freedom for those without property in a market economy is a very restricted one (Cohen 1981; Roemer 1996). For instance, Cohen (1981) asks if private ownership of one's own skills and talents is compatible with equality of con-dition, both of which are prima facie desirable goals. His answer contains an important critique of writers like Nozick. Cohen begins by remarking that most right-wing philosophers believe that freedom and equality are conflict-ing ideals, and when the two come into conflict, freedom should be preferred. The response of leftists is that th ere is no n ecessary conflict, or if so, "free-dom must give way to equality since justice demands equality and justice is superior to all other political values" (13). By asking if freedom and equality are compatible, Cohen presents a critique of Nozick's notion of self-ownership and claims that a union of self-ownership and unequal distribution of worldly resources leads indefinitely to great inequality of private property in exter-nal goods of all kinds and, hence, to inequality of condition (115). The point is that the discussion of material distribution of resources simply cannot be restricted to the questions posed by economists. Efficiency arguments entail moral dilemmas just like those of equity.

Evading the normative issues described above, a great deal of research—especially within comparative politics—examines the impact of the welfare state and transfer spending on the relationship between equity and economic performance and growth, but there is more conflicting and contradictory evidence than systematic and conclusive findings (Castles and Dorwick 1990; Flora and Heidenheimer 1981; Korpi 1985; Weede 1986; Huber and Stephens 2001; Swank 2002; Kenworthy and Pontusson 2005).[12] Furthermore, as Kenworthy has shown, transfer spending only modestly correlates with income inequality (1995, 231). Esping-Andersen, one of the most influential scholars of the welfare state, cautions us to avoid confusing the welfare state with equality precisely because there is such diversity among their goals, because there are numerous methods of measurement, and because welfare states "pursue different conceptions of equality" (1990, 262). Chapter 3 will discuss the welfare state literature and its relationship to the broader body of work on comparative democratic institutions as well as the most recent work of comparative scholars dealing with income inequality.

In addition to the lack of systematic empirical findings from either economists (see Levy and Murnane 1992, and Gottschalk and Smeeding 1997 for surveys) or the literature on the welfare state, there is no general theoretical framework available for examining income inequality in cross-national perspective. In a recent overview of the stylized facts coming out of research on income inequality, Gottschalk and Smeeding point to the need for a more unifying theoretical structure from which to study income inequality cross-nationally. These authors claim that prior research has been of a "rough and ready nature and did not stand up to close scrutiny," but they suggest that continued research on "international comparisons of income distribution can provide important benchmarks of how one nation differs from or is similar to other nations" (1997, 634). This is precisely where comparative political economy and comparative analysis more generally makes its most valuable contribution to political and social inquiry. Gauging income inequality from a broad level of generality can be much more beneficial than the narrow approaches that focus on single causes of increasing income inequality such as the change toward higher skilled workers (Juhn, Murphy, and Pierce 1993), the impact of international trade (Krugman 1995; Rodrik 1997), the shift in age composition (Blackburn and Bloom 1987), the role of education (Katz and Murphy 1992), or the shift toward a service-oriented and information economy (Ryu and Slottje 1998). Although there are obviously a multitude

12. An important exception here is the work of Bo Rothstein. See especially his book *Just Institutions Matter* (1998), which I discuss in Chapter 3.

of contributing factors, none of these alone can tell us very much about the overall trends and deeper underlying causes of the growing income gap.

Economist Frank Levy concludes that there is a great deal of myth about what causes inequality and that even the best research in economics is missing one of the most fundamental issues: the role that perceptions of fairness plays. As he puts it, "popular beliefs about how the economy distributes its gains will go far in determining public policy" (1998, 163). In other words, what is missing in research on income inequality is the impact of citizens' views on issues of rising income inequality, especially during a period of general prosperity. This study contributes to the literature on income inequality by bringing this element directly into the explanatory framework. In the age of increasing globalization, it is important to analyze how citizens in different societies conceptualize the relationship between capitalism and democracy because it is precisely this relationship and its changing nature in the context of a more interdependent world that shape a number of large-scale outcomes such as income inequality. As neoliberal discourse spreads and policymakers everywhere seem inclined to embrace the "liberal orthodoxy" (Hall 1997), it is important to see if this trend is reflected in citizens' attitudes and societal preferences. Fred Block pointedly sums up the consequences of what he refers to as marketization: "Increasingly, public debate has come to hinge, not on what kind of society we are or want to be, but on what the needs of the economy are. Hence, a broad range of social policies are now debated almost entirely in terms of how they fit in with the imperatives of the market" (1990, 3).

The following discussion is meant to show the problems of associating marketization with democratization (evident in much of the globalization literature) or of more broadly sublimating politics to economics and the ramifications of this tendency for political scientists and citizens who are concerned with growing problem of income inequality. The normative and practical implications of such ideas bear directly on questions of the sources of economic inequality and, thus, are of central importance to my argument. Such a discussion follows John Dryzek's lead in having "political theory supply the conceptual resources to counteract the imaginative deficiencies of empirical work. The latter in its turn would supply empirical resources to counteract the idealism of political theory . . . [and to deploy this combination] to discover and enumerate spaces for freedom in political innovation amid structural necessity" (1992, 518).

## Globalization and the Dialectic of Democracy and Capitalism

By now there is a rather unwieldy literature offering a wide variety of con-
ceptualizations, empirical analyses, and theoretical interpretations of the processes of globalization. Despite this diversity, it is possible to distill a more or
less encompassing definition of what is meant by globalization. According to
Louise Amoore and colleagues, most scholars agree "that globalization en-
compasses a broad range of material and non-material aspects of production,
distribution, management, finance, information and communications technol-
ogies, and capital accumulation" (1997, 181). This inclusive and rather uncon-
tentious perspective serves to c onvey the extensiveness of th ese processes.
Most of the scholarly work could be mapped out according to which of these
activities is the central focus, whether authors depict globalization as something qualitatively new and/or inexorable, and whether it is conceived as a
relatively uncertain, positive, or negative phase in human development and
world order.

Such varied positions highlight the epistemological ramifications and
normative challenges of the broader globalization debate that are of central
concern in c onsidering both the ideational as well as empirical impact on
questions of distributive justice. The approach I take derives from my view of
globalization as a dialectical process (Birchfield 1996, 66).[13] This entails rejecting the notion that globalization is an external phenomenon that one may
observe objectively, recognizing ourselves as implicated in an d inseparable
from "the world out there" and focusing on the contradictions extant in any
given historical moment—not merely for critique, but to challenge the myth
of inexorable forces and thereby theorize and actualize progressive change. I
agree with Robert Cox that this mode of thinking is employed "as much to
arouse consciousness and the will to a ct as to diagnose the condition of the
world" (1996, 66). A practical definition of globalization will clarify the relevance of this perspective in g rounding the following critique. To this end,
Held's conceptualization is useful: "Globalization can be taken to denote the
stretching and deepening of social relations and institutions across space and
time such that, on the one hand, day-to-day activities are increasingly influenced by events happening on the other side of the globe, and on the other,

13. For a broader discussion of the dialectics of globalization, see Anthony Giddens's *The Consequences of Modernity* (1990, especially 64). See also the special section, "On Dialectic and IR Theory"
in *Millennium: Journal of International Studies* 2, no. 2 (1997): 403–16.

the practices and decisions of local groups or communities can have signifi-cant global reverberations" (1995a, 20).

Such an interpretation makes the implications for democratic politics quite clear because new forms of power are being created and exercised in ways that undermine traditional notions of legitimate authority and accountability that are tied to the territorially bound state. A tension emerges, however, from the asymmetrical possession and exercise of this new power by what some scholars have termed the "transnational capital class" (Gill 1990; van der Pijl 1997) or, in other words, the relatively few who benefit most from the dereg-ulation of world financial and labor markets and increasing trade liberaliza-tion. Dani Rodrik put it quite cogently: "Globalization is exposing a deep fault line between groups who have the skills and mobility to flourish in global markets and those who either don't have these advantages or perceive the expansion of unregulated markets as inimical to social stability and deeply held norms" (1997, 2).

Despite such enormous power imbalances, the triumphalist ethos of mar-ket ideology seems to prevail. As Gill put it, "the present world order involves a more 'liberalized' and commodified set of historical structures, driven by the restructuring of capital and a political shift to the right. This process involves the spatial expansion and social deepening of economic liberal definitions of social purpose and possessively individualist patterns of action and poli-tics" (1995, 399). While this emerging "market civilization" is contradictory or even "oxymoronic," the ideological dimension has not been adequately exposed or problematized in the recent literature. Consequently, its contesta-tion can be most propitiously waged on its own terms—that is, by subjecting market ideology to the core concepts of democratic theory.

When market logic is applied to more and more areas of human life, as is the case with neoliberal globalization, what essentially results is an increasing sublimation of politics. The dominant assumption that human nature and behavior can be characterized as economizing, thereby maximizing utility to secure self-interest, gains acceptance as an inviolable truth. One result of this is a loss of an appreciation of other values that are completely devoid of eco-nomic rationale—such as respect, tolerance, and social growth—or a deepen-ing of community as opposed to merely its spatial expansion. And now, as we seem to be moving into an era in which the market becomes a chief rallying cry (and the key metaphor for world dis/order) and is asserted as the best guarantor of freedom, it is incumbent upon democratic theorists and citizens to take stock of its repercussions for the democratic experiment. Those who insist that there is no democracy without a free market need to be reminded that the two forms of human organization are not entirely interchangeable and do not n ecessarily coexist peacefully. As Earl Shorris argues, "political democracy is a relation among human beings who control themselves. Market democracy is a competition in which people try to control each other. . . . This one is a misnomer, for the control of one human being by another, no matter how subtle the means, is no democracy" (1994, 137).

Assessing the relations between capitalism and democracy in light of globalization is rendered all the more pertinent when recognizing that existing within a single world economy are diverse models of capitalist political economies underlying which are competing visions of democracy.[14] Cognizance of this diversity serves to challenge the myths and exaggerations as well as the threats and possibilities of globalization. Therefore, no approach to u nderstanding the global economy can afford to ignore the valuable contributions that comparative political economists have made in demonstrating that capitalism is not a monolithic structure but rather one taking on different qualities in diverse domestic settings that reflect important historical and cultural particularities. Likewise, students of comparative politics must be ever more attuned to the exigencies of the world economy. If we have learned anything from comparative political economy, it is that the market economy is not a uniform structure; rather, its heterogeneity can be understood as historically conditioned variations in state-society relations. Moreover, this is why developed capitalist democracies exhibit different sizes and forms of welfare states and contending models of state-market relations.[15] The neoliberal model and

14. This idea is captured quite nicely in Michel Albert's *Capitalism vs. Capitalism* (1993). It is worth noting the similarity of Albert's argument of "capitalism as threat," in spite of its victory over communism, to that of the later published article by George Soros, "The Capitalist Threat" in *The Atlantic Monthly,* February 1997.

15. David Harvey's conceptualization of this problem is useful here. In *The Condition of Postmodernity* he argues that "the tension between the fixity (and hence stability) that state regulation imposes, and the fluid motion of capital flow, remains a crucial problem for the social and political organization of capitalism. This difficulty is modified by the way in which the state stands itself to be disciplined by internal forces (upon which it relies for power) and external conditions—competition in the world economy, exchange rates, and capital movements, migration, or, on occasion, direct political interventions on the part of superior powers. The relation between capitalist development and the state has to be seen, therefore, as mutually determining rather than unidirectional" (1989, 109). The various homogenization or "convergence" theses within the globalization debates seem to suggest that only what Harvey refers to here as the "external conditions" are eroding state power. It is ironic that these arguments emanate from a tradition that was formerly critical of Marxist approaches for economic determinism.

its attendant free market ideology belie this complex reality. As Stephen Gill points out, the political project behind the rhetoric constitutes an attempt to "make transnational liberalism, and if possible liberal democratic capitalism, the sole model for future development" (1995, 412). Thus, it is important to first expose the implications of this model to construct a more compelling contestation of it.

When the market mechanism—a method of organization or social coordination designed to render more efficient the exchange of goods and services—is associated with a fundamental democratic value—liberty—one necessarily presupposes a narrow and materialistic conception of both freedom and the aims of democracy itself.[16] Hannah Arendt captured this effect as she observed, "the development of commercial society . . . , with the triumphal victory of exchange value over use value, first introduced the principle of interchangeability, then the relativization, and finally the devaluation of all values" (quoted in Harvey 1989). This effectively subordinates actors to rules. For the market mechanism to function, certain rules must be established. Private property must be guaranteed and incentives to compete for scarce resources are encouraged and described as natural. Communal values and cooperation are not nurtured because that would undermine the role of scarcity, which is the idea underpinning the whole system. By giving primacy to rules and, more importantly, venerating and reifying property to such an extent that it acquires the status of personhood, it excludes other potential ordering principles of society and diminishes the importance of social values and distributive justice, which are vital to democratic participation and decision making. It should be noted that the hegemony of the market is achieved by its representation as an uncontroversial metaphor for a society at liberty to do with property as it pleases without interference from the state. In the context of globalization, this becomes increasingly convenient for capital because the state may abdicate its former responsibilities of regulation and provision of social welfare by claiming global competition and market forces dictate such action.

This issue raises the deeper problem of the relationship between capitalism (which requires supposedly "free markets") and democracy. An overview of the argument made by Bowles and Gintis (1986) regarding this relationship is helpful here in eliciting the incompatibility of market ideology with the

16. See, for example, the writings of Friedrich A. von Hayek, *The Road to Serfdom* (1944); Milton Friedman, *Capitalism and Freedom* (1962); and Milton and Rose Friedman, *Freedom to Choose* (1980).

aims and principles of democracy. For these authors, the relationship between democracy and capitalism is an uneasy one because the economic system has as an imperative the privileging of a certain set of rights over others. Bowles and Gintis forcefully articulate the idea that the liberal democratic model and what they refer to as "capitalist governance" necessitate that property rights prevail over personal rights. They proceed to critique both liberal and Marxist political theory and propose a theoretical and practical agenda for expanding the scope of both liberty and individual choice, but in a framework consonant with the notion of popular sovereignty. What is useful in their argument for the development of this critique of market ideology is the recognition that both liberal and Marxist theories have too unitary a conception of power that ignores the fundamentally political nature of economic life and undertheorizes the role of the state.[17] In other words, in a manner strikingly similar to Karl Polanyi (1944), they argue that although the economy is a site of social conflict, the underlying sources of tension are inherently political. It is worth remembering that it is the capitalist wage relation that necessitates the conceptual separation of economics and politics, respectively, into private and public spheres of activity, which in turn becomes the defining feature of the liberal state.[18] The main thrust of the argument presented by Bowles and Gintis is that the democratic experiment involves the enlargement of popular sovereignty and liberty, but the process has been inhibited as capitalism and the liberal creed have produced a collision course between two fundamental rights: property rights and personal rights. The clash of these rights facilitated what the authors refer to as an "institutional modus vivendi" of the two forces, which entailed a series of accommodations (from Lockean

17. Bowles and Gintis argue that whereas liberalism reduces social action to mere means toward an end, Marxism denies the relevance of instrumentality and thereby the role of individual choice (1986, 19). This is essentially why they argue that neither tradition is an adequate approach to democratic theory. The primary objective of the former is liberty and the latter is equality or classlessness. What Bowles and Gintis seek to construct is both a post-liberal and post-Marxist agenda that acknowledges that individual action and social structure are mutually determining. I believe what these authors are aiming for is something that the whole of Gramsci's thinking actually achieved. Augelli and Murphy seem to grasp this in their appropriation of Gramsci for their 1988 work titled *America's Quest for Supremacy and the Third World*; see their introduction and especially pages 4–6, where they claim that "Gramsci's ideas help bridge the gap between Marxist and liberal social science."

18. Mark Rupert (1995) reconstructs this crucial element in Marx's thinking (and what I believe is the core of a Marxian political theory) to present a "radicalized social ontology" as the basis for critical international political economy (IPE). See pages 16–31 in his work titled *Producing Hegemony*.

to Keynesian) that attempted to resolve the contradictory logic of capitalism while "simultaneously promoting the process of economic growth and containing the explosive potential of coexistence of economic privilege and representative political institutions" (1986, 34).

The above quote contains a very significant insight into the ambiguities involved when relating the market to freedom and democracy, particularly as it must be sustained in light of increasing globalization. The economic privilege the authors refer to is the status that liberal theory grants to the capitalist economy as a private realm of property. Bowles and Gintis argue that this is an untenable position, as a sphere cannot be considered private if it involves the "socially consequential exercise of power" (1986, 66–67).[19] I would add that the whole notion of privilege hinges on this vital segmentation of public and private. For instance, the private status granted to corporations, despite their enormous social power, effectively removes from political discourse a whole host of issues that from the democratic perspective should be subjected to public debate—not the least of which is the wage labor system and the asymmetries between the power of labor and the power of capital. In countries where free market ideology is not so pervasive, values such as social justice and worker democracy is a more frequent part of discourse (e.g., Germany, France, and the Nordic countries). Yet, as capital is becoming more mobile and globalized, there is an even greater threat to the idea and practice of social democracy—which at its root has a conception of justice that derides this false separation of economics and politics. This is precisely why democratic theorizing must encompass nonterritorial notions of popular sovereignty and solidarity as well as contest the false separation of economics and politics.

One of the strongest non-Marxist critiques of market society was that offered by Karl Polanyi writing in the wake of World War II.[20] Challenging Adam Smith and the assumptions of eighteenth century political economy, Polanyi argued that the establishment of laissez-faire economics *required* state intervention and that market society did not emerge naturally as a result of man's propensity to "truck, barter and exchange," nor was market expansion

19. The authors define a socially consequential action as one that "both substantively affects the lives of others and the character of which reflects the will and interests of the actor" (67).

20. Polanyi's most important work detailing the rise of market society and its consequences for the social fabric of humankind is *The Great Transformation: The Political and Economic Origin of Our Times* (1957; originally published 1944).

impersonal or inevitable. He notes, "The road to the free market was opened and kept open by an enormous increase in continuous, centrally organized and controlled interventionism. To make Adam Smith's 'simple and natural liberty' compatible with the needs of a human society was a most complicated affair" (1944, 140).

The fundamental legacy of Polanyi's work and its relevance here is the author's introduction of the idea that the "self-regulating market" was largely a myth because deliberate political action was required to pave the way for such an approach to economic organization. Though he wrote from the perspective of an economic historian, his account of the emergence of market society entailed astute, if subtle, political analysis as opposed to understanding it as a strictly economic phenomenon. By applying Polanyi's perspective to the present situation of global capitalism and the growing gap between the rich and the poor, we gain insights into how the process of global marketization unfolds and in what ways it suppresses other important societal values that seem central to the life of a democratic society—both domestic and international.

Two specific places in Polanyi's writing where he grasped the antithetical nature of markets and popular sovereignty are his excursus on the rise of the "self-regulating market" and his account of society's "double-movement." In the former, Polanyi distinguishes the move toward free markets or self-regulating markets from previous economic systems. He emphasizes that never before had markets been more than accessories of economic life, where "as a rule, the economic system was absorbed in the social system"; in contrast, the market economy is one in which markets alone direct the production and distribution of goods ( 1944, 68). Polanyi outlines the assumptions of this system and identifies what he saw as a harbinger of its negative consequences for social and moral life:

> An economy of this kind derives from the expectation that human beings behave in such a way as to achieve maximum money gains. It assumes markets in which supply of goods (including services) available at a definite price will equal the demand at that price. . . . Under these assumptions order in production and distribution of goods is ensured by prices alone. . . . Nothing must be allowed to inhibit the formation of markets, nor must incomes be permitted to be formed otherwise than through sales. . . . Neither price, nor

supply, nor demand must be fixed or regulated; only such policies and measures are in order which help ensure the self-regulation of the market by creating conditions which *make the market the only organizing power in the economic sphere.* (68–69; emphasis added)

Polanyi forcefully articulated the mythic proportions of the assumption of human nature and behavior underlying the market economy and its centrality to the "disembedding" of the economy from social relations and institutions where values other than profit had previously prevailed. The author structures his argument around an analysis and critique of the commodification of land, labor, and money, which he decries as an artificial process producing "fictitious commodities," the consequences of which subordinate the substance of society to the mechanism of the market. The implications of this system for democracy are woven throughout his analysis but are most emphatically relayed in his discussion of the double movement, which he empirically substantiates with his account of the Chartist Movement. Two primary points of his account are the constitutional separation of economics and politics and the observation that this was essentially designed to "separate people from power over their own economic life" (225). Thus, consistent with my critique of market ideology, Polanyi illustrated that it is the tendency of market economics to insist that all other rights and values be subordinated to the sacral realm of property, and that it is only through humanity's struggle to protect itself against the vagaries of the market that civilization is rescued and the reality of society is rehabilitated. One scholar summed up the moral and social ramifications of the transition to laissez-faire economics as a shift from Gemeinschaft to Gesellschaft that "entailed a loss of a certain vital human quality . . . [replaced with an] atomized society in which the interdependency of individuals was not mediated through political, social, or religious institutions but via the market and contract" (Booth 1994, 656–57).[21]

Neoliberal globalization might be seen as another grand-scale attempt at laissez-faire economics that more than anything else demonstrates the power of market ideology: why else would its disastrous consequences be risked again? This question is precisely why Polanyi's exposition of "the self-regulating market" as a dangerous myth is so critically instructive at this moment in history.

21. Another current recapitulation of Polanyi's ideas appeared in *Politics and Society* 21 (1993) in an article by John Lie titled "Visualizing the Invisible Hand: The Social Origins of Market Society" in England, 1550–1750."

But Polanyi did more than offer this critical interpretation of the fallacies and travesties associated with laissez-faire economics. He also implicitly planted the seed of a radical democratic theory that is aptly summed up in his idea of the "double-movement."

Polanyi's concept of the "double-movement" refers to society's "inevitable self-protection against the commodification of life" (Mendell and Salée 1991, xiii). Polanyi writes, "For a century the dynamics of modern society was governed by a double movement: the market expanded continuously but this movement was met by a countermovement checking the expansion in definite directions" (Polanyi 1944, 130). He argued that there were two basic organizing principles in society at work simultaneously. On one hand, economic liberalism was "aiming at the establishment of a self-regulating market, relying on the support of the trading classes and using largely laissez-faire and free trade as its methods." On the other hand, social protection was "aiming at the conservation of man and nature as well as productive organization, relying on . . . the support of those most immediately affected by the deleteriously action of the market—primarily, but not exclusively, the working and the landed classes" (132).

The discernment of the double movement intimates how Polanyi's ideas could be employed to invigorate political economy with democratic theory. This is not only useful for theoretical purposes but also because, as Polanyi has shown, it is the natural, spontaneous response of individuals and collective society to preserve not only their own autonomy but their very existence by trying to shape their destiny through a more democratically controlled, socially embedded economy. Such a view also resonates with the thesis of Bowles and Gintis—that the rights necessary to make capitalism work and those required to fulfill democratic ideals are often in direct conflict. Thus, a dire consequence of the hegemony of market ideology is that rather than the norm of market forces conforming to the principles of democracy, this ideal is supplanted by a norm that delegitimatizes political demands construed as infringements on market freedom.

Global capitalism renders the dualities of public/private and politics/economics all the more problematic because national governments may now justify disengagements of social welfare commitments in the paradoxical terms of preserving national sovereignty in an increasingly interdependent world. For example, note the following argument by Wolfgang Streeck regarding the European Union:

National political systems embedded in a competitive international market and exposed to supranationally ungoverned external effects of competitive systems are tempted to protect their formal sovereignty by devolving responsibility for the economy to the "market"— using what has remained of their public powers of intervention to limit, as it were constitutionally, the claims politics can make on the economy, and citizens on the polity. . . . If citizens can be persuaded that economic outcomes are, and better be, the result of "market forces," and that national governments are, therefore, no longer to be held responsible for the economy, national domestic sovereignty and political legitimacy can be maintained even in conditions of tight economic interdependence: with the nation-state having offloaded its responsibility for its economy to the "world market," its own insufficiency and obsolescence in relation to the latter ceases to be visible. (1996, 307–8)

If indeed "persuading citizens" is effected, then the hegemony of market ideology will be achieved. Of significance here is that it is an ideological struggle and a debate over values that should, from a democratic point of view, be taking place in the public sphere. I develop this argument more fully in the next chapter. From the dialectical perspective, this period of shifting social relations is historically produced and politically contestable. As this critique of market ideology has illustrated, resistance to the market as the key metaphor and organizing principle of society requires both a rejection of the market model of society that is grounded in democratic theory and a recognition that the hegemonic battle of neoliberal globalization is to reiterate—at this stage— primarily on the terrain of ideology.[22] A more fruitful way of conceptualizing the relationship between capitalism and democracy would be to understand each as mitigating the excesses of the other. Democratic deliberation may not always produce just or ethical results, and the private sphere should be jealously guarded from state action that excessively impinges on economic and personal rights. Likewise, capitalism and the market economy in general may be like Churchill's description of democracy as the worst form of government

---

22. Empirical evidence is pouring in—compliments of what might be called the backlash globalization literature—taking the claims of the globalists to task with hard data such as the following: Boyer and Drache 1996; Berger and Dore 1996; Garrett 1998; Hirst and Thompson 1996; Gill and Mittelman 1997.

except for all th e others, replacing government with socioeconomic order. The risks of chronic social dislocation and of the collapse of capitalism itself are too great if democratic deliberation does not keep its excesses in check.

Recognizing that democracy and capitalism exist in dialectical tension is not new, but specifying variation in the models of developed countries according to how societies negotiate this tension serves to crystallize the link between democratic theory and political economy. If the economy is the site of action concerned with producing, consuming, and distributing the material resources in a given society, and if the polity is the arena wherein decisions are made about "who gets what, where, and how" (the famous Lasswellian definition), then the overlap between these two becomes more obvious and directly relevant to our understanding of income distribution. However, this by no means necessitates a view of reducibility of one sphere to the other. Instead, when political economy is conceptualized as applied democratic theory, it places primacy on the core principles of d emocratic thinking as the normative grounding that I have referred to above. In other words, how we conceive of the separation, inseparability, or interrelations of e conomics and politics is directly related to how we envision democracy. Of course, one may argue that this tactic may simply replace one controversial ambiguity for an other because there are as many definitions of democracy as there are of political economy. Indeed, as David Held observes, "within the history of democratic theory lies a deeply rooted conflict about whether democracy should mean some kind of popular power . . . or an aid to d ecision making" (1995a, 5). Nonetheless, the very questions that orient democratic theory—what is the nature of individual rights and citizenship, the proper form and function of the state, the meaning of liberty and equality—are fundamentally and inextricably linked to the concerns of political economy. Understanding income distribution and, more specifically, income equality and how and why it varies among capitalist democracies requires a focus on how the economy and polity interconnect in ways that influence the meaning and relevance of these questions.

If democratic politics is genuinely about free persons deciding their fates through their own individual volition and collective actions within a certain set of agreed upon rules and norms, then the relationship between economics and politics is not to be decided from above by either scholars or policymakers but by the citizens themselves. Instead of presupposing what this relationship is or sh ould be, this political cultural or id eational dimension should be brought directly into our analytic framework. Applied democratic theory entails both translating the abstract, philosophical concerns into the real issues and problems faced by citizens and taking seriously the views and preferences of those individuals who comprise these democratic societies. It is essential to recognize that varying conceptions of justice may be a considerable force behind how much distributional inequality a given society is willing to tolerate. After all, the presumption when studying long-standing capitalist democracies is that th ere is some significant relationship between the values and preferences of cit izens and the kinds of p olicy outcomes that c haracterize their societies.

Before concluding this chapter, it is u seful to contra st my formulation of political economy as applied democratic theory with the thinking of one of—if not the—most preeminent democratic theorist, Robert Dahl. Dahl is perhaps most widely known for his definition of democracy as "polyarchy" (1966) and for his justification for a p rocedural versus a substantive understanding of what constitutes a democracy. Yet, what is less widely appreciated is how much effort Dahl devoted to exploring the scope of democracy and democratic theory when confronted with questions of economic justice. For instance, in his 1985 work, *A Preface to Economic Democracy,* Dahl questions the relationships between political equality, political liberty, and economic liberty, fundamentally reconsidering the way in which equality and liberty have been cast as locked in an inescapable trade-off. In particular, he offers an analysis and critique of how Tocqueville's view of equality as a potential threat to liberty is mistaken and profoundly misleading. In contrast, he sets out his own conception of the relations between democracy, political equality, and economic liberty and searches for a superior alternative to the system of American corporate capitalism that might produce greater equality without sacrificing liberty. Although he recognizes some of its problems, it is obvious that he is committed to considering the impact of the economic structure of society and how this may distort democratic politics. Dahl's work with Charles Lindblom (1977) also presents a similar critique of democratic theory in light of the interrelations of e conomics and politics and consequently the limits of s eparating substantive and procedural democracy. Both scholars ultimately agree that the inequalities inevitably created by market capitalism will also generate inequalities in the distribution of political resources. In turn, this imbalance of political resources allows certain citizens to exercise more influence over government than others, and as a consequence, the principle of political equality is violated th ereby shaking the moral foundation of representative democracy. It is precisely this insight that makes the growing trend toward higher income inequality a pressing matter for democratic theory and practice, and it in fact bolsters my formulation of political economy as applied democratic theory.

Applied democratic theory is not concerned with establishing a priori whether economic rights or social justice are intrinsic to our estimation of democracy, but it does insist that just because the questions have to do with economic issues does not mean they can legitimately be siphoned off from democratic debate. A central preoccupation of applied democratic theory, then, is to ask how citizens in democratic societies conceive of the relations between politics and economics and the actions of markets and governments. The following chapter demonstrates how this theoretical perspective can provide the basis for a conceptual and empirical model that requires us to take ideas and values seriously as causal forces driving distributive outcomes and explains the way those outcomes vary across capitalist democracies.

# — 2 —

## POLITICAL JUSTICE VERSUS MARKET JUSTICE: WHY VALUES MATTER

> The central conservative truth is that it is culture, not politics, that determines the success of a society. The central liberal truth is that politics can change a culture and save it from itself.
> —DANIEL PATRICK MOYNIHAN, *The New Republic,* 7 July 1986

In the previous chapter I argued that political economy and, especially, comparative analyses of capitalist democracies could and should be usefully conceived as studies in applied democratic theory. Applied democratic theory requires both a normative framing and an empirical treatment of problems of political economy. In the case of explaining variation in income inequality among sixteen different countries, the normative aspect acknowledges that distributive outcomes in established democracies—presumably free and open societies—indubitably reveal some degree of judgment, prioritization, and choice by citizens and policymakers. The empirical element is obvious in that political economic outcomes are quantifiable, material phenomena. However, the key distinction of my approach is the insistence that these material realities also be construed as manifestations of a society's values. The normative and value dimensions inevitably associated with distributive outcomes should be examined empirically while maintaining that the empirical nature of income distribution is inescapably normative. Put dialectically, we can observe the normative empirically while recognizing the empirical as imbued with normativity. Here I am concerned with translating this theoretical argument into a conceptual model that will actually demonstrate what applied democratic theory entails analytically to better explain variation in income inequality.

This chapter shows why the values and preferences of citizens with regard to income inequality and redistribution must be a central part of the investigation. In essence, I am following in the footsteps of the pioneering work of Thompson, Ellis, and Wildavsky (1990), who showed how perceptions and preferences of individuals have causal impact in the social world by sustaining certain types of institutions and social relations. The cultural theory they elaborate centers around how people choose to live; it insists on asking how individuals come to know what their interests are and pays attention to ideas about competing ways of life within a country. A significant parallel between the goals of this study and the approach developed by these scholars is captured by the following statement in the opening of their book *Cultural Theory*: "Instead of a social science that begins at the end—assuming values and beliefs—our theory makes why people want what they want and why people perceive the world the way they do into the central subjects of social inquiry" (1990, 2). Too often social scientific theories have forced a false dualism between the study of culture and values and that of structure and institutions rather than bringing these two dimensions of social life and the human condition together and exploring how they might be either mutually constitutive and interdependent or in dialectical tension. Although this chapter focuses on the ideational as manifested through social values and attitudes, this element of the causal story is inherently connected to the material and institutional aspect of sociopolitical life. Based on principles of democratic theory, values matter in a normative sense, but they have empirical weight as well.

The chapter is divided into four sections. I begin with a brief discussion of the role that values have played in social scientific research generally and more specifically in the comparative political economy literature, and I show why these ideational factors should matter. Having established the importance of taking values seriously, I then identify the specific values and ideas that are most relevant to this comparative study of income inequality. I offer a critique of the theoretical and philosophical debates about distributive justice primarily generated by Rawls (1971) and Nozick (1974) and introduce a different model of popular conceptions of distributive justice that is more congruent with my notion of applied democratic theory. Moving from the realm of abstraction into more empirical territory, the final section presents an analysis of survey data collected to construct the value orientation that characterizes the prevailing socioeconomic and political-cultural ethos in each of the sixteen countries included in the study.

## The Values Debate in Social Science

What is the possible link between values and growing income inequality in capitalist democracies? The thesis of this book is that this link lies primarily in the relationship between societal values and political institutions; thus, this chapter addresses the first part of the analytical puzzle—"why" values matter. At the outset, it is necessary to defend a rather loose definition of values and justify why I use values, ideas, and culture somewhat interchangeably throughout this study. When I invoke the term *ideas*, I mean to imply the opposite of material forces or "structural" variables and, generally speaking, ideas are what serve to formulate worldviews and beliefs from which values are constitutive. At the societal level, values reflect shared understandings and underlying assumptions, provide meaning and orientation to individuals, and may bolster some notion of collective identity. As such, these concepts could be assumed under the rubric of culture as emphasized by Clifford Geertz (1973) as "thick description," but I wish to be somewhat less open-ended in my conception of culture. Ronald Inglehart puts it the following way: "Value systems play an important role in any society. They provide the cultural basis for loyalty to given economic and political systems. And value systems interact with external economic and political factors in shaping social change" (1997, 52). As I will show in this chapter, this is precisely the way in which causation may be imputed to culture and values. Culture in the general sense that is used throughout this book means the values, ideas, and beliefs prevalent in a given society. I tend to employ the term *culture* as a broad explanatory force and the term *values* when I speak of the specific way in which culture is operationalized in the study. Furthermore, I would add that when I refer to culture and values, I in no way mean to describe either as monolithic or immutable factors of social and political life. A comment on the opening quote of this chapter provides greater clarification of this point.

If we replace the word *culture* with *values* in the statement made by the late U.S. senator Patrick Moynihan, the "why it matters" question is reflected in his first truth: values shape the success of a society—however one may define success. Thus, culture or values can be construed as having independent or explanatory power in their own right. With regard to a broad outcome such as income inequality and understanding its comparative context, these specific values might be characterized as those that reveal whether a society prioritizes egalitarianism relative to other attributes of its economy and society.

Reflecting his second truth—that politics can change culture or values—such factors are viewed as more contingent, or we might say values in this sense are dependent variables that are molded by the forces of politics. Whether embracing the first or second truth or both (which is the position I take), the point is values matter because they lie at the real core of democratic deliberation, resistance and contestation, consensus building, and, ultimately, social change. But values or culture broadly speaking are hard to define, even harder to measure, and intrinsically subjective. None of these characteristics is easily absorbed into the goals of social scientific explanation. Yet prominent political and social theorists from Alexis de Tocqueville to Max Weber have posited values, ideas, and culture as key causal forces that drive momentous changes in human development. These two thinkers alone exercise an enduring influence on such grand, metatheoretical questions as what makes democracy work, how do individuals and societies interrelate, and why has capitalism emerged in the Protestant West. Nonetheless, with exception of the recent constructivist interventions in both comparative politics and international relations,[1] the social sciences have had somewhat of a "one step forward, two steps back" relationship with ideational or cultural categories of explanation. Why?

Ideas, values, beliefs, and norms—collectively referred to as "culture" or "ideational forces"—undoubtedly play an important role in shaping human and social phenomenon, but they have had a much more controversial history as explanatory factors in the social sciences than materialist or structural ones for two reasons. The first explanation lies in the scientific evolution of the study of politics and society. The development of the social sciences generally has centered on the need to build theories capable of producing generalizations that can be subjected to systematic, replicable testing. Many have argued that cultural or ideational categories of explanation are in fact antithetical to this tradition. As Ian Shapiro has remarked, "appealing to culture to explain a political outcome is a bit like appealing to upbringing to explain why a person does something[.] Unless we are told which aspect of culture is supposed to account for the outcome in question, there is no way to begin systematic evaluation of the claim" (1998, 40). Shapiro goes further by suggesting that

---

1. A fuller discussion of the impact of constructivism and how it relates to more conventional approaches to integrating ideas and values in our research is beyond the scope of this chapter. For general guides, see Daniel M. Green, ed., *Constructivism and Comparative Politics* (2002), and Peter Katzenstein, ed., *The Culture of National Security* (1996).

cultural approaches are by default a last-resort attempt at explaining phe-nomena and that culture as a causal variable tends to yield merely "residual" explanations. In this light, culture is seen as too broad, too ill-defined, "soft" or "spongy," and resistant to narrow specification to incorporate into cause-and-effect equations. In fact, David Laitin, in a review of cultural approaches in political science, labels research of this nature a "degenerate research pro-gram" according to Lakatos's criteria. He coincidentally cites Lijphart's review of *The Civic Culture Revisited* to note that "precise specification of mecha-nisms linking culture to structure" is the primary lacuna of the research tra-dition engendered by Almond and Verba's classic work (Laitin 1995, 168). Whether for ideological or methodological purposes, ideas and cultural values posited as sources of behavior and policy outcomes have in the final analysis been much less commonly exploited than other more readily quantifiable variables. Discussing the degree of discomfort many political scientists feel with regard to the concept of culture, Marc Howard Ross writes:

> For many, culture complicates issues of evidence, transforming hopes of rigorous analysis into "just so" accounts that fail to meet widely held notions of scientific explanations. Culture violates canons of methodological individualism while raising serious unit of analysis problems for which there are no easy answers. Culture to many neo-Marxists and non-Marxists alike seems like an epiphenomenon offer-ing a discourse for political mobilization and demand-making while masking more serious differences dividing groups and individuals. (1997, 43)

Before elaborating further on this point, a brief comment on the second reason for the relative paucity and less respectable status of ideational/cultural arguments is in order. This second explanation could be characterized as a political one whereas the first might be summed up principally as method-ological or epistemological. By political here I mean to underscore the racial, gender, and class prejudices, as well as the imperialistic implications of some of the previous works that assigned culture a causal role in explaining phe-nomenon as wide-ranging as economic underdevelopment, ethnic violence, authoritarianism, political instability, educational performance, and competi-tiveness. For instance, Orlando Patterson (2000) suggests that many academics criticize works of cultural explanations because they have often been employed by conservative reactionaries wishing to exonerate governments and other public agencies from bearing any responsibilities for social problems. Ironically, this resulted in the "liberal mantra" that cultural explanations tend to produce an invidious "blame the victim" tendency; therefore, even more benign intentions of exploring the effect of culture are often avoided. Patterson adds that another reason cultural arguments are shunned is because policy specialists and analysts assume nothing can be done about culture. In other words, if no policy recommendations can be proffered, the research has no merit or usefulness. Nathan Glazer (2000) has also shown how cultural explanations are associated with judgments tinged with inferiority claims (even if unintended) about race or ethnicity, especially when it comes to explaining development, which illustrates the reluctance many feel about adopting cultural approaches. It is clear why such objectionable associations would deter analysts who might otherwise want to investigate cultural or values-based explanations. Both of these authors, however, seem to agree that these suspicions and rejections of cultural explanations are often based on misunderstandings and presumptions about the invariability of culture and values. For example, it is asserted that identity politics and multiculturalism have paradoxically contributed to a degradation of the general study of culture and its deployment as an explanatory category in human affairs.

Summing up the impact of *The Bell Curve* debate and its effect on African American studies, Patterson argues, "If cultural factors are to be given prime explanatory status in the IQ wars, they cannot be reduced by multicultural and liberal sociological critics to what Margaret Archer has called 'a supine dependence.' This selective censorship of the causal use of the culture concept has distorted the study of Afro-American social history and contemporary issues" (Patterson 2000, 207). In a similar vein, summarily criticizing some of the classic cultural works in political science as explaining culture with culture or avoiding structure-agency problems make for an all-too-easy dismissal of further work deploying culture as a causal variable. These debates, although very important, are a bit too far astray from the main concern here; however, they illustrate the point that culture and ideational explanations have had an uneasy trajectory in the academy for both ideological as well as methodological reasons. However, this should not leave us with a "throw the baby out with the bathwater" solution but rather a determination to improve the way in which culture as a concept and a causal factor is used in social science research. Now I will turn to the specific uses of values and culture in comparative politics, and especially in comparative political economy, to show how this deficiency can be overcome.

## Culture and Values in Comparative Politics

The following discussion is not meant to be a survey of the literature of cultural approaches but a selective analysis of some of the most significant recent contributions to our knowledge and understanding of how cultural factors exercise causality in social, economic, and political life. The single most important work on political culture since Almond and Verba's landmark study in 1963 is arguably Robert Putnam's *Making Democracy Work* (1993). Although many criticisms were lodged against Putnam's argument, most would agree that Putnam's study has done more to ignite a resurgence of political cultural approaches than any other recent work in comparative politics. The study is of particular interest for my argument in that it focuses on the relationship between culture and institutions and mass rather than elite beliefs (although Putnam and his research associates also include interviews with some political elites). Putnam enlisted a range of data on governmental performance, aggregate economic and political participation data, and surveys to explain regional differences of governmental effectiveness and institutional success between Southern and Northern Italy. Despite identical institutional structures, Putnam observed a remarkable difference in regional governance in Italy. Analyzing data from the nineteenth century to the 1980s, the author and his team of researchers found that cultural factors were the most important determinants of success defined as economic development and political stability. Those regions that exhibited greater civic engagement characterized by a high degree of social capital and "generalized reciprocity" or a belief that one's efforts to participate and promote the common good would be reciprocated by others were the most stable and successful examples of flourishing democracy. Although many critical views of Putnam's theory have appeared (Laitin 1995; Tarrow 1996; Levi 1996), few would disagree that his work makes an important theoretical and empirical contributions to our effort to disentangle the linkages between economic, cultural, and institutional factors.

Another contribution that has now survived more than two decades of continued research, empirical refinement, and criticism is that of Ronald Inglehart (1977, 1988, 1990, 1997). Culminating in the publication of *Modernization and Postmodernization* (1997), Inglehart has produced a theory of intergenerational value change that has explained in cultural ter ms the political and personal lifestyle differences between individuals who emphasize materialist values versus postmaterialist ones. His thesis, which has largely b een supported through extensive analysis of survey data, is that people value most that which they have been deprived of in their childhood and youth. This "scarcity hypothesis" explores the crucial relationship between values and the socioeconomic environment and is complemented by his "socialization hypothesis," which holds that one's basic values reflect the conditions that prevailed during one's pre-adult years. The combination of these two hypotheses produces his general model of value formation upon which he bases his argument that younger generations are shifting their attention away from traditional material goals such as law and order, economic security, a strong defense, and so forth that are emphasized by older generations. Having grown up in a climate where those goals were relatively secure, newer generations are embracing postmodern or postmaterial goals of self-expression, personal freedom, and quality of life issues. In other words, only in a period of relative abundance can citizens afford to think about new forms of political participation and a wide variety of new issues such as women's rights, the environment, identity politics, and so on.

What is most significant about Inglehart's findings for the purpose of my argument is that h e shows with empirical evidence that mass belief systems are changing in patter ned and systematically discernable ways and that th is value change has serious and predictable economic, social, and political consequences. According to Inglehart, such changes affect economic growth rates, political party strategies, and the prospects for democratic institutions. Thus, the overall finding is that th ese new value orientations are linked to generational differences that are fundamentally reshaping the nature of politics in advanced industrial societies. Such beliefs and values are "not mere consequences of economic or social changes, but shape socioeconomic conditions, and are shaped by them in reciprocal fashion" (1997, 8). Tapping the extensive database of the *World Values Surveys* conducted in more than forty societies over a twenty-five-year period, Inglehart confirmed that the goals and values of both in dividuals and societies are changing reflecting a sh ift from modernization to p ostmodernization because of th e diminishing marginal utility of economic determinism and growth. Economic factors are decisive under conditions of economic scarcity and physical insecurity, but there is an observable postindustrial, postmaterial syndrome that is no w resulting in a shift away from traditional to rational-legal values and transforming the political agenda of advanced societies and fostering new political movements, new issues, and new parties. Such findings have enormous implications for what we might call the "values matter" school of thought.

In terms of Inglehart's contributions to the progress of social science, he has done the most to advance the civic culture tradition by emphasizing cultural values in his use of cross-national survey data for theory-building purposes. Additionally, both the measures used and the data compiled have widespread applicability as well as predictive and interpretative power and certainly confirm the rich potential of using survey data to study ideas and cultural values among mass publics. Though the postmaterialism thesis has revealed the way in which worldviews and values may influence future economic development and democratic institutional stability, Inglehart is insistent on avoiding both cultural and economic determinism, which is a methodological virtue I aspire to in the design of this study as well.[2] I return to this point in the concluding paragraphs of this chapter.

Cultural variables, or more specifically, values, as causal factors have been largely omitted from most empirical analyses of comparative political economy. According to Peter A. Hall,

> In the field of comparative political economy, approaches that emphasize the role of ideas or the importance of cultural variables to economic policy and performance are less developed than those that place more stress on interests or institutions. However, they have been far from unimportant. The literature that accords a prominent role to such ideas or culture can be divided into three groups, distinguished by the importance each attaches to such variables relative to other causal factors. (1997, 183)

Interestingly, Hall's first two categories describe authors and works that could be classified as more on the institutionalist side of the ledger. In the first group, Hall in fact refers to Goldstein and Keohane's (1993) caution that whereas

2. On this point precisely, Inglehart comments: "as both Marx and Weber argued—belief systems, economic, and politics are intimately related. Their linkages seem to reflect neither a simple Marxian causality (with economics driving culture and politics) nor a simple Weberian causality (with culture driving economics and politics) but reciprocal causal relationships. Cultural, economic, and political systems tend to be mutually supportive in any society that survives for long. They help shape each other, and they are changing the world in ways that are to some extent predictable" (1997, 9).

ideas are important, they should only be incorporated into the causal analyses after all other variables have been given preeminence. Such a position is precisely why the image of cultural explanations as a last resort tends to prevail. From the very outset, culture or ideas as having causal power proceeds from a weak foundation and an assumption that the explanation offered is second best. The second group assigns greater causal priority to ideas. Here Hall includes scholarship on epistemic communities led by the work of Haas and Sikkink on the process of ideational transmission of best practices or strategies within given professional communities, especially economic organizations and government agencies. Goldstein and Keohane's (1993) explanation of U.S. trade policy is also included in this category, but their work is still very cautious about imputing causality to ideas in that her emphasis is primarily on the way in which ideas about trade become institutionalized. Again, although such works unquestionably seek explanatory power from the role of ideas, these scholars are primarily focusing on idea formation and not on values per se. They are generally restricting their analyses to the elite level, not how ideas and values in mass society effect political and economic change, which is the level of analysis most relevant for the purposes of this study. Hall's (1989) earlier work on the power of economic ideas incorporates a broader view in that he and various other contributors to his collected volume trace the appeal of certain economic ideas (in this case, Keynesianism) beyond politicians and experts to show how they resonate with the partisans of particular ideologies as well as with the electorate. As Hall puts it, "ideas are assigned causal force because they can make kinds of social or political coalitions possible" (1997, 184). The real causal force or impact of ideas is identified at the level of institutionalization into what Hall calls the "standard operating procedures" of key organizations and absorbed into the worldviews of those who manage them.

The last group Hall identifies as idea-oriented scholars are the most ambitious in assigning cultural variables causal primacy. Such status stems from the proposition that ideas are believed to be constitutive of basic meaning systems that underlie both individual and collective action. The works falling into this category range from Ziegler's (1997) comparative work on French and German industrial policies to those such as Boyer and Hollingsworth (1997) and Shonfield (1965) who explain differences in national economic policies largely in terms of embedded cultural practices stemming from national historical experience and deep-seated views on the economy. My approach to incorporating ideas and values falls somewhere between the second and third categories.

On the one hand, I am interested in exploring how values may influence a complex economic problem such as income inequality and believe that deeply held beliefs, ideas, and values and how they differ from one society to another might help us understand why income inequality is growing in some countries and not as much in others. I also believe that the values most likely to influence this phenomenon stem from deep-seated historical and cultural notions about the proper roles of markets versus governments. On the other hand, however, if we are to speak in terms of causation, I am not persuaded that "ideas all the way down" can yield satisfactory results. Consequently, the second category in which the ideas and values are essential to identify but not exclusively sufficient to explain is closer to the strategy I pursue. Thus, the conceptual model I construct is one in which ideas are conceived as important independent variables and certainly not ones that should be relegated to a default position when all other possible causal factors have been eliminated. But ideas are also not sufficient in their own right to establish precise causal links to broadscale outcomes of the political economy.

One approach that stands out as having achieved an important breakthrough in confirming the critical, causal role of norms and values in explaining economic change is the work of Vivien Schmidt. Schmidt has produced a wealth of theoretical and empirical scholarship that deepens our understanding of state-business relations and the transformation of the French economy (1996), explains the impact of internationalization on (and adjustments and responses of) advanced welfare states (2000), and generally expands our knowledge of the political economy of Europe and the complex relationships between domestic economic policy and the processes of Europeanization and globalization (2002). Here I will focus specifically on how she has used values as an explanatory factor in some of her work, and in the following chapter I will comment more broadly on her analysis of different forms of European capitalism and contrast it with the Varieties of Capitalism (VOC) school and their respective insights for institutional analysis.

In a collected volume co-edited with Fritz Scharpf (2000), Schmidt and the contributing authors focus on the challenges and responses of advanced welfare states arising from the pressures of the international economic environment.[3] Schmidt examines the role of values and discourse in the politics

---

3. There are only two other contributing authors besides Schmidt and Scharpf in *From Vulnerability to Competitiveness,* volume 1 of their two-volume work, *Welfare and Work in the Open Economy* (2000).

of adjustment and more specifically seeks to explain how governments managed to overcome (or not) intense and narrow, interest-based opposition and persuade electoral majorities of the merits of new policy programs. It is worth quoting Schmidt at length to show how she articulates the values and discourses that facilitate successful adjustment.

> [Values and discourses] involve forms of p olitical communication which, in the continuum between "bargaining" and "arguing," are located closer to the arguing pole. To describe them, I will use the term of "policy discourse." While this discourse must necessarily provide the cognitive definitions of the problem and the cause-and-effect relationships defining effective solutions, the emphasis here is o n the normative content of th e arguments proposed to ju stify unpopular policy initiatives. The reason is worth spelling out. The welfare state itself is a socio-p olitical construct which, since it involves insurance and redistribution, could not exist witho ut the support of strong normative arguments and moral convictions. (Schmidt 2000, 230)

Thus Schmidt sets out to show that no w elfare-state reform could succeed without an effective appeal to values and a shift in the underlying definition of moral appropriateness. To further elaborate what her objectives are and how she structures her analysis, Schmidt states that she will

> explore the democratic legitimization of reform of the welfare state by considering how governments actively sought to j ustify policy change through normative discourse. By focusing on moments of crisis or transition when values are generally made explicit in public debates as opposed to continuing as unquestioned background assumptions embedded in inst itutional practice, this chapter seeks to offer comparative insights not only into the values that remain central to d ifferent polities' notions of social ju stice but also into the discourses that appeal to the values in their efforts to legitimize policy change. Moreover, it considers not only the substantive content of those discourses but also how the national institutional context affects the locus of d iscourse as well as the course of reform. Finally, it raises questions about whether there is a n ew emerging

value consensus about the appropriate kinds of policies for a new, less vulnerable, more competitive welfare state in the open economy. (Schmidt 2000, 231)

Through extensive case studies of several countries among each of the three families of welfare states, Anglo-Saxon, Scandinavian, and Continental, Schmidt executes this strategy to powerful effect. Employing tightly compared analyses of matched pairs of countries or the same country at different time points to control for other variables, she is able to demonstrate that in the face of similar events (economic crises), ideas, values (specifically the core values differentiating each of the three broad types of welfare states), interests, and institutions (single actor or multiactor systems), the presence or absence of a coherent legitimizing discourse (what she characterizes as coordinative or communicative) is what made the difference in determining successful adjustment.

I value most in Schmidt's work the thoroughness with which she tackles the issues that Hall and others have raised as being the most difficult challenge facing scholars working in the idea-oriented tradition: the need to disentangle ideational or cultural factors from other kinds of causal variables. Enlisting authoritative knowledge of specific countries, deploying the logic of comparative methodology and detailed empirical accounts of the economic situation in each case, bearing in mind the institutional constraints and differences between countries, and weighing interest-based explanations against her arguments, she is able to show how crucial values are in terms of how the discourse (that appeals to such value orientations) is instrumentalized in a decisive way over and above competing factors that could account for policy change. In this way she specifies the causal links and does so using an analytical model that is highly dynamic. Her findings are of particular interest here in that she has carefully demonstrated with empirical evidence why values matter and precisely how they shape economic outcomes. Thus there is a great deal of similarity in the way we conceptualize the role of ideas and the causal influence they can have. One important difference, however, is that I examine actual survey data of mass publics to measure values whereas Schmidt uses discourse analysis of elite rhetoric and gauges it against more static definitions of the core values that presumably undergird each type of welfare state. A second difference is that I focus in my study on the actual relationship between value orientations and specific institutional settings to determine if we get greater explanatory power from seeing both as independent but also highly interactive causal forces. The point of this discussion has been to affirm that when studying democracies, there indeed should be a meaningful link between these value systems and outcomes.

We have established why values need to be considered as independent or explanatory factors in our study of political economic outcomes; it is now important to specify which values or which aspects of political culture are most significant for establishing a causal link to patterns of income inequality. If we follow the straightforward injunction of Roger Keesing that it is best "to narrow the concept of 'culture' so that it includes less and reveals more" (1974, 73), we can avoid many of the perils of previous cultural approaches and at the same time assert with greater clarity and confidence that values matter. In the case of searching for the causal roots of variation in income inequality among well-established capitalist democracies, the specific attributes of political culture that identify citizens' values and beliefs about income inequality, distributive justice, and the proper roles of markets and governments are what matter most. Before turning to a discussion of how the values question relates to theoretical discussions of distributive justice, it is important to delimit the nature of the dependent variable. Studying comparative patterns of income distribution is a particularly useful way of assessing the overall quality of life of a society as well as the real situation or life chances of individuals who comprise it. The growing tendency of scholars to prefer the Human Development Index to gross domestic product (GDP) figures is indicative of this compulsion to enlarge our conception of the economic indicators and the depth of information they can convey about a society. An anecdote recounted by Karl Deutsch to describe the importance of analyzing income inequality helps draw out this point. He tells the story of a man eating a whole, roasted chicken in a room, and a hungry man looking on. A statistician looking in through the window reported that on average there was a half a chicken per capita in the room. This observation did nothing to relieve the man who was starving, yet it is taken as an objective and useful account of resources available in society, and in some instances it is the sole measure that purports to describe the general welfare of a society. Studying income distribution reveals more about general welfare in that we learn how equally or unequally those resources are shared throughout society.

Amartya Sen (1992) suggests that the central question underlying work on equality is really "equality of what?" He insists that most empirical and philosophical work done on the issue of equality assumes away fundamental interpersonal diversities to simplify the analytics but that this is done at a high cost because substantial inequalities in well-being and freedom may result from an equal distribution of income given individuals' variable needs and circumstances (29–30). In reviewing Sen's contribution to theories of distributive justice, Roemer recalls his argument (1980) that Rawls's reaction against welfarism went too far in the other direction. Sen did not completely reject Rawls, but as Roemer characterizes it,

> [Sen] claimed that primary goods were not the appropriate maximanda. The focus should be on what goods do for people, and they do things for people to escape morbidity, to be adequately nourished, to have mobility, to achieve self-respect, to take part in the life of the community and to be happy (Sen 1993, 36). These "doings and beings" Sen calls functionings. Rawls's theory suffers from a "fetish handicap" (Sen 1980) in focusing on goods as such. If the various institutional primary goods were being equally supplied (prerogatives and powers, the social bases of self-respect), then Rawls would call for equalizing the remaining one, income: but, Sen says, that is wrong. Incomes should not be equalized, but distributed in such a manner as to equalize the functionings that persons can achieve. (Roemer 1996, 188–89)

I associate my view of the significance and meaning of income inequality with the relevance that Sen attributes to it in his "capability approach." Sen notes that the evaluation of inequality is closely linked with an assessment of poverty, which he sees as the "deprivation of some minimum fulfillment of elementary capabilities" (Sen 1993, 9). He argues that this consideration is particularly relevant in understanding the nature of poverty in the richer countries. Just as for Sen, the relationship between "the incomes and the capability to lead secure and worthwhile lives" most interests me. To force the issue of why an examination of income inequality facilitates—or perhaps requires—a view of political economy as applied democratic theory, one need only briefly consider how persistent inequalities in one domain—the economic—may filter into and inhibit or jeopardize equality in the other domain—the political. This is increasingly evident given the growing influence of money in politics (especially in the case of the U.S. elections), but regardless of that particular phenomenon, the simple fact is that the democratic polity is built upon an egalitarian principle whereas the capitalist economy is premised on inequality.

David Cameron (1988) refers to this tension as "one of the great and enduring political-economic paradoxes" (219) and describes its potential consequences as follows:

> Even if the economic inequalities do not spill into the political realm and thereby distort, corrupt, and otherwise emasculate democratic politics, their existence may erode the legitimacy of the polity. The public may, with some reason, take the perpetuation of economic inequalities as indicative of the confinement of the egalitarian principle to one domain of life rather than its generalization to all of social life. Or it may conclude from the continued presence of economic inequalities that the polity, although founded upon and committed to an egalitarian principle, is weak and politically emaciated because it appears to be incapable of enacting and implementing policies that are consistent with its organizing principle. (220)

The relationship between political equality and economic equality has long been a central concern of democratic theory, but it should also be of significance to students of political economy and particularly comparative political economy. In this vein, it is instructive to review how theoretical debates about distributive justice have developed and what relevance they may have for our study of income inequality—in other words, how we can use these debates to help shape and confine our analytical specification of cultural values to those most germane to the causal argument being made here.

## Theoretical and Popular Conceptions of Justice: What Matters More?

I do not intend to examine in great detail the whole substance of the debates generated by Rawls's seminal work *A Theory Of Justice* (1971) but rather to highlight how these theoretical debates have reached an impasse that can be broken by taking a more applied approach and one that can be fruitfully derived from the work of Robert Lane. One should be concerned with theoretical discussions or philosophical debates about justice because ideas matter, and even academic debates affect public thinking about one of the master concepts of both political science and democracy itself.[4] Do theories about justice filter down to the public and help inform ordinary citizens and shape their views on the implications of certain economic phenomenon? Or, do public debates and what is actually transpiring in civil society and the political sphere influence theoretical work? Put another way, is there any relationship between popular conceptions of justice and debates within the academy? As the Rawls-Nozick debate reveals, there are some links, however tenuous, between theoretical and popular conceptions of justice, but ultimately my main interest is in establishing what matters more for clarifying how values about distributive justice may impact actual outcomes or help explain comparative differences in degrees of income inequality.

The topic of income inequality forces questions about justice even if the way it is being studied is geared toward empirical questions. As Chapter 1 showed, underlying normative assumptions about how market distributions of income occur pervade all of the various approaches in political economy. In the realm of political philosophy and at least since the writings of John Locke, understandings of the origins and rights of private property and the various ways to account for or to justify economic inequality has long been the central preoccupation of those concerned with matters of social or distributive justice. No other work of moral and political philosophy of the twentieth century has done as much to propel debates about justice as that of the publication of John Rawls's *A Theory of Justice* in 1971. Primarily motivated by a concern to counter utilitarianism and offer an alternative view to the utility maximizing principle, Rawls identifies principles of social justice as normative standards that apply to what he refers to as the "basic structure of society." Rejecting utilitarian aggregation as too weak to provide a strong foundation for liberal democratic freedoms, individual rights, or distributive considerations, the author articulates a set of liberal egalitarian principles that share a common foundation and a prioritized order that cannot be compromised. In societies that have attained a certain level of development, the first basic liberty principle prioritizes civil liberties, freedom of conscience

4. For instance, Friedrich von Hayek, Nobel laureate for the prize in economics of 1974, became lionized by many business and political leaders. Ironically, this is what he had to say about justice: "I have come to feel strongly that the greatest service I can still render to my fellow men would be that I could make the speakers and writers among them thoroughly ashamed ever again to employ the term 'social justice'" (1976, 97). Prime Minister Margaret Thatcher would be of the same mind when she made an appeal to the values of self-reliance and the need to banish the notion of society from the British political lexicon. More discussion of this appears in Chapter 5.

and expression, and rights to freely associate and participate in the political process.

The second principle is that of democratic equality; it is most consequential for our concern with income inequality. The principle is divided into two subprinciples with the first, the "principle of fair equality of opportunity," requiring the elimination of formal discrimination but also of inequalities that stem from what he calls the "social lottery" of family situation or class background. The "difference principle" is an evaluation for just differences in income and wealth and requires that such inequalities be arranged to benefit the least advantaged members of society as much as possible. Next, Rawls deploys a hypothetical contractarian argument to show the soundness of his two principles as emerging from rational agreement between parties in an original position whose goal is to advance the good of those they represent, but who are fairly situated behind a "veil of ignorance" and thus oblivious to both the specific conceptions of the good or the particular situations of other individuals. Aware only of their own needs as free and equal citizens, the parties then proceed in two stages. They first consider the effects of the principles on the individuals' share of "social primary goods" (by this Rawls means basic liberties, opportunities, self-respect, income, wealth, etc.). Because of the implied assumption that principles of social justice are more plausible if social cooperation can be secured, the parties then consider ways the competing principles shape individual motivation and generate their own support once implemented. In other words, the intuition is that the conception of "justice as fairness" should prevail as the parties enter into agreement voluntarily, and it is presumed that everyone's well-being depends on a form of cooperation without which no one could enjoy a satisfactory life.

In his later work, Rawls would substantially elaborate and modify these earlier statements, but before discussing his final formulations, let's turn to his chief critic.[5] Also rejecting utilitarian positions but strongly opposed to Rawls's theory of "justice as fairness," Robert Nozick's *Anarchy, State, and Utopia* (1974) defends a historical entitlement conception of justice. Nozick's objective is to show that a state might be just even if it fails to meet basic

5. See especially John Rawls, *Political Liberalism* (New York: Columbia University Press, 1996) and Erin Kelly, ed., *Justice as Fairness: A Restatement* (Cambridge, Mass.: The Belknap Press of Harvard University Press, 1999). For a survey of the literature spawned by Rawls's work, see Henry Richardson and Paul Weithman, eds., *The Philosophy of Rawls: A Collection of Essays* (New York: Garland, 1999).

needs or pursue other political objectives and performs only such minimal functions as protecting individuals from theft and fraud and ensuring contracts are upheld. For Nozick, it is illegitimate to use the coercive power of the state to ameliorate the social or economic situations of some, for it would inevitably involve the violation of rights and liberties of others in so doing. In fact, he proclaimed that "taxation of earnings from labor is on a par with forced labor" (1974, 169). In his framework, private property is the cherished value to be considered in any understanding of distributive justice. The central task of a theory of justice is to explain wh y and how individuals attain certain entitlements. Nozick concludes that principles of justice must be historical; therefore, making the justice of a distribution dependent on its origins—as long as it was generated by means of a voluntary process—arrangements and outcomes could be declared just. Moreover, any principles of justice requiring distribution based on merit, need, or productivity are ill-conceived or unsound because such would necessitate a denial of individual liberty to transfer their holdings as they see fit. Finally, Nozick also justifies a principle of acquisition according to which individuals can unilaterally acquire entitlements in un-owned resources if doing so does not make others worse off than they would have been had those resources remained unowned. Thus vastly unequal distributions produced in capitalist economies are entirely consistent with such views of justice because they presumably and minimally uphold the Lockean proviso of leaving "enough and as good" for others.

Many prominent theorists would enter these debates with some attempts at reconciling the two conceptions, such as Dworkin (1981), who argued that liberty and equality are interdependent elements of a single political ideal. Even though he endorsed Nozick's views on private property in the means of production, he ultimately sided with Rawls in his conviction that something could legitimately be done to regulate economic inequalities. G. A. Cohen would challenge Rawls's, Dworkin's, and Nozick's conceptions and articulate an alternative view that "justice requires an ethos governing daily choice which goes beyond one of obedience to just rules" (2000, 136). Despite the plethora of articles and books responding to the justice debates as staked out in these two enormously influential publications, no resolution or consensus evolved as to what standard or conception of justice might be the most appropriate or morally superior. Instead, after three decades of various iterations of the Rawls-Nozick debates, we are essentially left with an ideological stalemate. As one commentator referring to the ongoing political conflict has summed it up, "Rawls supplied the philosophical framework for the side of the debate that advocates public policies directed at improving the relative distributions of the least advantaged, Robert Nozick's *Anarchy, State, and Utopia* (1974) supplied a framework for the other. Nozick's is a theory that gives primacy to liberty over any attempts to undermine distributive inequality; Rawls seeks to construct a theory in which commitment to liberty and equality are compatible" (Young 1998, 482)

One of the most novel works that transcends such a binary theoretical predicament is that of Ross Zucker's *Democratic Distributive Justice* (2001). Zucker has produced a refreshing new perspective on the relationships between democratic theory and economic justice and a compelling argument for a more egalitarian distribution of income. It is refreshing in the sense that he offers a moral argument for limiting income inequality that is stronger, and in my view more persuasive, than any argument hitherto provided by liberals, critical theorists, Marxists, or communitarians. Zucker thoroughly examines the assumptions of liberal and neoclassical theories—in particular the concept of the autonomous person—that justify unequal distributions of income and wealth in liberal theories of property. In the next phase of his argument, he constructs a competing view of the "socially formed" person that he claims affects calculations of dueness in ways that would result in a more egalitarian form of property rights than found in either classical or welfare state liberalism. Zucker then develops an argument that shows how the social theory perspective allows an interpretation of capital-based markets as having a community dimension that is often denied in liberal political theory as well as by economists. In challenging the premises and assumptions of other theories of property and distributive justice and introducing his alternative, Zucker contends that

> excessively individualistic and unsystematically social premises about the person, when used in justificatory arguments, warp principles of distribution by skewing them in an inegalitarian direction. While a weakly formulated social concept of the person may point toward an egalitarian distribution of income and property, it cannot ground this principle firmly enough to prevent backsliding. But if the social concept of the person is strengthened and the correct inferences are drawn from it, it can securely underpin the egalitarian principle. (2001, 7)

Complementary to h is social th eory of th e person, Zucker proceeds throughout the book to mount a case for a substantive as opposed to a procedural view of democracy, and from all of this he derives a democratic distributive property right that is forcefully summarized in the following sentences. "As a condition of basic freedom, the redistributory property right accrues the supreme ethical worth possessed by other rights of basic freedom. Having supreme ethical worth, the redistributory property right is indispensable to the core of a democracy that internalizes justice" (2001, 292). Although I believe this argument advances notions of justice and economic democracy in the best tradition of Dahl and Lindblom and one that certainly resonates with my development of a perspective of political economy as applied democratic theory, the problem remains that it is an e xclusively theoretical argument. Although I agree with Zucker in principle, it is not clear how his contributions may affect public conceptions of justice or policy debates at this point; therefore, his argument remains at a l evel of abstraction that is aloof to th e causal chains I am trying to elucidate.

Much more pragmatic and generally consistent—in spirit if not letter— with the argument I am making is the seminal study by Jennifer Hochschild (1981). Her study explored American beliefs about distributive justice by conducting in-depth interviews with a small but diverse number of participants from different socioeconomic backgrounds and political ideologies to probe values concerning the fairness of existing income distributions and other economic resources. Contrary to conventional wisdom, Hochschild found that these values were not so m uch determined by a respondent's social st ation or ideology but rather varied according to the three domains she specified— social, economic, and political. In general, Americans were more egalitarian and supportive of public assistance than one might think, given the assumptions of r ugged individualism and suspicion of big go vernment. However, this egalitarianism depended largely on the extent to which public effort was couched in ter ms of basic needs, investment, or contingent upon results. As we will see shortly, these finding are consistent with the claims that R obert Lane makes about the American preference for market justice, but it is significant to point out that both of these scholars have discovered the perceptual contingency of such values. Similarly, Lockhart's (1989) conception of socioeconomic rights drew on Hochschild's work as he proposed that support for any government redistribution in the U.S. context had to be needs driven. This conceptualization of socioeconomic rights would have no explicit goal of achieving substantive equality through redistribution from rich to poor but would merely ensure basic material needs of those individuals who are unable to contribute to and participate fully in society or who confront unexpected hazards of life. In essence, socioeconomic rights as theorized by Lockhart would not "threaten marketplace norms . . . and would mesh with the work-ethic principle of effort and reward" (44). The work of these scholars underscores the critical role that values play in debates about distributive justice, whether at the elite or mass level. But their contributions are primarily directed to understanding the American public because both scholars are concerned either with understanding the roots of American views of fairness or with showing how a particular conception of socioeconomic rights could be tailored to American beliefs and values.

Despite this level of abstraction, the defining contours of the theoretical debates continue to revolve around what the legitimate realm of state action is when it comes to regulating the economy in distributive matters. Rather than a stronger philosophical/theoretical defense of egalitarianism, this overview has revealed that what is necessary now (particularly in an age of increasing globalization that is rendering domestic policy priorities inseparable from international economic realities) is a more grounded conceptual vision of the legitimate right of citizens—and, by extension, their societal values—to determine what the boundaries of government and market behavior should be. It is possible and desirable from a pragmatic point of view, then, to develop a conceptual model that would integrate both normative and empirical questions of distributive justice into our analytical framework for understanding why income inequality varies in capitalist democracies. The work of Robert Lane is an enormously useful resource in this endeavor.

Robert Lane's (1986) "Market Justice, Political Justice" is an effort to explain why the American public displays an apparent preference for market justice over political justice when comparing the way governments and markets serve different purposes, satisfy wants and needs, and distribute valued goods in society. Lane's elucidation of how individuals make justice-based defenses of the functionings of markets and governments is directly relevant to how opinions are formulated about the distribution and redistribution of income. Given that unimpeded market processes will inevitably produce income inequities, it is important to identify to what extent individuals accept market distributions as just or, conversely, prefer that market allocations be altered through some form of "political justice." Lane's very thorough and complex analysis of the structural and ideological roots of Americans' preference of market justice does not easily lend itself to br ief summary; what follows instead is a r econstruction of his argument that merely highlights the value it brings to the present study of income inequality. It is cr itically important to show the potential effects of the preference of market justice for distributive outcomes and its causal link to in creasing income inequality in some countries compared to relatively stable and more egalitarian distributions in other countries where market justice is not a dom inant or prevailing sociocultural norm.

Lane's aim is "not to clarify philosophical justice; [but to] illuminate concepts of the legitimacy of markets and politics, to contribute to an u nderstanding of the forces of social change" (384). His analysis begins by probing the "origins and elements of a sense of injustice" and offering the following conceptual formula of distributive justice: "*Who* distributes *what to whom,* in virtue of what *criterial characteristics,* by what *procedures,* with what *distributive outcomes?*" (italics in or iginal, 385). The author then analyzes ea ch of these italicized terms and compares their market and political expressions. Lane draws on various surveys and previous studies of American attitudes to illustrate why Americans can be said to prefer market methods to political methods. He concludes:

> On balance, therefore, it seems that the public tends to believe that the market system is a m ore fair agent than the political system. People tend to include the problem cases in the political domain and exclude them from the market. They ignore many of the public benefits and, with certain exceptions, prefer market goods to political goods. They prefer the market's criteria of earned deserts to the polity's criteria of equality and need, and believe that market procedures are more fair than political procedures. (387)

The connection between the belief that the market follows natural laws and the notion that individuals are responsible for their own fate (the political culture of individualism) is quite important and helps to explain why the market in effect eludes criticism and becomes insulated from complaints of injustice. The belief in the laws of supply and demand and the resulting perception of a "harmony of interest" means that individuals never attribute injustice to the market mechanism itself. For example, Lane describes a worker who assesses his contribution to productivity not in ter ms of it s intrinsic worth but by what he is actually paid. To paraphrase, a worker gets exactly what he deserves and a firm must pay what it pays. This form of attribution requires a person to believe that if he is unemployed, it is by his own discretion, but if a firm lays him off, it is because it had no choice. Lane remarks, "No system could develop a more elegant device for avoiding attributions of injustice to the rewards and punishments it distributes" (392). It follows also that if it is widely believed that the market produces a supposed harmony of interest, the problem of distributive justice is moot. Any government interference with a m arket outcome such as particular distributions of in come would be prohibited because the original distribution is s een as more fair (even if it is h ighly inegalitarian) than would be the resulting redistribution of an already conflictual, thus tainted, political procedure.

As for the broader consequences of a prevailing tendency to favor market justice, I argue that this ideological predisposition effectively de-legitimates collective political action, which is required for market-produced hierarchies and inequities to be challenged and perhaps corrected. For example, the degree to which the class compromise becomes institutionalized through various models of the welfare state depends in part upon how entrenched market logic is in the public psyche. Esping-Andersen's (1990) typology of welfare states in essence reflects this interpretation. His trifold clusters of welfare states are categorized according to the main ideological tendencies assumed to underlie each model. The conservative, liberal, and social democratic welfare state regimes vary in terms of how extensive the process of de-commodification is with the social democratic version, of course, exceeding the others—a direct result, one might argue, of its citizens' rejection of the market metaphor for all domains of well-being. For my purposes, the effect of the welfare state on reducing income inequality is gauged at this deeper ideological level.[6]

If there is some degree of truth to the idea that the market distributes and the state redistributes, a third dimension should be identified (for our purpose here) that falls in between the state and the market—politicized civil society. As Karl Polanyi poignantly remarked, "The separation of p owers, which Montesquieu (1748) had meanwhile invented, was now used to separate the people from power over their own economic life" (1944, 225). Polanyi argued

---

6. Walter Korpi and Joakim Palme (1998) have developed a model that addresses more fully the empirical effect of different models of welfare state institutions on inequality and poverty.

that the attempt to implement the utopian idea of a "self-regulating market" involved a devastating disembedding of the economy from social life. His reminder that this effort was in itself an enormous political maneuver shed light on the ideological blinders of market justice and it would seem to resonate with those skeptical of the turn toward a neoliberal as opposed to a more social democratic model of political economy. The following passage reinforces the significance of giving weight to this aspect of political culture, labeled broadly the prevailing sociocultural norms or values about distributive justice and the legitimacy of politics versus markets:

> What happens in a political economy in which the market is regarded as "fair and wise" and political practices, at least, are regarded as neither? In such a society, however much people sympathize with the unemployed, the handicapped, and even children, they will regard these nonproductive others as externalities, for in the market they are undeserving. People tend to prefer somewhat more egalitarian outcomes than the market provides, but their love of market methods inhibits them from advocating any solutions that seem to frustrate these methods. . . . Astigmatism of this sort also weakens collective effort, through unions and labor parties, to alter life chances. Minimal government is assured and people are endowed with more commodities and fewer collective goods. (Lane 1986, 397)

Thus, the key insight of Lane's analysis of varying conceptions of justice and its relevance to my argument here is that cultural norms or societal values viewed in this light have obvious ramifications for what democratic politics may have the ethical authority to do versus what activities or outcomes are deemed best left up to the market mechanism. Where market justice is strongly ingrained in the collective conscience, state intervention in the economy is less likely; thus, one would expect to find more inegalitarian income distributions compared to societies whose acceptance of the moral authority of democratic politics is stronger than the belief that justice is rightfully meted out through market forces. Robert Boyer's (1990) work on market theory lends support to this claim; he has argued that the "market" has never been as widely embraced by continental Europe as it has been by the Anglo-American tradition, which in turn is generally confirmed by Esping-Andersen's discernment of different worlds of welfare regimes. Accordingly, if one is concerned with bringing democratic theory to bear on our study of political economy or our deployment of the tools of political economy to explain sociopolitical and economic outcomes, a primary compulsion should be to take citizens' views about the legitimate roles of politics and markets seriously.

Furthermore, Lane's analysis is useful because it provides a conceptual lens whereby these cultural attitudes may be neatly specified in a way that is broadly generalizable across all capitalist democracies. It is reasonable to assume that individuals in democratic societies have varying predispositions about the proper functions of government (or politics) and the market. It is also likely that general attitudes about inequality and justice may be at least partially captured by this distinction of market and political justice, which then allows us to gauge and aggregate the sociocultural element that may contribute to a causal explanation of income inequality. Yet despite the important role that political culture may play in determining how much discretion a government may or may not have in terms of altering market processes or outcomes in a manner that may affect income distribution, without qualifying this perspective, we risk reifying culture and imbuing it with the properties of agency that cannot be sustained empirically. Furthermore, although placing primacy on the role of ideas and norms is extremely important, privileging this element to the exclusion of other factors would assign too much causal weight to culture. Similarly, to emphasize that inequality is endemic to capitalism gives preference to structure, belies the mediating role of welfare state institutions and policies, and neglects the wide-ranging impact of the diverse models of political economy.

For strong theoretical reasons, I examine the independent effect of values on income inequality. As it has been hypothesized earlier, a prevalence of attitudes in support of political justice should be linked to lower income inequality. From a methodological point of view, however, to posit culture alone as a driving factor behind income inequality is to reify this powerful but indirect force. Ideas and norms may influence behavior and shape the content of public policies as well as individual and collective choices, but ideas alone cannot act. Thus, one of the two core independent variables deployed in this study—values, broadly defined here as attitudes toward the competing roles of states and markets in determining a society's distributional outcomes—needs further qualification. To take culture seriously as having a causal role in shaping distributional outcomes, we must first conceptualize the specific aspect of culture that is salient with regard to how income gets distributed and then specify the linkage between this ideational element and the concrete world of behavior or action. It is the latter that has proven to be the greatest deficiency in "culturalist" research. Thus, imputing causation to cultural factors without attention to specification issues linking the realms of superstructure and structure, to paraphrase Antonio Gramsci, has been the biggest flaw in this approach to political science and one I seek to redress in this study. The way in which I conceptualize political culture for the purposes of this study stems from my identification of Robert Lane's notions of political justice versus market justice as being the salient attribute of culture that might contribute explanatory power to our attempt to understand cross-national variation in income inequality. Although theoretically innovative and extremely valuable in pointing toward the critical role that the perceptions of citizens play in shaping justice claims and—by extension—outcomes in a society, Lane's claims are based on secondary and random accounts of survey research in which there is little more than a random collection of various studies that can at best represent weak proxies of his otherwise theoretically powerful concepts.

Highlighted earlier but worth reiterating here is the implicit theory of social change embedded in Lane's analysis. Toward the end of the article he writes:

> We have argued that the preference for market justice over political justice has deep structural roots in the purposes and values of the two institutions, in the way they satisfy wants, in their differential employment of justice criteria, and in the levels of popular justice assessments in the two domains. We have seen how the attributions of causes, how the differences between initial distribution and redistribution, and how the application of rights differentially affect justice claims. The perceived harmony of interest in the market was contrasted with the perception of conflict in politics. While these structural effects are indeed significant, at an even deeper level they are themselves partly perceptual, ideological. (1986, 397)

Hence, social change can take place through little or no institutional or structural change but rather a shift in perception, especially one that restores political justice to favor and adopts what Lane refers to as a "community point of view." This is precisely the insight embodied in the second truth articulated by Moynihan, addressed at the beginning of the chapter—with political action, perceptions can be altered and thus value change induced. I return to this idea of perceptual or ideological shift in the Conclusion of this book.

## Analysis of the Survey Data

I seek to strengthen and extend Lane's conceptualization through a more formal and direct operationalization of what he refers to as popular conceptions of justice. In attempting to capture this important distinction between preferences for market justice and political justice, I proceeded by examining the body of survey research pertaining to individual attitudes on the role of government and welfare spending or income redistribution. Consistent with an understanding of political economy as applied democratic theory, we should be concerned with th is political cultural d imension of what is oth erwise conventionally perceived as strictly an economic outcome. Because all of the cases reviewed here are long-established democracies with market economies, it is reasonable to assume that individuals in these societies have values and preferences about whether income distribution should be left up solely to the market or whether some type of intervening and redistributive governmental action should attempt to ameliorate inequitable market outcomes. As I described earlier, Robert Lane's notion of political justice and market justice captures an important distinction that serves to map out such public conceptions or sociocultural attitudes about the respective roles of markets and politics in distributing material resources such as income.

As an empirical indicator for this potential explanatory variable, I located specific survey data that addressed individual attitudes about the proper scope of government activity in the redistribution of income. This was no easy task because much of the survey literature focuses solely on one country, conducts two-country comparisons, or uses the Eurobarometer database to examine opinion among western Europeans.[7] In contrast to such common strategies in survey research, this research design necessitated identical survey questions

7. The European Science Foundation has sponsored "Beliefs in Government," which is the most exhaustive collection of mass surveys of attitudes in Western Europe to date. The goal behind the original project was to examine the changes in mass opinion about the proper scope and roles of government, which is precisely the kind of question I am addressing here. Unfortunately, there is no corollary collection of the same magnitude for the United States, Canada, Australia, and New Zealand. For reviews of the multivolume work, see *West European Politics* 21:194–201 and *The American Political Science Review* (1998).

systematically applied across the set of sixte en countries. Additionally, the time span had to be consistent with the measurements of the other variables in the analysis. The final constraint was ensuring that enough lead time for such cultural variables to have a causal impact on the dependent variable was taken into consideration to avoid the problem of backward causation.[8]

To operationalize and measure the preference for political or market justice, I needed specific survey data that registered individual attitudes about the boundaries of legitimate governmental action with regard to income distribution. Using cross-national individual level surveys, I am able to connect individual attitudes to the broader societal level of analysis and thereby identify whether coherent sociocultural patterns exist regarding public conceptions of distributive justice. Again, given the most basic assumptions of democratic theory, one would expect these prevailing patterns of citizen opinion to have some bearing on policy outcomes. Opinion on political justice versus market justice in relation to income inequality is measured by using survey data from the cross-national component of the General Social Survey (GSS), the International Social Surveys Programme (ISSP) module index on Social Equality and the Role of Go vernment (1985, 1987, 1990, 1992, and 1999) and the cumulative file of the European Community Studies, otherwise known as the Eurobarometers (1970–99). Though I had to employ data from two different sources, the sampling techniques were virtually identical.[9]

An additional complication encountered in comparative survey analysis is the consistency and the phrasing of the questions across countries and time. This problem was minimal because the different surveys I located were very comparable and captured the essence of my use of Lane's conceptualization and, with the exception of several countries in my sample, were repeated in identical form over the time period necessary to correspond adequately with the three time points at which the dependent variable was measured.[10] The

8. It is noteworthy that one of the most recent and widely cited scholarly works using survey data to forge a cultural explanation of economic and political change as well as democratic stability is the work by Inglehart (1997), which in fact is guilty of this methodological flaw. For example, the author uses attitudinal data on motivation and postmaterialism in the 1990s to explain e conomic growth rates from the period of 1960–88. See Duane Swank's (1998) review of *Modernization and Postmodernization* in *Comparative Political Studies* for a more in-depth critique.

9. Data from both org anizations derive from cross-sectional surveys with a r epresentative sample of adults aged eighteen or over, with approximately two thousand respondents from the ISSP surveys and one thousand from the Eurobarometers, and with all figures weighted according to population in each country.

10. For New Zealand, Norway, Sweden, and Switzerland, the surveys were only available for one time point.

following survey items were selected as the most appropriate representations of the cultural variable used here:

1. "It is the responsibility of the government to reduce the differences in income between people with high incomes and those with low incomes." (ISSP)
2. "Do you agree or disagree that greater effort should be made to reduce inequality?" (EB)

Both of these very straightforward survey items are congruent with my conceptualization of market justice versus political justice with regard to the problem of income inequality. Another issue in comparing items across two different survey instruments is the degree of compatibility in the response categories. Fortunately, the Likert scale was used in each of the surveys, thus simplifying the coding of the data.[11] I selected the surveys prior to the time at which income inequality was measured and then aggregated the data to get the percentages of each response. The coding scheme employed maximized the information available and put more weight on the two extreme response categories. Polarization of the information in this manner is a reasonable approach if one is interested in the relative strength of attitudes as in this study. Both the "strongly agree" category and the "strongly disagree" category were multiplied by two, and added to those sums were the "agree" and "disagree" responses. The total sum for the disagree category was then subtracted from the total sum for the agree statements. For example, for political justice for the period between the mid 1980s and the mid 1990s, the data for Canada recorded the following: strongly agree (15.4) $\times$ 2 + agree (30.6) = 61.4;

11. The Likert scale format is a general approach to surveys that provides respondents with statements and asks them to indicate how strongly they agree or disagree. One important difference between the Eurobarometer surveys and those of the GSS is the absence of a neutral category in the former. Respondents to the GSS had an opportunity to select a "neither agree nor disagree" category. The difference in a five-point versus a four-point scale is a matter of theoretical importance, which potentially complicates the data analysis. However, because the basic essence of the question is comparable and the theory being developed and tested requires a diversity of political institutional settings and, thus, the necessity of pooling these two sets of surveys to acquire information on each country in my sample, the sacrifice had to be made to drop the neutral category from the GSS responses. On average, that category was selected about 15 percent of the time. While this is valuable information to sacrifice, omitting it is theoretically justified because the central concern is identifying the actual distribution of formulated and relatively firm opinion on the issue of government intervention when addressing the question of income inequality. Thus, although the data may not be ideal, the indicators are generally highly comparable, and the research design is sound.

strongly disagree (9.3) $\times$ 2 + disagree (20.4) = 39. So, 61.4 − 39 gives Canada a score of 22.4. The numbers found in Figure 1 are average scores for each country over the three time points in the study. The top box in Figure 1 provides a continuum from the most market justice-oriented societies to the most political justice-oriented societies, with Switzerland and France anchoring the two extremes. In the index, the higher the number is, the stronger the propensity toward political justice. Below the continuum, the countries are divided into three categories: strong market justice societies, moderate political justice, and strong political justice societies. The middle category is termed moderate political justice rather than moderate market justice because there is such a stark difference in the numbers for the strong market justice societies and the other two categories. Thus, the 68 score for several countries falling in the middle category is a good deal closer to the strong political justice countries than the extremely low numbers found in the strong market justice countries.

On one hand, this analysis and the resulting ranking of these countries are fairly consistent with expectations and the conventional views of the general political culture of these countries, but on the other hand, there are some striking curiosities that merit discussion. Unsurprisingly, most of the Anglo-Saxon countries are more market justice in orientation, whereas the continental European and welfare states tend to be more inclined toward political justice. A notable exception is that the United Kingdom, long deemed a bastion of economic liberalism, is in fact not among this group but rather displays a stronger inclination toward political justice. Because the Swiss and British cases are explored in greater detail in Chapter 5, I will not conjecture here about their rankings except to foreshadow my argument that these two countries are the "exceptions that prove the rule" and are the critical cases that illustrate my thesis that neither institutions nor values singularly or in isolation can yield a full explanation of cross-societal outcomes. It is also surprising to find the Nordic countries in the moderate rather than the strong political justice category given their stature as paragons of egalitarianism. Likewise, one might find it counterintuitive that Canada, also considered a society predisposed toward greater egalitarianism, is as strongly market justice oriented as demonstrated through these surveys. A consistent logic can be offered to account for each of these curiosities. That logic lies in the nature of the survey questions that tap into theoretical notions of whether the state should redistribute income and address inequality as well as perceptions about the actual

| SZ | A | C | US | NZ | SW | N | D | F | G | UK | NL | B | IT | IR | FR |
|----|---|---|----|----|----|---|---|---|---|----|----|---|----|----|----|
| **Strong Market Justice Societies** | | | | | **Moderate Political Justice Societies** | | | | | | **Strong Political Justice Societies** | | | | |

| Strong Market Justice Societies | Moderate Political Justice Societies | Strong Political Justice Societies |
|---|---|---|
| Switzerland (4.10) | Sweden (44.5) | Netherlands (85.6) |
| Australia (14.9) | Norway (48.6) | Belgium (109.1) |
| Canada (16.5) | Denmark (56.8) | Italy (111.8) |
| United States (22.4) | Finland (68.3) | Ireland (112.5) |
| New Zealand (27) | Germany (68.6) | France (113.4) |
| | U.K. (68.9) | |

★ The abbreviated country names that appear in the continuum are organized in the same order vertically in each of the three columns above from left to right. The numbers in parentheses represent averages of the justice values scores for three time periods between 1974 and 1999.

FIG 1 Political Justice Versus Market Justice: Value Orientations in Capitalist Democracies

need for state action based on existing levels of inequality. Because Sweden has the least amount of income inequality among the countries examined here, perhaps it is not so sur prising that r espondents there might be less inclined to ag ree that go vernments should do m ore to a ddress inequality. This would hold for the other Nordic countries as well as Germany, where indeed we do find lower levels of inequality. The same may hold for Canadians, who do in fact have lower levels of income inequality than some of the other Anglo-Saxon countries (although st ill relatively high compared to the Nordic states). This, combined with the widely held assumption by Canadians that their government is far more generous when it comes to social welfare than they know to be the case for their neighbors to the south, may provide at least a partial explanation for why they answered negatively in such high numbers.

Ideally, we could more accurately capture this dimension of values if we were able to create a set of questions that could disentangle perceptions from reality and clearly disassociate support for government redistribution from understandings—whether accurate or assumed—of the degree of inequality extant in society. Because this is not a possibility, it is best to acknowledge the limitations of opinion data while also asserting their relative validity and usefulness for capturing what I conceive as a forceful agent in helping to explain cross-societal variation in income inequality.[12] This exercise also reinforces the need to avoid assuming that just because social scientists have classified countries as LMEs (liberal market economies) or CMEs (coordinated market economies) (Hall and Soskice 2001) or organized them into three worlds of welfare capitalism (Esping-Andersen 1990) public values in these societies don't necessarily map onto those types of welfare regimes and political economies in such a neat and categorical fashion. In the next chapter, I raise this point again with r egard to pol itical institutions as opposed to typ es of pol itical economy, but the argument is the same: we need to assume less and do more, both theoretically and empirically, to define and analyze u nderlying public

12. I am grateful to an anonymous reviewer for drawing my attention to this problem. Although I acknowledge this as one of the more difficult challenges of dealing with survey data and the sometimes fuzzy nature of public opinion, I nonetheless maintain that the benefits of paying attention to what the public thinks (using the best resources possible, despite their limitations) outweigh the costs of imprecision. It should be noted that Kenworthy and McCall (2008) have attempted to address this problem, but the data they employed (using calculations by Jonathan Kelley and comparing perceived pay levels of different occupation categories—a reasonable strategy) was not extensive enough or complete enough to use in my own analysis.

values and their relative congruence with the types of institutional environments within which they exist.

This index serves as the empirical core of the conceptual model that takes values seriously as potential causal factors shaping income inequality and therefore explaining variation in levels of disparity among these capitalist democracies. Almond and Powell defined political culture as the "patterns of individual attitudes and orientations towards politics among members of a political system" (1996, 23). Although I have used attitudes and values somewhat interchangeably throughout this book, it is important to make a distinction between the two for theoretical clarity and particularly with regard to imputing causal weight to ideational factors. I rely on Seymour Martin Lipset's distinction first and then briefly discuss how such a distinction bears on Lane's conceptualization and the way in which I am using the concept of culture in this study. Lipset notes:

> It is important to distinguish between attitudes and values. Attitudes are much more malleable; they vary with events and contexts. They may change to reflect current social developments, recessions, corruption scandals, or violent periods, and therefore, may counter assumptions about deep-rooted variations among nations. Values are well-entrenched, culturally determined sentiments produced by institutions or major historical events.... They result in deep beliefs, such as deference or antagonism to authority, individualism or group-centeredness, and egalitarianism or elitism, which form the organizing principles of societies. (1996, 24–25)

Lipset adds that values may have a bearing on "behavior outcome," such as the propensity to rely on government for addressing social welfare problems. And, as his research relies heavily on opinion surveys to forge his "centrality of culture" thesis,[13] it is not surprising that Lipset later states that surveys provide adequate indicators of values. The important question is whether the way in which I have operationalized Lane's conceptualization of justice represents what we might call values or attitudes. Profound notions about the proper roles of states versus markets would seem to capture more than malleable

---

13. See Lipset's article by this title in the *Journal of Democracy* (Fall 1990): 80–83, for a representative idea of how this author pits cultural factors against institutional ones. The article is also reprinted in Lijphart's edited volume, *Parliamentary versus Presidential Government* (1992).

attitudes subject to frequent change and, thus, more appropriately be desig-
nated as values according to Lipset's distinction. However, consistent with the
spirit of Lane's ideas, all that would be necessary to produce significant changes
in society are "shifts in perception" and, thus, what we might consider to be
more likened to attitudes than entrenched or difficult to change values. For
instance, Lane describes a change likely to occur if the "community point of
view" (or political justice) were to prevail: "As in the harmonic view of the
market, benefits to others are also, if in lesser degree, benefits to the self, partly
because of the market itself: the grocer, made unhappy by the taxes he pays
to support welfare, is happy to receive the custom of his welfare clients. The
community point of view makes the connection" (1986, 400).

Presumably, as such attitudes become more commonplace, the greater a
society's propensity to support the workings of the polity to redress the inequities of the economy. Thus, I propose that attitudes be interpreted as con-
stituent parts of what we mean by values. In either case, what we are broadly
interested in is th e ideational or cultural e lement that influences individual
preferences and public policy priorities. I wish to avoid the notion that cultural factors are mere manifestations of the structural or institutional settings
in which they are formed (Althusser 1971) as well as the idea that culture is a
"persistent and unalterable" force in society (Schiller 1969). Instead, I reiterate Lane (as well as Gramsci) in claiming that there are reciprocal as well as
independent relations between the two and therefore argue that the symbio-
sis between them may provide greater understanding of social an d political
phenomena than a focus on one to the exclusion of the other. Although this
is only one measure, it is a very precise indicator of the values most relevant
as a causal factor in this study. By defining these broad values as an indicator
of political culture that represents the aggregation of individual orientations
and attitudes, I hope to have overcome some of the conceptual and methodological issues that have impaired previous cultural approaches.

Values around notions of distributive justice and ideas about whether the
state should do something about growing inequality underscore the underlying and in escapably normative concerns associated with stu dies of inc ome
inequality. The point of the model I have constructed, derived from Lane's
insights and operationalized through survey data, acknowledges this, but rather
than working on the theoretical plane as Rawls, Nozick, Zucker, and many
others, I deploy the notion of applied democratic theory and actually let the
citizens—not the theoreticians nor the elites—convey what the cultural values

and preferences are in a given society. To return briefly to Inglehart (1997), it is interesting to recall that, with regard to economic behavior, he detected a shift in peoples' emphasis on maximization of income and job security to a growing desire for meaningful employment and participatory styles of management and work, and at the same time a reversal in the inclination to seek government solutions and a growing acceptance of capitalism and market principles. Being content to show patterns of a shift toward market values, however, would not really unravel the causal links between value change and economic change or growing income inequality. Likewise, structuralist accounts of new patterns of capitalist accumulation seem incognizant of the complex realities of how democratic politics interfere with the ideal workings of the market economy.

I propose that institutions be construed as mediating forces in this epistemological chasm. In other words, I wish to formulate next an analytic framework that depicts institutions as the workhorses that negotiate cultural norms and the structural constraints (or opportunities) extant in capitalist democracies.[14] A broader view is that institutions are embodiments of the way in which the relationships between culture and structure or democracy (politics) and capitalism (economics) have been historically and socially constructed. In thinking about institutions in this particular light, I am drawn to the work of Arend Lijphart and his well-known typology of democracy. Whereas the reemergence of institutional analysis in political science during the past decade or so has produced convincing analytical argumentation and empirical evidence that "institutions matter," Lijphart's approach is more encompassing in that its preoccupation lies more with "how" institutions matter.[15] The values question as I have articulated it here makes the "how" dimension and, therefore, Lijphart's approach all the more compelling. The next chapter offers an overview of institutional analysis in comparative political economy, assesses the congruence of the theoretical arguments made so far with the substance of the consensus-majoritarian model, and elucidates the model's analytical usefulness for understanding patterns of income inequality among capitalist democracies.

14. Robert Grafstein's (1988) characterization of political institutions as "both human products and constraints on those participating within them" and his attempt to reconcile these constraint and creation features of institutions is particularly insightful.

15. Knight 1992, Koelbe 1995, and Ostrom 1995 provide excellent reviews of the new institutionalist literature with emphasis placed on the divisions and the possible complementarity of the rational choice and historical institutionalist approaches.

# — 3 —

THE POWER AND THE LIMITATIONS OF POLITICAL INSTITUTIONS:
RETOOLING THE CONSENSUS–MAJORITARIAN FRAMEWORK TO
"BRING CULTURE IN"

Under certain institutional conditions, a strict economic rationality may prevail,
while under others, social norms may achieve a critical importance. The task
of social science is therefore to discover how this relation between political
institutions and the logic of individual action actually functions.
—BO ROTHSTEIN, *Just Institutions Matter*

Chapter 2 presented the first stage of the analytical and causal schema I propose by developing a conceptual model that specifies the key societal values
that represent the most salient ideational factor underlying varying patterns of
income inequality among capitalist democracies. However, while maintaining
the position that values matter, I also acknowledge that these normative and
ideational forces alone cannot produce necessary and sufficient causal explanations. Instead, we must conceptualize values as independent but contingent
factors. Viewing societal values as independent—that is, not merely reflective
of structural conditions—is essential to my perspective of political economy
as applied democratic theory in that political economy requires greater attention to agency and takes the firm normative position that values should matter in democratic polities. The contingent factor comes into play when we are
concerned with explaining why and how values matter in shaping concrete
outcomes such as income distribution. The empirical side of the coin is introduced in this chapter by arguing that political institutions are the vehicles by
which values are transformed into material realities. More specifically, I posit
that values can have critical causal influence, but the weight and direction of
that influence depends upon the political institutional environment within
which they operate. Thus, the present chapter is concerned with the next

logical piece of the puzzle—the impact of political institutions as well as their relationship to societal values. As Bo Rothstein argues, "political institutions are both empirical and normative orders" (1998, 216).

Sharing this view, one aim here is to identify what the linkages might be between these two conceptions of institutions. Drawing on Robert Lane's insights, I articulated the kind of normative order (specified as justice values) that I believe to be theoretically relevant for understanding broad socioeconomic outcomes such as income inequality, but here the purpose is to focus on the role of political institutions. Although I do further articulate the notion of institutions as empirical embodiments of values, I do so primarily in broad terms of democratic governance showing how in effect Lijphart's composite index for his two types of democracies may also be construed as a cultural model. It is crucial to distinguish this objective from the following more specific task of integrating well-defined values or value orientations into our institutional and empirical analyses. Once again, this is where the independent role of values resurfaces. We can argue that certain types of political institutions coalesce to offer an approach to governance that tends to better aggregate and reflect public attitudes and values, but we remain agnostic with regard to the actual content of those values.

As previously stated, the institutional approach that I am drawn to and the one I find most fitting for this study is that of Arend Lijphart's consensus-majoritarian framework. Nonetheless, I believe it is necessary to situate Lijphart's model within the broader scholarly literature on institutional analysis. The first section briefly discusses the various approaches with a special focus on what I call the competing institutionalisms in comparative political economy. Here I examine the rational choice and historical institutionalist schools of thought as well as the burgeoning scholarship on the varieties of capitalism (VOC) and recent trends in welfare state research. Next, I focus specifically on the current works that have addressed the phenomenon of growing income inequality in the advanced industrial democracies. The point of this discussion is not to present an exhaustive overview of the comparative political economy or institutionalist literatures but rather to paint in broad strokes what some of the analytical deficiencies are and to elucidate why none offers the best strategy for uncovering the deeper normative and democratic theoretical questions driving this particular study. The second half of the chapter argues that we need to retool our institutional approaches so ideational factors or "culture" may be brought in—both in an empirical sense and in a manner consistent with the framework of applied democratic theory proposed in Chapter 1. Although I argue that Lijphart's widely used typology of democracy is the approach most conducive to bringing values in, I find the model itself to be empirically overstretched because it packs in too many variables and is theoretically underspecified in normative democratic terms. Although Lijphart has recently commented on the degree to which consensus democracy might also be conceived as a cultural model as well as an institutional one, very little attention has been paid to such a notion. I develop this perspective more fully while remaining true to Lijphart's original typology but extending it to include a cultural dimension. Engaging with Lijphart's work and some of his most severe critics, I reconstruct the consensus-majoritarian framework in a way that bridges institutional and cultural variables or, to refer back to my use of the Rothstein quotation earlier, connects the empirical and the normative. In doing so, the groundwork is in place for an empirical analysis of the relationship between the cultural values of a particular society and its ensemble of political institutions to see how this interplay affects distributional outcomes.

## Competing Institutionalisms in Comparative Political Economy

As Thomas Koelbe, has usefully reminded us, "the study of institutions has been central to political science since its inception" (1995, 231). However, the manner in which institutions have been conceptualized and studied by political scientists has changed dramatically. In some ways the evolution from the "old institutionalism" to the "new institutionalism" charts these major developments, but in other ways it reveals certain similarities and abiding concerns. The "old institutionalism" for the most part preceded the behavioralist revolution of the 1950s and 1960s and thus was not driven by the positivist logic that encouraged scientific approaches to the study of politics, such as the Eastonian "systems" approach and the proliferation of statistical and survey methods. Instead, the focus was primarily on description, classification, and formal legalistic studies of political institutions. The inauguration of the term "new institutionalism" appeared with the publication of March and Olsen's seminal *American Political Science Review* article of 1984 in which the authors provided a general perspective on institutions that placed an emphasis on the "logic of appropriateness" as a means of shaping the behavior and guiding the actions of the actual members of institutions (25–28). Ironically, the authors called for somewhat of a return to the roots of their intellectual forebears in the sense that they contested the growing dominance of rational choice and behavioral approaches in political science research characterized by "contextualism," "reductionism," "utilitarianism," "functionalism," and "instrumentalism."[1] The resulting effect treated the state and other governing institutions as a mere "black box" into which inputs could be made and from which outputs became their main object of inquiry. What March and Olsen urged as the replacement of these methodological tendencies was a "new institutionalism" that would place collective action at the center of analysis with a conception of politics that is as much a shaper of society as it is shaped by it. In other words, the relationship between political collectivities and their socioeconomic environments should be seen as reciprocal. Within one year of this call for both a new way of thinking about the significance of institutions as well as a return to some of the virtues of the older form of analysis, scholars "brought the state back in" (Evans, Rueschmeyer, and Skocpol 1985), and as many as six new strains of new institutionalism would emerge.[2] Major innovations would lie in the degree to which theory and methods became more refined and capable of employing institutions as the key variable to explain political life. As B. Guy Peters characterizes it: "Whereas the older version of institutionalism was content to describe institutions, the newer version seeks to explain them as 'dependent variables' and, more importantly, to explain other phenomena with institutions as the 'independent variables' shaping policy and administrative behavior" (1998, 206).

The two most pertinent strands of institutionalist analysis in the subfield of comparative political economy are rational choice and historical institutionalism, and just as in the broader comparative politics field, the two approaches tend to compete for pride of place in the scholarly literature. The sociological variant is also gaining prominence, particularly among constructivists (Green 2002), but it has not attained the status of the two other predominant versions in political science. Despite the fact that March and Olsen singled out rational choice as a principle antagonist and an obstacle to the development of a

---

1. Each of these characteristics was a target of their criticism in the article as well as in their subsequent writings. For an excellent synopsis of their arguments, see Peters 1999 (chapters 1 and 2). For other reviews of the different versions of the new institutionalism, see Koelbe 1995 and Hall and Taylor 1996.

2. See Peters 1999 for a lengthy description of each of the following: normative, rational choice, historical, empirical, international, and societal institutionalism. The author devotes a chapter to each of these versions of the new institutionalism.

collective, institutional perspective, a rational choice school of institutional analysis has flourished. Both Douglass North's *Institutions, Institutional Change, and Economic Performance* and Elinor Ostrom's *Governing the Commons* were published in 1990, a propitious year for the rational choice approach; although these works are very different, they each establish a similar definition of institutions as norms or rules—be they formal or informal—that govern human social interaction, constrain behavior, and reduce transaction costs. Individual utility maximization is the source of explanation, so scholars generally stress the role of institutions as decision rules that can s upply information that structures behavior to facilitate some form of realization of the collective good. In the rational choice institutional framework, various scholars have invoked such an understanding of institutions to explain decisions by government regarding the extraction of resources through taxation and conscription (Levi 1988; 1996); to identify how and when cooperation will occur (Axelrod 1984); to account for agg regation of in dividual, self-interested preferences (Shepsle 1989; Weingast 1996); and to explain the capacity for policy change in different political structural settings (Tsebelis 1995), only to name a few well-known and often-cited studies. In all of these various models, institutions are posited as the mechanism by which rational egoists can achieve a state of equilibrium, which is in essence the antithesis of the March and Olsen conceptualization of inst itutions and their version of what ha s now become known as "sociological institutionalism." In a subsequent section, we will see how rational choice models have addressed the question of income inequality.

In stark contrast, "historical institutionalism" could be interpreted as maintaining the general spirit of March and Olsen's call to reorient the discipline by addressing the problem of ahistoricism and individualism/reductionism so prevalent in political science. In this mode of analysis, institutions are somewhat ambiguously and variably defined, but the overarching commonality is the attention paid to the role of institutional choices made early in the development of specific policy areas and the argument that these initial choices will have pervasive influence on subsequent policy decisions. Thus, "path dependency" is the central analytic concept, and the starting assumption is that once a government or organization begins down a certain policy trajectory, there is a tendency for it to p ersist.[3] Laying out their strategy in *Structuring Politics*

---

3. It is interesting to note that Douglass North (1990) also emphasized the idea that the historical creation of economic institutions matters in terms of how it might shape future economic outcomes. In fact, he was awarded the Nobel Prize for his work in this area.

(1992), Steinmo, Thelen, and Longstreth argue that their approach should have broad applicability in the discipline and even in certain affinities with other institutionalist approaches because institutions are understood as the elemental forces of politics in their ability to shape goals, define means, and provide evaluative criteria for policies (see specifically the chapter by Thelen and Steinmo).

Although Peter Hall does not invoke the term *historical institutionalism*, his 1986 work comparing the development of economic policies of France and the United Kingdom is clearly an early example of this research approach. His basic argument is that to fully understand the patterns of policy choices and differences between these two countries, it is essential to understand their respective political and policy histories. On the role of institutions, Hall states that they are "the formal rules, compliance procedures, and standard operating procedures that structure the relationships between people in various units of the polity and the economy" (1986, 7). One of the most significant influences of Hall's work that has since come to be a distinctive feature of historical institutional analysis is the independent role that ideas play in shaping policies as well as defining institutions. For example, an important work that clearly specifies the influence of ideas is Immergut's (1992) comparative analysis of h ealth policies in three European countries. Immergut shows that what most determines health policies in different national systems are the ideas that medical practitioners hold about best practices in c onjunction with the institutionalization of p otential veto points that impact the policy process and determine the influence of various interest groups. Other important works include analyses of social identities in politics (Anderson 1991; Lustick 1993), cultural and ideational legacies of colonialism (Laitin 1986), and the origins and strategies of union movements in the United Kingdom and the United States (Hattam 1993).

According to Pierson and Skocpol (2002), three important features characterize historical institutional scholarship: "tackling big, real-world questions; tracing processes through time; and analyzing institutional configurations and contexts" (713). In a sometimes subtle manner and in other times less so, these authors seem to contrast these attributes of h istorical institutionalism with their opposite tendencies in rational choice scholarship. For example, in noting that some rational choice theorists have begun to use historical case studies, they argue that "the past enters only in a highly restricted sense, as what might be termed 'illustrative history'" (705), effectively accusing these scholars of mining history to find outcomes that can b e explained through rational choice reasoning. This is often contrasted with the analytic advantages of the historical institutionalist approach, which analyzes conjunctures and slow-moving macroprocesses behind a broad range of large-scale social phenomena like democratization, industrialization, state building, and welfare state development. Although Pierson and Skocpol acknowledge with Thelen (1999) that different types of institutionalists have converged on some similar questions and general findings about the significance of institutions, crucial differences remain. For instance, Pierson and Skocpol argue that

> Rational-choice scholars tend to focus on rules of the game that provide equilibrium "solutions" to collective action dilemmas. Historical institutionalists, meanwhile, probe uneasy balances of power and resources, and see institutions as the developing products of struggle among unequal actors. Rational-choice scholars often focus on one set of rules at a time. Historical institutionalists, by contrast, typically do meso- or macrolevel analyses that examine multiple institutions in interaction, operating in, and influenced by, broader contexts. (2002, 706)

Further revealing how the two strands indirectly vie for influence, Levi, an influential rational choice scholar, expresses that although she is of the view that convergence might be possible, others continue to hold to the superiority of another approach. In spite of her apparent openness to the possible insights of different approaches, her estimation of the superiority of rational choice is evident in the following sentence: "A line in the sand remains, nonetheless. Rationalists are almost always willing to sacrifice nuance for generalizability, detail for logic, a forfeiture most other comparativists would decline" (1997, 21). Furthermore, in pointing to the comparative advantages of the rational choice perspective, Barry Weingast (2002) says the approach has the potential to provide the microfoundations for the macropolitical phenomena that are incidentally often the object of study for the historical institutionalists. Although neither these scholars nor others who write entries in manuals surveying the political science literature or elsewhere have overtly stated as much, I believe that rational choice and historical institutionalist approaches tend to be engaged not only in original and important political research but also in theoretical and methodological battles over which approach is the most powerful or more scientifically progressive. As these passages reveal, there is a sort of competition under way, and the implications for how we understand the various ways in which institutions shape our political and economic lives seems to be of major consequence. So, where does the Lijphartian mode of institutional analysis fit within this competition?

In contrast to some of the more abstract and theoretical work of the rational choice and historical institutionalist modes of analysis, B. Guy Peters (1999) classifies Lijphart as an "empirical institutionalist," which he describes as those who tend to be motivated primarily by the general question—do institutions matter? The bulk of this literature has revolved around the relative differences between presidential and parliamentary regimes and their respective impact on the performance of the political system. Performance here has been conceptualized in a number of ways ranging from stability in newly democratized regimes (Riggs 1988; Linz 1990, 1993) to the types of policies enacted (Weaver and Rockman 1993). Singling out Lijphart's approach, Peters discusses how his work has also been concerned with the impact of choices of institutions on the relative effectiveness of governments. Specifically, Lijphart has attempted to assess whether majoritarian parliamentary systems such as the United Kingdom govern more effectively than consensual systems like that of his native country, the Netherlands, where coalitional governments tend to trade some degree of effectiveness for representativeness. As is widely known, Lijphart's empirical analyses have led him to conclude that consensual systems are able to provide both greater effectiveness as well as better representation. Peters, however, questions this finding as well as other works that attribute success to specific forms of political institutions. However, in suggesting the relative advantages that accrue to majoritarian systems, Peters claims that the "institutional structure of majoritarian systems appears more likely to enable a prime minister to shape policy than does that of consensual systems" (1999, 82). But he goes on to say that the "differences in outputs such as economic performance may be as much a function of poor policy choices as the structural features of the system" (82). This is an important critique and one that I will reconsider in a later section of this chapter when I review other problems of Lijphart's model.

Despite raising this red flag, overall Peters seems to hold the empirical institutionalist approach in high esteem. He claims that one factor that distinguishes this version of institutionalism from the rational choice and historical institutionalist variants is that the institutional design question appears to be more central to Lijphart and others working within the empirical institutionalist tradition. Much less interested in theoretical development, these scholars are more concerned with being able to use empirical evidence about the probable implications of certain institutional choices to better advise governments faced with institutional design questions. Surprisingly, Peters concludes by arguing that in fact this strand of institutionalism more than any of the others is ultimately driven by normative questions, or what he clarifies as the attempt to identify "what works"—especially the capacity of institutions to make decisions, and by determining what impact a specific institutional arrangement may have on the performance of government (94–95). This is a very apt characterization of the thrust of Lijphart's work and serves to clarify how his approach in general contrasts with other forms of institutional analysis. Whereas the rational choice variant is oriented around microlevel explanations of institutions, and the historical institutionalist version tends to focus on deep, historical and macrolevel roots of political phenomena, Lijphart generally pursues a more mesolevel of analysis concentrating on existing political institutions and their impact on democratic governance. Although I share Peters's overall assessment, perhaps Bernard Grofman's claim that Lijphart's comparative institutional analysis "deserves separate recognition as an important and separate strain of new institutionalism" (2000, 44) is well founded. Offering a more in-depth account of the distinctiveness of Lijphart's approach and how it differs from other versions of institutional analysis, Grofman concludes that

> Lijphart's work can be distinguished from the positive political theory approach with its emphasis on institutions as game-theoretic equilibria and ways of avoiding preference cycling; from that of the sociological approach to organizational theory, with its emphasis on nonsystematic and unanticipated consequences of organizational choice and/or insistence that preferences are shaped by institutions as well as shaping them; and from the narrative historical approach, with its emphasis on institutions as organic growths whose understanding requires "thick description." Lijphart's work also may be contrasted with authors who focus so tightly on formal rules and constitutional jurisprudence as to exhibit relative disregard for empirical evidence about the extent to which rules do matter. (2000, 46)

Although such a characterization portrays the advantages or the different emphases of a Lijphartian approach to institutional analysis in a general sense, it is now important to elucidate what this implies if we compare his conceptualization of institutions with the newly emerging theoretical paradigm in comparative political economy, the Varieties of Capitalism (VOC) approach, and consider its implications for the comparative analysis of income inequality.

Just as comparativists such as Lijphart and legions of others have long been preoccupied with different forms of democracy, another predominant trend in comparative research is to identify and explain different forms of capitalism. Although this is not a particularly novel development, its growing hegemony in the field and the way in which it subsumes the broader institutional questions addressed above portend significant theoretical consequences that have been largely ignored. I will return to this point after providing a general overview of the origins, main insights, and contributions of this new literature and research program. In his overview of the state of the subdiscipline of comparative politics, David Laitin (2002) claimed that the historical institutionalists set the research agenda for the study of the political economy of the advanced industrial states with the classic text of Peter Katzenstein (1978) defining the dependent variable as the varying political strategies of OECD states in adjusting to the collapse of the Bretton Woods system and the oil shocks. Specific institutions arising from distinct historical trajectories constituted the key independent variable, and, according to Laitin, historical institutionalists depicted a continuum of different types of capitalism ranging from strong states relative to society to strong societies relative to state institutions (651). Neocorporatism became one of the central organizing concepts through which major differences in advanced political economies would be understood.

By the 1990s, with the publication of Esping-Andersen's *Three Worlds of Welfare Capitalism*, all of the various outcomes capturing the attention of comparative political economists could be more or less interpreted as coalescing around three types of capitalism, or as Esping-Andersen put it, welfare regimes that he identified as liberal, corporatist, and social democratic. For almost another decade most studies of comparative political economy, regardless of whether they specifically addressed welfare state or social welfare policy questions, would be compelled to reference this landmark work because its implications extended far beyond narrow public transfer policy and welfare programs. Ironically, no sooner than this seminal work made its mark did global economic crises provoke a spate of literature on the retrenchment of the welfare state (Swenson 1992; Cable 1995; Schmidt 1996; Schwartz 1994) followed by a backlash literature with no real resolution about the actual state of the welfare state (in generalizable terms). Furthermore, as noted by Peter Hall, we did not yet have a "clear understanding of how these different kinds of welfare states interact with different models of the economy" (1997, 196.) Both the changes in the global economy" and the incremental theoretical development of the VOC literature might be characterized as beginning to make those connections and overshadowing the previous "worlds of welfare" and, indeed, most other prevalent comparative political economy approaches.

Although other works have played an important role in pioneering the varieties or diversities of capitalism perspective (Shonfield 1965; Berger and Dore 1996; Crouch and Streeck 1997; Boyer and Hollingsworth 1997; Coates 2000; Kitschelt, Lange, Marks, and Stephens 1999), the Hall and Soskice (2001) edited volume bearing the title *Varieties of Capitalism* expresses the central theoretical statement of the approach. The authors state that the main objective of the book is to elaborate a new framework for "understanding the institutional similarities and differences among the developed economies" (2001, 1), to offer an account of how the "institutions structuring the political economy confer comparative advantages on a nation" (v, vi), and, perhaps most importantly, to call into question "the presumption that increasing international economic integration will force the institutions and regulatory regimes of diverse nations into convergence on a common model" (vi). Drawing on the new economics of organization, the approach locates the firm at the center of analysis because they are after all the "crucial actors in a capitalist economy" and the "key agents of adjustment in the face of technological change or international competition whose activities aggregate into overall levels of economic performance" (6). And, as Hall and Soskice argue, previous alternative approaches have overemphasized the state and labor. Further articulating the basic elements of their approach, Hall and Soskice specify five spheres in which firms must develop relationships to resolve coordination problems: (1) industrial relations or bargaining with labor over wages and working conditions; (2) vocational training or securing a workforce with appropriate skills; (3) corporate governance and access to finance and investment; (4) inter-firm competition and cooperation; and (5) employee relations and adverse selection issues (6–7).

The way in which firms resolve these various coordination problems largely reveals what type of political economy is in operation. In the VOC analytical framework liberal market economies (LMEs) and coordinated market economies (CMEs) constitute ideal types at opposite ends of a spectrum along which nations can be arrayed. Distinguishing the two types, the authors further elaborate:

> In *liberal market economies,* firms coordinate their activities primarily via hierarchies and competitive market arrangements. . . . Market relationships are characterized by the arm's-length exchange of goods or services in a context of competition and formal contracting. . . . In *coordinated economies,* firms depend more heavily on non-market relationships to coordinate their endeavors with other actors and to construct their core competencies. These non-market modes of coordination generally entail more extensive relational or incomplete contracting, network monitoring based on the exchange of private information inside networks, and more reliance on collaborative, as opposed to competitive, relationships to build the competencies of the firm. (2001, 8)

What are the implications of this new analytical framework for understanding distributional issues? As data presented in their introduction conveys, there is systematic variation between these types of political economy on a multiplicity of performance indicators. In particular, in the LMEs, the adult population tends to be engaged in higher numbers in full-time equivalent employment and income inequality is high, whereas in the CMEs, working hours tend to be shorter for larger segments of the populations and incomes are more equal (20–22). As it relates specifically to Lijphart's typologies of democracies, there is an almost mirror reflection of consensus–majoritarian patterns of countries and the way the countries cluster according to distributional outcomes across political economies. LMEs such as Australia, the United Kingdom, Canada, New Zealand, and the United States are all encircled as high income inequality cases, which also happen to be examples of Lijphart's majoritarian democracies. Likewise, CMEs or Lijphart's consensus democracies such as Finland, Sweden, Norway, and Germany are those with lower income inequality (22, fig. 1.2).

Furthermore, if one focuses on the characteristics of each political economy type, the connections become even stronger from a cultural norms point of view. The overarching principle of competitiveness predominates in LMEs in that equilibrium outcomes of firm behavior result from demand-and-supply conditions in competitive markets, whereas a more cooperative or coordinative ethos prevails in the CMEs where equilibria on which firms co-ordinate are more likely the result of strategic interaction among firms and other social actors (2001, 8). To those familiar with Lijphart's verbiage about the major distinctions between consensus and majoritarian democracies, the parallel is striking. Both in terms of his description of the nature of multi-party coalition building or his defense of the inclusion of corporatism as a compatible dimension of consensus democracy, Lijphart is clearly interested in showing how certain institutions structure cooperative as opposed to adversarial and competitive approaches to solving political problems. I return to this apparent correlation in more detail later when Lijphart's model is the center of discussion.

Although data are presented by Hall and Soskice in their introductory chapter to demonstrate the relationship between LMEs, CMEs, and income inequality, the topic is not a strong focus of the volume. In fact, comparative distributive outcomes are not specifically addressed anywhere, and only two or three of the chapters out of fourteen are devoted to a further exploration of social policy issues more broadly. Estevez-Abe, Iversen, and Soskice examine the relationship between specific varieties of capitalism and social policy regimes and show that social protection actually aids the market by helping economic actors overcome market failures in skills formation (chap. 4). They show in their analysis that collective bargaining at the industry or higher levels brings diverse income groups into a collective decision-making process, which gives low-income groups an opportunity to influence the distribution of wages that they would not enjoy in less coordinated systems. The chapter by Mares (chap. 5) develops a theoretical link between the Varieties of Capitalism approach and the varieties of welfare regimes approach by showing how social policies offer distinct institutional advantages to employers, an element typically left out of welfare state analyses. In particular, her analysis suggests that "the incidence of risk will generate significant cleavages among employers, between firms who gain from highly redistributive social policies and firms who lose from the participation in a broad pool of risks" (Hall and Soskice 2001, 212). Mares's analysis is important because it goes beyond the typical "welfare state as constraint" (on firms) point of view and demonstrates with theoretical rigor the specific conditions under which particular firms will actively support social policy arrangements.

One of the major achievements of the VOC approach is that Hall and Soskice have presented a coherent theoretical and empirical argument against the one-model-fits-all orthodoxy of neoliberalism, which predicts all countries will eventually converge around the Anglo-American model of political economy. One of the political consequences of this intellectual achievement, however, is that they deduced only one other alternative model of political economy, that of the CME as exemplified best by Germany; in fact, the bulk of the chapters use Germany as the prime example. This has led some critics to charge that it really is a "tale of two countries dressed up as a typology of general applicability" (Goodin 2003, 205). Robert Goodin's concerns about this point, however, were allayed by subsequent work by Hall and Gingerich (2001) that produced an index of "Coordination" that indicates there really is a dimension of difference among the other advanced industrial countries. Goodin is more pessimistic about the very logic of the VOC that seems to predict that CMEs "are doomed to extinction" because, as he shows, they are based on "relations of trust" that are long and difficult to establish but easy to destroy, and therefore, many middle-ground countries will naturally gravitate toward the LME model (2003, 211–12).

My reproach of the VOC in general is that despite Hall and Soskice's implicit commitment to the CME model and more social democratic orientations, at the end of the day, they seem to privilege a singular economic logic that has more in common with neoclassical thinking (also somewhat evident in the choice-theoretic methodologies common to many of their contributors) than the Keynesianism or post-Keynesianism assumptions that formerly underpinned some of these scholars' work. The result, I fear, is a loss of the "primacy of the political" approach to political economy that I highlighted and argued against earlier in Chapter 1. Chris Howell is very direct in his critique of this aspect of the VOC:

> The theoretical framework of *Varieties of Capitalism* offers an extremely thin notion of politics and state action, in which governments, whose function is essentially to encourage coordination among economic actors, act largely at the behest of employers. States do not appear to have interests distinguishable from those of employers, nor do they have the capacity to act independently of, still less against, employer interests. Managing the political economy is a fundamentally cooperative venture: coordinating activities, facilitating information flows, and encouraging cooperation. This approach betrays a latent functionalism in which capitalist political economies and the

social relations that undergird them are fundamentally nonconflict-
ual; the interests of different actors can be effectively coordinated for
long period by sets of institutions. (Howell 2003, 110)

At the outset of this overview of VOC, I commented on its growing hegemony in the field and the theoretical consequences of the way in which it
subsumes the broader institutional questions that have been driving research
for at least the last two decades. If the VOC indeed becomes the paradigmatic
approach for the way in which comparative political economists conceptualize and study institutions, then the imperial reach of economics will have
conquered one of the last vestiges of intellectual resistance. It is noteworthy
that the explicit definition of institutions used in the VOC is derived from
that of an economist and is articulated in terms of "the support they provide
for the relationships firms develop to resolve coordination problems" (Hall
and Soskice 2001, 9). If the state and labor are no longer central, and political
parties are not even mentioned (Iversen's subsequent work notwithstanding,
as I discuss below), our world of politics according to VOC's line of argument
is being driven entirely by one set of actors: business. Many scholars and commentators across a diverse ideological spectrum would readily agree with this
but would profoundly disagree about the implications of a world driven by
one group of actors, no matter how heterogeneous. Fortunately, such a perspective belies the complex reality of societal responses to capitalist economic
development.

Contrasting VOC with Coates's *Models of Capitalism* (2000), which explicitly integrates labor movements and different forms of class compromises and
industrial relations in France, Germany, and Sweden into its analysis and classification scheme, Howell takes a broad swipe against the VOC approach. He
writes:

> The danger of the perspective of the *Varieties of Capitalism* is that it
> flattens history, explaining the failure of these more radical political
> economic projects as overdetermined, a restoration of equilibrium
> rather than a result of political conflict and the exercise of power
> in a contingent historical process. It is not clear what is gained by
> redefining the ubiquitous workplace conflict between employers
> and workers as a coordination problem. What is lost is the sense that
> power is exercised by actors with different interests and unequal

resources and capacities. In working within the framework of a smoothly functioning, self-adjusting political economy, the approach of the *Varieties of Capitalism* finds it difficult to describe, still less explain, the moments of crisis and conflict that are a central part of comparative political economy. (2003, 112)

Vivien Schmidt's contribution to the debates about convergence and competing models of capitalism infuses more of a politics-and-power perspective into her analysis and offers a refreshing theoretical and empirical alternative to the two worlds of the VOC. Surprisingly, her work is rarely considered in the various reviews and critiques of the larger VOC literature. In her co-authored two-volume work with F. Scharpf (2000), *Welfare and Work in the Open Economy,* and followed by her book, *The Futures of European Capitalism* (2002), Schmidt has provided extensive and authoritative accounts of political economic change in the advanced capitalist economies. Schmidt largely refutes the convergence thesis and argues that different models of European capitalism will persist, showing that even where national economic policies have converged, there is still variation in the timing and the degree of change. Perhaps her most original contribution is the attempt to bring the role of ideas (through discourse analysis) into a causal argument about the dynamics of policy change. After carefully differentiating Europeanization and globalization and assessing the pressures each force exerts on domestic governments, Schmidt examines the dynamics of economic adjustment strategies in Britain, France, and Germany from the mid-1970s to the late 1990s. Her main argument is that although there is a general trend toward greater market orientation, economic policies and practices in Europe continue to diverge and thus represent three distinctive models of European capitalism: Britain's market capitalism, France's state-enhanced capitalism, and Germany's managed capitalism. Using a diverse set of methods and a rich theoretical framework, Schmidt provides a convincing empirical account of how institutions, interests, and cultural norms function together to produce or impede political economic change.

In Part II of *The Futures of European Capitalism,* Schmidt charts the different configurations of government, labor, and business relationships in each country and argues against proponents of globalization who contend convergence is occurring in Europe as well as against the varieties of capitalism scholars who specify only two broad models of capitalism as opposed to the three models that she has discerned. As an expert on French political economy, she argues that the statist model and the distinctiveness of French capitalism is lost by the firm-centered and dualistic approach of Hall and Soskice and other VOC scholars. Part III addresses the "why" question of policy change and is the most original and compelling part of her argument. Particularly innovative is her willingness to assign causal weight to ideational factors such as discourse, which she defines as "whatever policy actors say to one another and to the public in their efforts to generate and legitimize a policy programme" (2002, 210). She refers to this as "discursive institutionalism." In her move to attribute interactive causation to discourse, she frames the following question to guide her empirical analysis: "when does discourse serve to reconceptualize interests rather than just to reflect them, to chart new institutional paths instead of simply following old ones, and to reframe cultural norms rather than reify them" (212).

Next Schmidt analyzes the discursive strategies of Thatcher in Britain and both Chirac and Jospin in France, as well as the "social market" policy paradigm and accompanying discourse in Germany. With these in-depth case studies, she sheds light on how discourse becomes a critical explanatory factor in generating and legitimizing the various liberalizing changes that have transpired in all three countries. She describes the importance of discourse in the following way:

> As the conveyor of a set of ideas and values, discourse represents the policy concepts and norms, methods and instruments, objectives and ideals contained in a policy programme. As such, it performs two functions. As part of its cognitive function, it serves to justify a policy programme by demonstrating its superiority in providing effective solutions to current problems and in anticipating, and thereby avoiding, future problems. As part of its normative function, it serves to legitimize the policy programme by demonstrating its appropriateness in terms of national values, whether long-standing or newly emerging. (2002, 213–14)

Thus, in Schmidt's analysis and in the real world of politics, people and values still matter and play a central role in explaining both stasis and change in the political economies of capitalist democracies. Her incorporation of ideational factors as causal influences is very adept, and her painstaking empirical work to substantiate her claims lends strong—albeit indirect—support to the arguments I make about the role that values play in understanding differences among capitalist democracies with regard to income inequality. One of the major differences in our conceptualization lies in how we capture this values dimension. For Schmidt, elite rhetoric reflects underlying norms and values held by the mass public. In my study, I measure those values directly by examining mass surveys. Nevertheless, the common intuition and emphasis is that we both appreciate that differences do exist among nations with regard to ideas and discourses about issues of social justice, and we both believe that this element should be a central part of our empirical analysis. Whereas Schmidt has been vigilant in demonstrating the empirical importance of ideas and values, I am principally motivated to elucidate their normative significance as vital to the integrity of democracy and secondarily to incorporate this dimension into my empirical analysis and comparative study of income inequality.

Cultural factors or, more specifically, values have generally been largely omitted from most empirical analyses of comparative political economy. Even those scholars who have taken values and norms seriously, such as Goodin and colleagues (1999) and Rothstein (1998), do not really try to uncover what, if any, causal role values might play in shaping outcomes such as predicting the viability of the welfare state in an increasingly competitive global economy. Goodin and colleagues, for example, are concerned with how the three different welfare regimes best deliver on the values they embody using panel data to trace how real individual lives fare over time in each of the three different types of welfare state. Although not intended in any way as a study of the causal role of values, the authors do, however, construe welfare institutions as "a distinctive set of fundamental values" along with other definitional characteristics (1999, 22, 37–38). On issues ranging from economic growth, poverty, and inequality to social integration and stability, they conclude that the social democratic regime, exemplified by the Netherlands, exceeds the performance of both the corporatist regime in Germany and the liberal model in the United States. Rothstein, conversely, seeks to defend the universal welfare state on both normative and empirical grounds by showing how social norms as well as moral and political logics produced certain institutions at formative moments in a nation's history and therefore continue to determine the level of political support for certain social policies. Rothstein concludes: "If it is true that the shape of welfare policy is decided by the social norms established among citizens, and if these norms in turn are determined by the type of political institutions we have analyzed, then the future of the welfare state of whatever type is something that lies in the hands of its political leaders and citizens, since they decide whether they want to change our political institutions or not" (1998, 222). Similarly, Scharpf and Schmidt complete their two-volume book on a note of democratic optimism when they note that even in the face of severe economic constraints, "the overall size of the welfare state and the extent of redistribution remain a matter of political choice" (2000, 336).

Also reconfirming the power of institutions and domestic political choice are scholars who are not necessarily wedded to any particular version of institutionalism but are especially attuned to the globalization debates and interested in assessing the state's capacity to govern the national economy in the face of growing internationalization (Swank 2001, 2002; Weiss 2003). Some of the more recent literature addresses specific linkages between welfare regimes and economic performance more generally (Huber and Stephens 2001; Swank 2001) and reaches positive conclusions about the capacity of national political institutions (conventionally construed) to maintain commitments to welfare provisions. Swank, in particular, provides strong empirical evidence that domestic political institutions of a certain kind are able to blunt the pressures of globalization. Although he sees the liberal market systems as likely to promote retrenchment, he finds the social corporatist form of interest group representation as opposed to the pluralist system and the "system of electoral representation, especially the degree to which it consists of inclusive institutions, not majoritarian institutions" most important in defending social protection schemes (Swank 2003, 72).

## Recent Comparative Scholarship on Income Inequality

One observation from the foregoing review is that very few comparative studies have focused specifically on the question of income inequality. If the welfare state literature has not generated much research on income inequality, what has been produced in the field as a whole? A decade ago, Peter Hall (1997) said in his assessment of the state of the field of comparative politics that relatively little attention has been paid to distributive issues or, in particular, national patterns of economic policy and performance and the impact on inequalities in the distribution of resources and life-chances (195). Although income distribution has been of central theoretical concern to students of comparative politics, the cross-national data have only recently become authoritative and widely available. Early work investigated the impact of tax and transfer policies, the influence of labor unions, and the ideological complexion of governments (Borg and Castles 1982. Katz, Mahler, and Franz 1983; Swank and Hicks 1985), but as Vincent Mahler (1989) pointed out, much of this literature was riddled with theoretical and practical problems stemming from inaccurate measurement and definitional inconsistency. Mahler (2004) has done extensive research on the impact of globalization and domestic political factors on income inequality and state redistribution in the developed world and has produced empirical evidence showing only weak and unsystematic relationships between economic internationalization and income distribution but reasonably strong relationships between domestic political variables and a more egalitarian distribution of income. The political factors he finds most influential and significantly related to lower inequality are higher levels of wage coordination, higher levels of union density, and stronger electoral turnout. Overall, his findings confirm the important role that domestic political factors continue to play in determining distributive outcomes in the advanced democracies. Supplying even stronger empirical evidence for the "domestic politics matters" thesis, previous research by Birchfield and Crepaz (1998) found specific constitutional structures and consensual political institutions to be systematically related to lower levels of income inequality. In contrast to the most recent comparative analyses of distributive issues, these works are much more general in their conclusions about the overall redistributive capacity of domestic political institutions (see also Crepaz 2002).

Pontusson, Rueda, and Way (2002) make an important distinction between the relative reductionary impact of political-institutional variables on the upper versus the lower halves of the wage distribution, showing that factors such as unionization, centralized wage bargaining, and public-sector employment primarily affect the income distribution of unskilled workers. In contrast, Left governments were found to have a more egalitarian effect on the upper end of the income or wage hierarchy. Also breaking new ground in research on the variations in income distribution is the *World Politics* article by Bradley and colleagues (2003) that divides the distributive process into two stages, the distribution of pretax and transfer income and the reduction in inequality effected by taxes and transfers. Most interested in vindicating the power resources theory, the authors test the relationships between distributive outcomes and union movement strength, leftist party mobilization, and leftist party governance. Consistent with power resources theory, they expected to find strong effects of union organization on pretax and transfer inequality, and of leftist government on governmental redistribution through the welfare state provisions. Breaking up the stages of distribution and redistribution, they find that pretax and transfer inequality is associated with high unemployment, a high proportion of female-headed households, and low union density. In contrast, political variables are the strongest determinants of reduction in income inequality. Ultimately, leftist governments drive the redistributive process through taxes and transfer and indirectly by increasing the proportion of GDP devoted to such mechanisms. Furthermore, Bradley and colleagues demonstrate that "there is great variation in time and space in the proportional reduction in inequality from the extremes of Switzerland in 1982 with only a 6.2 percent reduction in inequality to Sweden in 1995 with a 47 percent reduction in inequality" (2003, 225).

Finally, Kenworthy and Pontusson (2005) have most recently examined distributive outcomes in the advanced capitalist democracies using income data for working-age households rather than earnings data for individuals. They observe a trend in increasing inequality in most OECD countries with more significant increases among the liberal market economies. Unlike previous studies, their analysis illustrates the importance of differential access to employment as a source of income inequality. Examining changes in the redistributive effects of taxation and income transfers to households, their data reveal that welfare states have functioned as they were designed to, compensating for the rise in market inequality that partially flows from unemployment problems. Thus, they argue, "it is markets, not politics that have become more inegalitarian" (450). I find this insight extremely interesting and relevant to the main thesis of this book, which is seeking to get better traction on the relationship between the workings of the market, popular ideas about what markets and states can and should do in terms of distribution and redistribution, and the institutional contexts in which both take place. If certain institutional settings tend to default more to markets (or insulate them from political demands) and markets are becoming more inegalitarian, then we need to probe deeper and understand how values enter the picture and whether specific institutions reflect popular preferences better than others do.

If there is widespread support for redistribution, does this matter for actual outcomes, or does it depend on institutional context? According to Kenworthy and Pontusson, the United States is exceptional in that it stands out as the one country that has experienced increased market inequality without producing a corresponding increase in redistribution. This is not surprising given the negative record the United States has for effectively redistributing income and reducing poverty. For instance, Luxembourg Income Study data for 1994 indicate that tax and transfers in the United States only reduced poverty by 13 percent as opposed to Sweden, whose policies reduced poverty by 82 percent (see Iversen and Soskice 2006, 165).

What are the different institutional conditions and value contexts that explain such disparate outcomes? This particular question distinguishes my inquiry from the new and impressive body of work that has emerged in the past several years. Yet, there is a certain coherence and compatibility between our approaches as well in terms of the common interest in getting at both the economic and political factors driving income inequality. Our work points to the same causal factors, but I seek to draw out the normative questions by introducing values, and I attempt a broader institutional framework.

In addition to presenting the most current data on income inequality and showing the important relationship between distribution and employment, Kenworthy and Pontusson (2005) also generate quantitative analyses that suggest a potential synthesis or reconciliation of the median-voter theorem and power-resources theories allowing for an understanding of the changes in redistribution in terms of how unions, Left parties, and other actors mobilize low-income workers to participate in the political process (see especially, 460–61).

In a similar vein, the latest research by Iversen and Soskice (2006) introduces a model that captures the role that specific electoral institutions play in bringing the very actors Kenworthy and Pontusson are talking about into coalitions that then produce various redistributive outcomes. Employing panel data from 1945 to 1998 for redistribution, government partisanship, and electoral systems, they test their argument that the electoral system plays a key role in explaining why some democracies redistribute more than others do. Using a standard economic model that departs from many of the simple assumptions of the commonly employed Meltzer-Richard model, they introduce political parties as representations of classes or coalitions of classes and allow taxes and transfers to vary across these classes. In doing so, they portray redistributive politics as a multidimensional game that extends beyond the rich-poor model so that middle classes play a critical, if not determinative, role in shaping outcomes. What they are able to show is that a two-party majoritarian system is more likely to produce center-right governments that redistribute less than a m ultiparty proportional representation (PR) system where center parties are more likely to ally with parties of the left and redistribute more. This article very carefully lays out the logic of how specific electoral systems produce different coalitions of classes, which in turn shape redistributive policies and outcomes. Their argument lends support for the institutional argument I make here, that PR is a predominant feature of consensus democracies. In a previously published book-length treatment of similar issues but that focuses on broader social protection and welfare policies, Iversen (2005) also empirically established how preferences vary across electoral systems and, in particular, how preferences are represented in coalition bargaining in PR systems but not in majoritarian systems where the median voter is likely to ignore the distributive preferences of those with little income. Low-income voters may in fact threaten the interests of the median voter, encouraging a vote for the center-right as a result. Even in the event of a shock to the income distribution where the median voter desires more redistribution, there will also presumably be a fear of center-left parties where the "poor set the policy" (2005, 189–90). In the first scenario—a PR system—a compromise is produced between the center and the left parties, but this is not the likely outcome in a majoritarian setting with the net effect being a less significant shift in policies. In this book, Iversen presents what he calls a general theory of political economy that is grounded in microfoundations and what he calls an "asset theory of preferences" to offer alternatives to power resources models as well globalization arguments about the expansion of welfare. He explains individual preferences for social protection as a function of the level and composition of their skill specificity or human capital assets. Although my argument about values is a different one because I do not conceptualize preferences via economic theories of behavior (although he also tests his theory using survey data), there is no reason to see the end result as a competing or alternative explanation to what I offer in this book. In fact, Iversen even uses Lijphart's measure for consensual systems to capture the political-institutional element in his argument. He defines it in terms of the degree to which a political system encourages political compromise, which is perfectly congruent with my conceptualization as well.

From this brief overview of the most recent comparative analyses of income inequality, it seems that as we move closer and closer to greater methodological precision and measurement of discrete factors influencing distribution and redistributions issues, we seem to move further and further away from general theories of politics and comparative political economy about matters of distributive justice. Conversely, the recent research reveals an increasing sophistication of the data and methods employed to understand more fully what is taking place in the advanced capitalist world with regard to growing trends of income inequality, and there are some consistent findings that vindicate conventional welfare state and domestic politics theories. What is missing is the lack of attention to values and attitudes about rising inequality and the views of citizens on what, if anything, governments should do to ameliorate growing inequality. There is an implicit recognition that this value dimension might matter when Kenworthy and Pontusson acknowledge the norms that undergird institutions such as corporatist wage bargaining and the welfare state, but the point is only indirectly considered. Ultimately, these disparate findings do not produce strong theoretical knowledge about the capacity of democratic politics to shape economic outcomes. Instead, we are left with a sense of the power as well as the limitations of institutions to fully understand and explain these patterns of income inequality. The power of institutions in explaining political economic outcomes such as income distribution flows directly from the ability of very specific structures, such as wage bargaining, to negotiate more equitable income schemes in the first place and welfare state institutions to retroactively ameliorate inequitable outcomes associated with market income. What I find limiting about all of the previous studies that have essentially produced this knowledge about the relationship between income inequality and political institutions is that this leaves us with a very narrow conception of the broader forces of politics in potentially shaping socioeconomic outcomes. The next section inquires into whether a broader approach to institutions that combines both a political economic as well as a political cultural element may prove more satisfactory.

## Retooling Lijphart's Consensus-Majoritarian Framework to "Bring Culture In"

Lijphart's approach to institutional analysis is more encompassing than the other approaches we have reviewed here in that its central preoccupation lies with how institutions matter and which types of democratic institutions work best for particular policy outcomes. It is precisely the "how" question that proved to be one of the major weaknesses of many of the other variants

of institutionalism. Nonetheless, no analytical framework is without its deficiencies, and I argue here that Lijphart's institutional model, if more rigorously
theorized, may actually embody a political cultural dimension that if properly
specified can reinvigorate his typologies on both normative and empirical
fronts. In his first book, *The Politics of Accommodation* (1968), Lijphart illustrated with a single deviant case that the majoritarian approach to democratic
governance was risky in highly plural and divisive societies, and that conso-
ciation of elites was more effective in producing stability in deeply divided
societies. Not only did this book drop a bombshell because his conclusion
challenged predominant thinking generated by Almond's reigning typology,
it would also lead him to impart one of the classic and enduring methodological insights in comparative politics (1971).

In *Democracy in Plural Societies* (1977) Lijphart extended his argument and
showed that societal pluralism did not have to be an impediment to democracies and that certain types of institutions could enable divisive ethnic, religious,
and class groups to coexist peacefully. Here the insight was that institutions
had to facilitate consensual forms of power and responsibility sharing. He identified such institutions as the grand coalition, proportional representation,
multiparty politics, and various methods of elite accommodation and seg-
mental autonomy. Although these works had an important impact, *Democracies*
(1984) would become his true landmark work in political science, which was
later revised and published as *Pattern of Democracy* in 1999. The main scholarly
achievement of this work lies primarily in the establishment of two conceptual dimensions along which democracies organize their institutions and
his actual mapping of twenty-one (and later thirty-six) countries on these
dimensional axes, majoritarian-consensual and federal-unitary. After comparing systematically the different forms of executive power, executive-legislative
relations, parliaments, party systems, electoral systems, constitutions, and forms
of direct democracy such as referenda and organizing this information empirically along two main dimensions, Lijphart conducted a factor analysis to find
that there are only five countries with very strong scores on both dimensions.
These are the prototypes of the different categories: New Zealand and the
United Kingdom are the majoritarian prototypes, and Switzerland, Belgium,
and the Netherlands are prototypical of the consensual group (1984, 216–17).
As I will discuss in the following chapter, major refinements have been made
to the various empirical measurements, but the general integrity of the typology has remained intact.

One scholar describes Lijphart's stature in the field of comparative politics as "one of the foremost authorities . . . whose work has progressed over time from an inquiry into the conditions which gave rise to certain types of democracy to an inquiry into the consequences of certain types of democracy" (Rothstein 1996, 322). Such a comment makes it easy to understand why there have not been any major challenges or fatal critiques of Lijphart's body of work. In fact, one of the only such attacks on Lijphart's entire research program went largely unnoticed despite its publication in the prestigious, high-profile journal, *World Politics.* In his article "Lijphart, Lakatos, and Consociationalism," Lustick charges that "the success of the consociational research program cannot be explained on the basis of its explanatory power or heuristic value—the criteria for good science advocated in early Lakatos. Rather, its success bears witness to the late-Lakatosian claim that research programs can succeed by relying on the political and rhetorical skills of their leading practitioners and on alliance between those practitioners and political interests outside the scientific arena" (1999, 90). Lustick then proceeds to review the development of Lijphart's body of work, especially his earlier work on consociationalism. More than offering his own criticism, he cites the rather sparse critiques from other scholars to make a case that over the span of his career, Lijphart lost sight of his initial empirical rigor, constantly changed his methodological rationale, and began to rely on impressionistic and selective use of evidence to defend and promote a "utopian consociationalist myth" (112–14). This harsh and seemingly personal critique is puzzling to say the least, but I agree with one element in Lustick's critique. Lijphart's methodological contortions to classify countries such as South Africa and India, and possibly Mexico and Japan, as consociational are problematic because the idea and emphasis on the power-sharing principle with regard to dealing with ethnic conflict overshadows the various other elements of the typology. It risks becoming a case of the model becoming so flexible that almost any country may potentially qualify as long as the ostensible goal is the value of stability. This development is particularly unfortunate given the progress that has otherwise been made in the derivative work that conceptualizes the consensus-majoritarian typology as a broad differentiation in types of governance. More attention should be paid, perhaps, to distinguish features of the former notion of consociationalism and the newer model of consensus democracy.

One of the other principle sources of criticism of Lijphart's work is that of the prominent political theorist Brian Barry (1975), who provides one of the most thorough and systematic critiques of the consociational model. He argues that Lijphart's 1968 work is guilty of t autological reasoning because accommodation is simultaneously the method for successful negotiations of disputes between contentious cultural groups and the explanation for stable relations among those same culturally divisive groups. Barry also develops a cultural critique of consociational theory, arguing that institutions are not necessary to resolve certain conflicts. Perhaps most damaging is Barry's argument that some of Lijphart's key examples like Switzerland, are not really as deeply divided or conflictual in the first place. Although these criticisms are more well founded than those of Lustick, they may not be too consequential for the current trend in Lijphartian institutional analysis. Furthermore, I seek to redress one of the key issues Barry raises about Lijphart "packing too much unacknowledged theory" into his typology. Rather than interpreting it in this way, I argue that the consensus-majoritarian typology is in fact undertheorized; therefore, my reconstruction of the typology is based upon a deeper democratic theory that counterbalances the other tendency of the model being empirically overspecified by packing in too many indicators. My intention is to instead underscore the overarching nature of the typology as a model of democratic governance.

The manner in which Lijphart has classified and combined various dimensions of political institutional settings, such as executive-legislative relations (parliamentary versus presidential systems), unitary or fed eral dispersals of power, and electoral rules and party systems (proportional versus single member district representation), has made his typology one of the most analytically useful frameworks in comparative political analysis. In fact, an entire research program has coalesced around investigations of the impact of consensual versus majoritarian institutions on various policy outcomes, macroeconomic performance, magnitude of the welfare state (Crepaz 1996a; 1996b); how they exhibit differing propensities to provide for accountability, stability, and accommodative decision making (Powell 1982; Baylis 1989; Linz 1993); how they produce different levels of congruence between citizens and policymakers (Huber and Powell 1994); and, most recently, how the degree of satisfaction with democracy varies across the two system types (Anderson and Guillory 1997). I build on this previous research in two ways. First, I have previously employed Lijphart's framework to explore the relationship between these two broad approaches to democratic governance and the varying degree of income inequality across these societies (Birchfield 1996; Birchfield and

Crepaz 1998). Second, I retool the consensus-majoritarian institutional framework by showing that there is an underlying political cultural dimension that has so far been implicit but undertheorized, in both Lijphart's own work as well as the wider research it has generated. Integrating Lane's theoretical work on conceptions of justice and Lijphart's empirical formulation of types of democracy will help to clarify why making explicit the role of political culture is so crucial—particularly as it bears on the causal processes of income distribution. Although I refer to this dimension as political cultural, it is important to underscore that it is in fact an expression of a normative perspective on political economy as applied democratic theory.

There is an important affinity between Robert Lane's delineation of market justice and political justice and Lijphart's underlying conceptualization of democratic politics that, once fleshed out, may give empirical character to conceptions of justice and an ideational or cultural dimension to empirical classifications of political institutions. In this sense, I hope to make the linkage that Rothstein has elucidated between the empirical and normative character of political institutions. In the final analysis, Lane demonstrates that market justice denies a "community point of view" (1986, 399) insofar as both markets and politics serve as want-satisfying mechanisms, with markets satisfying individual wants and polities satisfying collective wants. If market justice prevails—as a result of perceiving political methods as ridden with conflicts of interest, injustice, corruption, and so on—the idea of politics as the "art of the possible" is essentially precluded. The result is to construe the purpose of politics in the most narrow of terms (what I have called winner-take-all politics), and even then it is viewed with suspicion. If one looks at the overall character of Lijphart's definition of consensus democracy, we can draw a parallel between market justice and majoritarianism and contrast it with the way in which consensus institutions are more reflective of political justice.

For example, majoritarian institutions such as a winner-take-all electoral system and a strong one-party executive typical of presidentialism deride a broad communal approach to politics in that it forces citizens to construe politics in a zero-sum manner. In contrast, Lijphart's often-quoted response to the question of who should govern is "as many people as possible" (1984, 4), which, in his view, epitomizes the inclusive nature of consensual political institutions. Guillory and Anderson's (1997) study further captured this effect as they showed with convincing empirical evidence that even those voters who essentially lose out in democratic competition display higher levels of satisfaction with the way democracy works than do lo sers in s ystems with majoritarian characteristics. Access and wider representation are the key features of consensually oriented political institutions, such as proportional representation and the multiparty system, as well as the shared or fused powers between the executive and legislative branches in parliamentary regimes that are conducive to coalition cabinets.

In a discussion of some of Rawls's later work, Bo Rothstein claims that the author came to the conclusion that "it is just institutions that can ge nerate a just society, not a just society that generates just institutions" (1996, 138). In other words, institutions are far more than simply the "rules of the game" because they directly affect what values and norms become established in a society. Seen in this light, it is clear that more consensually oriented political institutions impart a cultural ethos of politics as a collective endeavor and that, although certainly containing some elements of competition, the feature is not the defining or overarching one as it is in the adversarial, winner-take-all approach of majoritarian systems.

In work with Crepaz (1991), Lijphart added another feature to his original model, interest intermediation, which generally falls into two broad categories: pluralism and corporatism. Crepaz and Lijphart advanced a theoretical and empirical argument for incorporating the type of interest group system into the consensus-majoritarian typology and showed statistical evidence that the linkage between corporatism and the other elements of consensus democracy were quite strong. However, this association is not entirely without problems (Anderson 2001). There appears to be a dilemma between Lijphart's claim that consensus democracy is about the widest possible dispersal of power and his inclusion of corporatism, which has been characterized by the attributes that seem directly in conflict with of consensual institutions.

Corporatism is about th e centralization and conc entration of po wer in the form of monopoly representation (Schmitter 1982), and many criticize its lack of transparency and elitism. The extent to which Lijphart acknowledges this tension is quite l imited. He does qualify that he refers to "democratic corporatism" in contrast to its more authoritarian variants and remarks that Katzenstein's description of corporatism as "an ideology of social partnership" and the absence of a "winner-take-all mentality are characteristics that link corporatism to other characteristics of consensus democracy" (1999, 172). Giving such short shrift to this important element in his model is theoretically inadequate, and without a more thorough defense of the affinity between corporatism and consensus democracy, the empirical measurements and statistical analyses performed with this item risk serious problems of misinterpretation and spurious findings.

One of the best defenses of corporatism from a democratic perspective was articulated by Dryzek (1996) who made the sophisticated if subtle argument that corporatism is the representational form of a "passively exclusive state" that shuts out all interests except business and labor and by virtue of this exclusivity facilitates a "flourishing oppositional sphere" that is much more fundamental to democracy than an inclusive state. Dryzek argues:

> Theorists who seek democratization in the shadow of corporatism believe that corporatism's best quality is its ability to actively include particular interests; the problem is only that historically a very limited range of interests has been included. I will suggest, in contrast, that the real beauty of corporatism is in its passive exclusion of many interests in society—and that it does this with a state that seems quite good at promoting economic justice (at least in comparison to all the alternative forms of state organization that have been tried from time to time). (478)

This interpretation of corporatism makes a powerful contribution to alternative visions of the political economy and the role of government. It may also serve to justify Lijphart's inclusion of corporatism in his overall measure for consensus democracy. Once the broader view of democracy and meaningful participation in political life is brought forward, the inconsistency or contradictions mentioned above appear to dissolve.

The interest group dimension of Lijphart's framework is what essentially makes employing his framework for politicoeconomic analysis most meaningful, but without this clarification of why corporatism and consensus democracy are theoretically compatible, this association would be a case of overreaching, particularly in highly aggregated empirical analyses. Because corporatism can reasonably serve as a proxy for centralized wage bargaining, it will obviously have an influential role in explaining cross-national differences in income inequality. As Gottschalk and Smeeding reports, for example, "It is clear that the countries with the largest increases in income inequality—the United States and the United Kingdom—were also the countries with the most decentralized labor markets. Countries with more centralized wage-setting institutions either escaped the trend toward greater inequality, like Germany, or experienced relatively mild increases like Sweden and the Netherlands" (1997, 34). While this is an important fact, why those types of institutional constraints are there in the first place and whether they are widely perceived as constraints or opportunities by society as a whole need to be further examined.

Gottschalk's observations raise another question. There appears to be a strong correlation between the Anglo-Saxon countries and growing inequality, whereas the continental Europeans are managing or even closing the income gap. The former generally fall into Lijphart's majoritarian category whereas most of the latter are consensual political systems. Though economists Frank and Cook (1995) have documented the trend—especially in the U.S. economy—toward winner-take-all markets, there has been no discussion of the possible connection between winner-take-all politics and winner-take-all economics.

Majoritarian institutions (e.g., presidential systems, single-member district electoral rules, and two-party systems) are based on a winner-take-all approach to politics, which in turn produces a higher proclivity toward winner-take-all economics or, in the case of income distribution, a greater disparity between the rich and the poor. Consensual political systems, on the other hand, are by their very nature more inclusive (and representative of diverse socioeconomic groups) and thus tend to produce distributive outcomes that are more egalitarian. Given the predominance of consensually oriented countries in the sample of countries I examine here, one might expect social welfare policies designed to reduce the gap between the rich and the poor to be maintained even in the face of globalization pressures and rhetoric from powerful groups in favor of more market-led strategies of (non)governance. In the final analysis, national models of political economy or "competing capitalisms" actual embody profound conceptions of what democratic politics is all about; from this vantage point, there are more commonalties than divergences among western European states. It is precisely this broad consensus over fundamental questions of social justice and the legitimacy of the state vis-à-vis the market in this policy domain that should serve to reassure those wary of the ostensible relinquishing of sovereignty in certain areas, macroeconomic policy in particular (e.g., adherence to European Monetary Union [EMU] standards). Crouch and Streeck (1997) argue: "While economic globalization places strong pressures on national economic policies for deregulation and privatization, formally ratifying the loss of national control over the economy, surrender to such pressures may well be offered in the name of national interest and national sovereignty" (10). In other words, Europeans may actually preserve national prerogatives such as greater economic equality by unifying their economies to compete against the American, winner-take-all model of political economy. Again, Crouch and Streeck frame this predicament quite cogently:

> The all-important question today, we believe, is how to recapture public governance of the private economy at some international level, after the national one has become obsolete. Domestic democratic sovereignty over the economy, the one sovereignty that really counts, can be restored only if it is internationally shared, that is, if the reach of what used to be "domestic" political intervention is expanded to match an expanding market. National social institutions and national democratic politics can support internationally viable, egalitarian high-wage economies only in a conducive international context, and it is only within such a context that they can continue to generate and maintain capitalist diversity and its beneficial consequences for economic performance. Existing national institutions . . . can today be no more than the building blocks of a new, larger institutional structure that must supersede them in order to preserve their contribution to the task of civilizing a, by now, globally integrated capitalist market economy. (17)

Income (re)distribution provides an illustrative case of this point; although it is undoubtedly a policy outcome, in a broader sense it reflects a society's underlying commitment to distributive justice or, as the following empirical analysis will show in the case of winner-take-all systems, a tolerance for widespread economic inequality.

In Lijphart's more recent work, he claims that the overall "quality of democracy" is higher in consensus systems (1994, 149) and he includes greater income equality as one of his criteria. This point of view is largely consistent with the advantages that Lane proposes would accrue to a society that restores political justice to favor. A market-based conception of justice erodes the extent to which democracy may serve as a counterweight to the social inequities of capitalism. Although Lijphart and others intimate that consensus democracy may exude an ethos in sharp contrast to that of majoritarianism, nowhere is the cultural dimension (which also reflects the nature of the relationship between politics and economics, as I have discussed previously) made explicit; yet, I submit this is where the real causal weight lies. It is not the pure mechanics of certain institutions but the way in which institutions embody and actualize the values and norms of its citizenry. This element is what I believe is presently underspecified in the Lijphart's framework, but this can be corrected by integrating the political cultural dimension derived from Lane and a conceptualization of political economy as applied democratic theory. Although a propensity to favor political justice seems congruent with the vision of democratic governance captured by Lijphart's model of consensus democracy and the winner-take-all approach of majoritarianism resonates with market justice, this is merely an abstract association that remains to be explored further and empirically validated. As the survey data presented in Chapter 2 showed, there is an apparent affinity between the notion of cultural values—disaggregated to the very specific variable of attitudes about the legitimate role of government in redistributing income—and consensus democracy. This finding coupled with the foregoing theoretical argument indicates that certain institutional environments do seem to engender certain types of norms and values, although it is not a foregone conclusion and there are exceptions to the general patterns detected. The question to be addressed now is whether cross-national differences in the various combinations of values and political institutions are systematically related to outcomes such as income inequality. In the next chapter, I translate these theoretical propositions about the relationship between ideational and institutional factors into an empirically testable model.

# — 4 —

THE INTERACTION OF INSTITUTIONS, VALUES, AND
INCOME INEQUALITY: A QUANTITATIVE ANALYSIS

The theoretical foundations of this study suggest that the ideational and the
institutional forces shaping a society's income distribution should be understood in relation to—not in isolation from—one another. Whereas Chapters
2 and 3 were concerned with arguing *why* values and institutions matter, the
present chapter shows *how* both can be simultaneously enlisted in our effort
to unravel the causal mechanisms driving distributional outcomes in capitalist
democracies. Translating this theoretical perspective into an empirical model,
I estimate the joint effect of values and institutions on income inequality in
sixteen countries by deploying the quantitative data in multivariate statistical
analysis. As I have argued in the preceding chapters, a more realistic and comprehensive explanation of cross-national variation in income inequality must
address how the economy and polity are organized and linked to one another
both conceptually and practically. At the conceptual level and consistent with
principles of democratic theory delineated in Chapter 1, I refer to two distinctive value orientations—political justice and market justice—representing
prevailing cultural attitudes in a given democratic society that characterize
how citizens conceive of the legitimate roles of markets and polities in shaping distributional outcomes. In practical terms, specific constitutional structures and political institutions operate to channel those values and preferences
into actual political-economic outcomes.

Although previous research suggests that certain political institutional systems tend to produce particular types of macroeconomic outcomes (Crepaz
1996a; Birchfield and Crepaz 1998; Swank 2002), I believe the influence of institutions on such outcomes varies systematically according to the ideational
and normative environments within which they are embedded. Accordingly,

my theoretical argument can be most appropriately tested through a multi-variate analysis with an intera ctive term that captures the independent and joint effects of these two causal variables. In the case of income inequality in advanced capitalist democracies, I posit that consensual political institutions combined with a strong societal norm of political justice will tend to produce more egalitarian income distributions; in contrast, we are likely to find higher levels of income inequality in majoritarian systems where market justice orientations prevail. Although earlier chapters have described these patterns and largely confirmed these broad correlations as well as identified some interesting exceptions, this chapter explicitly models this conceptualization of the complex interrelationships between values, institutions, and income inequality. First, I explain my methodological strategy drawing especially on the insights of Henry Brady and David Collier (2004). Next, I describe the data and discuss various measurement issues. Finally, I provide an analysis of the statistical model and discuss the overall implications of the findings.

Before describing the data and the nuts and bolts of the research design, I wish to clarify my general methodological strategy and articulate the potential as well as the limitations of statistical analysis in political science research. As Gabriel Almond underscored in *A Discipline Divided* (1990), one of the most long-standing polemics in political science is the debate between those who view the discipline as a "hard science" and those who are more pessimistic about assuming the mantle of science and who prefer eclecticism in choosing among a variety of scholarly methods. The latest round in this ongoing debate was ushered in by the publication of King, Keohane, and Verba's *Designing Social Inquiry* (1994) wherein the authors argue that the basic logic of scientific inference is the same for both quantitative and qualitative research.

King, Keohane, and Verba provide the first of two justifications I make in employing statistical analysis to investigate the complex phenomenon of variation in income distribution. The authors comment that "the perceived complexity of a situat ion depends in part on how well we can simplify reality, and our capacity to simplify depends on whether we can specify outcomes and explanatory variables in a coherent way" (1994, 10). I hope to have achieved this at the outset by reconceptualizing political economy as applied democratic theory and adding a political cultural and ideational dimension to Lijphart's institutional framework. I theoretically specified variation in income inequality as a function of two encompassing and interactive explanatory variables, values, and institutions. And, as my theoretical framework derived a clear set of hypotheses, the complexity and multicausality associated with the distribution of income does not preclude but rather facilitates a rigorous and systematic empirical examination. The second justification relates to the nature of the dependent variable in that income distribution is, of course, a quantitative phenomenon. When explaining the variation in income inequality across a group of societies, which themselves can be assessed and compared quantitatively, a statistical analysis is a feasible and appropriate methodological strategy to employ. What is distinctive about this study of income inequality is that it has from the outset been equally concerned with the normative underpinnings of what now in this chapter will assume the form of more parsimonious, if not reductive, summary empirical measures of the potential causal mechanisms shaping income distribution.

In sum, my examination of why certain societies produce more egalitarian income distributions than others is guided by a research strategy that seeks an answer in a manner that is both theoretically and normatively grounded as well as empirically verifiable. As Thelen puts it, "There is, in other words, no dichotomy between theoretical and empirical work because good analyses have to do both. . . . The utility of a theory after all, cannot be assessed apart from the empirical material it is meant to explain" (1999, 10). Likewise, I believe statistical analysis in the study of politics can only be useful insofar as the theoretical concepts to which they are tethered are logically conceived and historically informed. As the previous chapters have illustrated, each of the core variables being studied—both the dependent and independent variables—are conceptualized in a much broader manner than understanding any of them as mere quantitative indicators.

Accordingly, my study pursues both a "data-set observations" approach conducive to statistical tests supplemented with "causal-process observations" derived from the focused comparative case studies examined in the following chapter. Brady and Collier (2004) contrast these two approaches and clarify their respective contributions to causal inference. Unlike King, Keohane, and Verba, these authors argue that the logic of inference is fundamentally different in quantitative and qualitative research, yet like Tarrow (1996, 2004) they are proponents of using both approaches through triangulation techniques such as process tracing and sequencing of different types of data. Rather than accepting the logic of statistical theory as the only means to divulge causal mechanisms, distinct but complimentary analytic and inferential leverage is gained when researchers employ multiple methods and diverse tools. By employing a combination of quantitative and qualitative methods, I seek to achieve the methodological breadth advocated by Brady and Collier (2004) and produce a deeper understanding of the variation in income inequality among capitalist democracies: "Cross-national regression analysis based on cross-sectional data has the virtue of providing a concise summary of the relationships about a set of variables across many contexts and of testing the 'comparative statics' of theories, that is, contrast among cases at a given point in time" (Brady and Collier 2004, 223). Chapter 5 enhances the quantitative analysis and variable oriented approach with comparative historical data and process tracing in case studies of two countries drawn from the original set of cases.

## Cases

The basic aim of this study is to identify general causal patterns of income inequality across this group of affluent capitalist democracies. Selecting only established democracies with market economies for my cases is a necessity dictated by theory. As I pointed out in Chapter 1, most studies of income inequality have consisted of either global studies done by sociologists examining income distribution across developed and developing countries or single-case studies, conducted primarily by economists, of income distribution in the United States. The methodological problems associated with the former category are typical of what comparativists describe as comparing apples with oranges. The advantage of a design that examines only similarly situated cases, such as the OECD countries, is that systematic investigation of this kind may identify key explanatory variables while implicitly controlling for other important variables that are judged to be more or less the same across the universe of cases (Przeworski and Teune 1970). The countries I investigate are those typically examined by comparativists of advanced industrial societies.[1] The sixteen countries for which I have obtained authoritative and comparable data for all of the variables are the following: Australia, Belgium, Canada, Denmark, Finland, France, Germany, Ireland, Italy, the Netherlands, New Zealand, Norway, Sweden, Switzerland, the United Kingdom, and the United States. The general pattern of income inequality in many of these countries began to widen noticeably during the mid to late 1970s and early 1980s and

1. Japan and Austria were eliminated from the traditional set of OECD countries because the data available were not fully comparable with the other countries.

appeared to be rising though the mid-1990s, yet there was a good deal of variation in the pace and degree of change. As a general rule, one cannot gauge change in income distribution for periods shorter than approximately a decade; thus, the three time points selected for this study are the periods from 1975 to 1984, 1985 to 1994, and 1995 to 2001. Attention to problem of income inequality by both policymakers and researchers is typically for mulated in terms of growing inequality and the widening of the gap between the rich and poor, thus implying change. However, to be clear, I am interested in understanding cross-sectional variation in income inequality in each time period, not the change over time in each country.

## The Dependent Variable

Measuring income distribution is an extremely complex matter, and attempting to compare measurements of income inequality cross-nationally has only very recently become possible through multiple and coordinated efforts such as those of the Luxembourg Income Study (LIS) and the UNU-WIDER World Income Inequality Database. The UNU-WIDER World Income Inequality Database (2005) reflects the most recent effort to bring together high quality data, including those from the LIS study, and standardize the calculation of income inequality in a wide sample of countries for many years.[2] The UNU-WIDER project often recalculates estimates of income inequality from the original microdata files and publishes estimates of the quality of the data published by the project. The estimates of inequality included in the UNU-WIDER database derive from disposable income or consumption estimates according to the source of the microdata.[3] Thus, the inequality estimates comprise either all consumption or income deriving from gross wages and salaries, cash property income and farm income, self-employment income, social insurance transfers, and factor income (such as sick pay, retirement benefits, child and family allowances, and unemployment compensation).[4] Such encompassing measures are appropriate for this study because I am interested in measuring the degree

2. The data can be found at http://www.wider.unu.edu/wiid/wiid.htm.

3. See UNU-WIDER (2005) World Income Inequality Database User Guide and Data Sources, V 2.0a, for further discussion.

4. For a more detailed description of the technical characteristics of the LIS database, see Atkinson, Rainwater, and Smeeding 1995. LIS Comparative Income Statistics and related information can be accessed electronically at http://lis.ceps.lu/inequality.htm.

of income inequality in a society after the "original" market distribution and the various forms of state redistributions have been made.

The UNU-WIDER project estimates inequality using the most widely reported measure, the Gini coefficient (also known as the Gini index or ratio), based on the Lorenz curve, which simply plots the share of population against the share of income received; thus, the higher the index, the greater the inequality. The UNU-WIDER project is the source of the final data used in the empirical analysis here because it permitted greater control over reconciling the time at which the dependent and independent variables were measured. Averages of the Gini ratios in each country from 1975 to 1984, 1985 to 1994, and 1995 to 2001 were calculated using only those data classified as the highest quality by the UNU-WIDER.[5]

For descriptive purposes, Table 3 presents some comparative data on income inequality for the sixteen countries included in this study.[6] There is quite an extensive and consistent range across each of these measures. For instance, the quintile share shows Sweden and Finland to be the most equal societies with approximately 31 percent of total income accruing to the top 20 percent of these populations, whereas the top 20 percent in the United States and Australia receive roughly 47 percent of total income, ranking these two countries as the least egalitarian in this group. Similarly, comparing the rich-poor ratios for Sweden and Australia, these two countries manifest the same rankings as examples of the most egalitarian and most inegalitarian societies, respectively. This pattern obtains as well when we examine the Gini coefficients. Summary measures such as the Gini index are not an appropriate gauge of what is happening at the extremes of the income distribution, for example, the bottom and top 1 percent. In some ways this is a very telling measure of how unequal certain societies are becoming; for instance, within the United States, income for the top 1 percent of earners skyrocketed more than 250 percent from 1979 to 1997, whereas it declined for the lowest 20 percent of households (see Atkinson 2005, 54). However, because this study is concerned with

5. Italy and Switzerland were missing highest quality data prior to 1985, so the next highest quality data were used instead to calculate the averages for 1975–84. For Germany, West Germany was used for the periods 1975–84 and 1985–93, and Unified Germany was used for 1994–2001.

6. Other possible statistical representations are the quintile measure, which reveals the proportion of income accruing to the top 20 percent of the population, and the rich–poor ratio, which provides a measure of the size of the gap between the rich and poor by dividing the amount of income received by the top 20 percent by the amount of income going to those in the bottom 40 percent. These latter statistics capture what occurs around the extremes of the population and reveals more information about change in income shares among these individual groups in society.

explaining broad cross-societal patterns of income inequality and not causes of extremes in wealth and poverty per se, the Gini is the most suitable measure.

## Core Independent Variables

The independent variables representing my core theoretical proposition are political institutions and societal values. The foregoing argument of this book demonstrates that we cannot take values for granted as we assess the impact of institutions on socioeconomic outcomes. If Lijphart is right that consensus democracies tend to pursue "kinder, gentler policies," then we would expect more egalitarian income distribution in consensual polities. However, the empirical data on income distribution reveal that although his assumption generally holds, there are some significant exceptions to this predicted pattern. Furthermore, as my critique of Lijphart emphasized, there is no reason to merely conjecture about societal values when we can find meaningful and reliable empirical indicators to convey this information.

Since the publication of Arend Lijphart's *Democracies* (1984), a great deal of research has been generated on the nature of different political institutions and types of democratic governance. Whereas much of the neoinstitutionalism

**Table 3** Comparative Measures of Income Inequality (1985–1994 averages)

| Country | Top Quintile Share | Rich–Poor Ratio | Gini Index |
|---|---|---|---|
| Australia | 42.2 | 2.74 | 31.7 |
| Belgium | 34.1 | 1.36 | 23.0 |
| Canada | 40.2 | 2.30 | 28.6 |
| Denmark | 38.6 | 2.22 | 24.0 |
| Finland | 31.2 | 1.15 | 22.6 |
| France | 41.9 | 2.41 | 32.4 |
| Germany | 40.3 | 2.14 | 30.0 |
| Ireland | 41.6 | 2.00 | 33.0 |
| Italy | 41.0 | 2.18 | 34.6 |
| Netherlands | 36.9 | 1.73 | 31.0 |
| New Zealand | 44.7 | 2.81 | 34.4 |
| Norway | 33.0 | 1.28 | 24.2 |
| Sweden | 31.8 | 1.18 | 22.2 |
| Switzerland | 41.1 | 1.96 | 36.0 |
| United Kingdom | 44.3 | 3.03 | 34.6 |
| United States | 46.9 | 3.53 | 37.5 |

literature is valuable for the empirical rigor that has been applied and the insights revealed about the critical role of institutions in explaining political phenomena, it is limited in two ways. First, it is very difficult to evaluate the overall progress of this body of research because there are many different institutions examined, and, second, there are at least three competing (and contentious) schools of thought: rational choice, historical institutionalism, and the sociological approach employed to quite diverse ends (Thelen 1999). As I have repeatedly emphasized, a key advantage of Lijphart's institutional framework is the encompassing nature of his typology of democracy. Lijphart is interested in the entire complex of institutions that comprise a democratic polity; as a result of his systematic classification of consensual and majoritarian democracies, comparativists have been able to generate theory, construct empirical models, and produce generalizations about these two distinctive approaches to democratic governance. Using Lijphart's measures for consensus and majoritarian democracies permits a more realistic and comprehensive gauge of the effect of political institutions on a complex policy outcome such as income inequality. The LC index (CONSCORP) formulated by Crepaz and Lijphart (1991) is a composite measure of consensus democracy and corporatism. As previously discussed, including corporatism effectively subsumes—albeit partially and indirectly—the impact of the welfare state on the dependent variable; work by Crepaz (1998) has empirically confirmed the systematic relationship between the magnitude of the welfare state and consensus systems. Furthermore, in Lijphart's revised and updated work, *Patterns of Democracy* (1999), an index measuring the degree of interest group pluralism/corporatism has been incorporated into the first dimension of his typology, which reinforces the insights of his findings with Crepaz that there appears to be a strong conceptual and empirical affinity between consensus democracy and corporatist interest intermediation. As Lijphart notes: "The typical interest group system of majoritarian democracy is a competitive and uncoordinated pluralism of independent groups in contrast with the coordinated and compromise-oriented system of corporatism that is typical of the consensus model" (Lijphart 1999, 171).

Lijphart adds to the observations of Peter Katzenstein (1985, 32, 157) that two other distinctive traits of corporatism, "an ideology of social partnership" and an absence of "a winner-take-all mentality" further reveal the linkage between corporatism and the other distinguishing features of consensus democracy. Thus, the impact of corporatism on income inequality can be reasonably assessed through the broader institutional index Lijphart has devised. Obviously, where labor has a more institutionalized role in political and economic decision-making processes, the less likely one is to find extreme wage dispersion and income inequality. In contrast, in the absence of tripartite concertation, interest group pluralism prevails, which is more likely to advantage groups who have the organizational and economic resources to influence government and thereby insulate it from the pressures of more numerous but disparate and less powerful labor groups.[7] Incorporating the impact of corporatism on income inequality, I believe, is congruent with my argument that there is a political cultural dimension related to understanding political economy as applied democratic theory that is implicit but undertheorized in Lijphart's typology.

With regard to the other institutions, ten major differences between majoritarian and consensual political systems have been deduced and found to cluster along the two separate dimensions. The first dimension, to which I have referred above, is labeled the "executive-parties dimension" and is the more salient of the two dimensions for the purpose of this study.[8] The following items comprise this dimension and represent the institutional element of my empirical analysis. The first description following each item refers to majoritarian systems and is followed by the contrasting definition or characterization of that element in consensual systems.

1. *Arrangement of executive power:* Concentration of executive power in single-party majority cabinets versus power sharing in multiparty coalitions.
2. *Executive-legislative relations:* Executive dominance versus executive-legislative balance of power.
3. *Party system:* Two-party versus multiparty systems.
4. *Electoral systems:* Majoritarian and disproportional versus proportional representation.
5. *Interest group system:* Pluralist interest group systems with "free-for-all" competition among groups versus coordinated and 'corporatist' interest

---

7. Along these lines and as early as 1965, E. E. Schattschneider argued that the flaw in the pluralist heavenly chorus is that it sings with a distinctly upper-class accent (see the Introduction.)

8. Lijphart's second dimension is the "federal-unitary dimension," which includes measures for centralized versus federal or decentralized government, unicameralism versus bicameralism, flexible versus rigid constitutions, judicial review, and central bank independence. As a whole, this dimension is less relevant to the central argument I am making about the impact of key political institutions on income inequality; thus, it is not included in the empirical analysis.

group systems aimed at comp romise and concentration" (as listed by Lijphart 1999, 3).

This composite measure expresses the institutional mechanisms through which private interests and social values may be converted into public policy, thus, capturing the core assertion of this study that political institutions play a powerful role in shaping distributional outcomes. Table 4 lists the key institutional features of each type of democracy and provides examples of the prototypical countries of each model. In terms of actual measurement and coding of the institutional variable, the Crepaz data used here have higher scores for more consensually oriented systems (e.g., Switzerland and Belgium are 1.87 and 1.66, respectively); likewise, the lower the score, the more majoritarian the system, such as scores of $-1.39$ for the United Kingdom and $-1.07$ for Canada.

The empirical relationship between political institutions and income inequality can be illustrated in a straightforward manner by plotting measures of consensus democracy against indicators of income inequality. Figure 2 is a scatter diagram of the institutional measure and the average level of income inequality for each of the countries. This figure illustrates the negative relationship between consensus institutions and income inequality. For instance, the bottom right cluster contains consensus democracies such as Belgium and Finland that also have low levels of income inequality. In the upper left quadrant, we find majoritarian countries such as the United States and Australia that have high levels of income inequality. An interesting pattern appears with

**Table 4** Lijphart's Typology of Democracy

| Institutional Elements | |
| --- | --- |
| Consensus | Majoritarian |
| Multiparty coalition executives | One-party majority executive |
| Executive–legislative balance | Executive dominates legislative |
| Multiparty system | Two-party system |
| Multidimensional party system | One-dimensional party system |
| Proportional electoral system | Disproportional electoral system |
| Corporatist form of interest mediation | Pluralist interest group system |
| Examples | |
| Switzerland | Canada |
| Netherlands | New Zealand |
| Finland | United Kingdom |
| Denmark | United States |

countries such as France, Canada, and New Zealand occupying a space characterized by majoritarian institutions and moderate to high income inequality,
reinforcing the idea that other factors are operative in explaining the relationship between institutions and income inequality. Most significant perhaps
is the location of Switzerland, a consensus system with quite a high level of
income inequality, underscoring the idea that institutions alone do not provide a full explanation of different patterns of income distribution.

The second core independent variable is the cultural or ideational factor,
broadly defined here as values and attitudes toward the competing roles of
states and markets in determining a society's distributional outcomes. The
way in which I conceptualize political culture qua values stems from m y
identification of Robert Lane's notions of political justice versus market justice as being the salient attribute of culture that might contribute explanatory
power to our attempt to understand cross-national variation in income inequality. Although theoretically innovative and extremely valuable in pointing
toward the critical role that the perceptions of citizens play in shaping justice
claims and—by extension—outcomes in a society, Lane's claims are based on

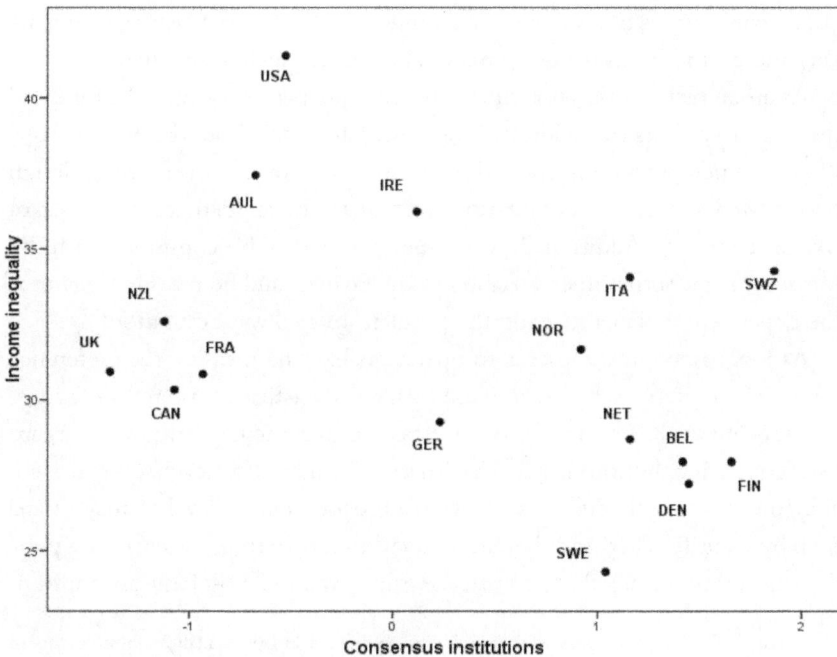

FIG 2 Consensus Institutions and Income Inequality

secondary accounts of survey research in which there is little more than a random collection of various studies that can at b est represent weak proxies of his otherwise theoretically powerful concepts.[9]

I strengthened and extended Lane's conceptualization through a more formal and direct operationalization of what he refers to as popular conceptions of justice. In attempting to capture this important distinction between preferences for market justice and political justice, I used survey data to generate an empirical indicator for what now will be treated as a causal variable. Consistent with an understanding of political economy as applied democratic theory, we should be concerned with this political cultural and ideational dimension of what is oth erwise conventionally perceived as strictly an economic outcome. Because all of my cases are long-established democracies with market economies, it is reasonable to assume that individuals in these societies have values and preferences about whether income distribution should be left up strictly to the market or whether some type of intervening, redistributive governmental action should attempt to ameliorate inequitable market outcomes. As I described in Chapter 2, Robert Lane's notion of p olitical justice and market justice captures an important distinction that serves to map out such public conceptions or sociocultural attitudes about the respective roles of markets and politics in distributing material resources such as income.

As an empirical indicator for this potential explanatory variable, I located specific survey data that addressed individual attitudes about the proper scope of government activity in the redistribution of income. This research design necessitated similar survey questions systematically applied across my set of sixteen countries. Additionally, the time span had to be consistent with the measurements of the other variables in the analysis and be measured prior to the dependent variable to avoid the problem of backward causation.

As I explained in Chapter 2, to operationalize and measure the preference for political or market justice, I used survey data that registered individual attitudes about the boundaries of legitimate governmental action with regard to income distribution. Using cross-national, individual-level surveys, I am able to connect individual attitudes to the broader societal level of analysis and thereby identify whether coherent sociocultural patterns exist regarding public conceptions of distributive justice. Again, given the most basic assumptions

---

9. Recall the implicit theory of social c hange embedded in Lan e's analysis, in which social change can take place through little or no institutional or str uctural change but rather a shift in perception.

of democratic theory, one would expect these prevailing patterns of citizen opinion to have some bearing on policy outcomes.

Opinion on political justice versus market justice in relation to income inequality is measured by using survey data from the International Social Surveys Programme (ISSP) on Social Equality and the Role of Government (1985, 1987, 1990, 1992, and 1999), the cumulative file of the Eurobarometer (1970–92), and Eurobarometer 52.1 (1999). Although I had to employ data from two different sources, the sampling techniques were virtually identical.[10]

The consistency and the phrasing of the questions across countries and time can sometimes be problematic; nevertheless, the surveys used were very comparable and captured the essence of my use Lane's conceptualization. With the exception of several countries in my sample, questions were repeated in identical form over the time period necessary to correspond adequately with the three time points at which the dependent variable is measured.[11] Although I presented these questions in Chapter 2, I list them here again and briefly remind readers of how I infer societal values from individual opinion data and the way in which the index was constructed.

1. "It is the responsibility of the government to reduce the differences in income between people with high incomes and those with low incomes." (ISSP)
2. "Do you agree or disagree that greater effort should be made to reduce inequality?" (EB)

The Likert scale was used in both surveys, thus simplifying the coding of the data.[12] The coding scheme maximizes the information available and puts

10. Data from both organizations derive from cross-sectional surveys with a representative sample of adults aged eighteen or over, with approximately two thousand respondents from the ISSP surveys and one thousand from the Eurobarometers, with all figures weighted according to population in each country.

11. For New Zealand, Norway, Sweden, and Switzerland, the surveys were only available for one time point.

12. The Likert scale format is a general approach to surveys that provides respondents with statements and asks them to indicate how strongly they agree or disagree. One important difference between the Eurobarometer surveys and those of the GSS is the absence of a neutral category in the former. Respondents to the GSS had an opportunity to select a "neither agree nor disagree" category. The difference in a five-point versus a four-point scale is a matter of theoretical importance that potentially complicates the data analysis. However, because the essence of the question is comparable and because the theory being developed and tested requires a diversity of political institutional settings and, thus, the necessity of pooling these two sets of surveys to acquire information

more weight on the two extreme response categories. Polarization of the information in this manner is a reasonable approach if one is interested in the relative strength of attitudes—as this study obviously is. Both the "strongly agree" category and the "strongly disagree" category were multiplied by two, and then added to those sums were "agree" and "disagree" responses. To refer back to the actual construction of the index and the specific rankings, see Figure 1. In the index, the higher the number is, the stronger the propensity toward political justice, which should coincide with less inequality.

To illustrate this relationship, I have graphed values and income inequality in Figure 3. This scatter diagram reveals general trends consistent with my theoretical expectations. The United States, Australia, and Switzerland all have strong market justice orientations and high levels of income inequality. In plotting political justice values against income inequality, we see that countries with stronger political justice orientations do indeed fall within the lower right quadrant. However, most interesting are the relative locations of Switzerland and the United Kingdom in Figures 2 and 3. Although both the United Kingdom and Switzerland have moderately high income inequality, inequality is greater Switzerland, a consensus system. But here in Figure 3 we see that the relative positions of the two countries are almost mirror images. Although the United Kingdom has higher political justice values than found in Switzerland, its level of income inequality is not as low as the values thesis alone would predict. Given the argument presented in Chapter 3 as well as additional supporting evidence (i.e., Huber and Powell 1994) that consensus democracies provide a closer relationship between societal preferences and policy outcomes, and given that Switzerland is a market justice society, its position in Figure 3 is indeed consistent with the core thesis of this study. Despite a general affinity between the norms of political justice and consensual political institutions—driven in part because of the role that corporatism plays— the message from Chapters 2 and 3 is that it is not so much which type of cultural norms prevail but rather that consensus democracies would tend to exhibit greater congruence between those preferences and actual outcomes.

---

on each country in my sample, the sacrifice had to be made to drop the neutral category from the GSS responses. On average, that category was selected about 15 percent of the time. While this is valuable information to sacrifice, theoretically it is justified because the central concern is identifying the actual distribution of formulated and relatively firm opinion on the issue of government intervention in the question of income inequality. Thus, although the data may not be ideal, the indicators are generally highly comparable and the research design is sound.

Again, these comparisons further underscore that neither the institutions nor the values separately or independently can fully predict income inequality; rather, the key explanation seems to lie in their interaction.

## Control Variables

Before moving on to a more complex exploration of these relationships through multivariate regression analysis, it is important to discuss the control variables commonly employed in other studies of income inequality. These controls fall into two categories, political and macroeconomic. The key political control variable is cumulative left cabinet rule.[13] The macroeconomic variables include economic growth and trade openness.[14]

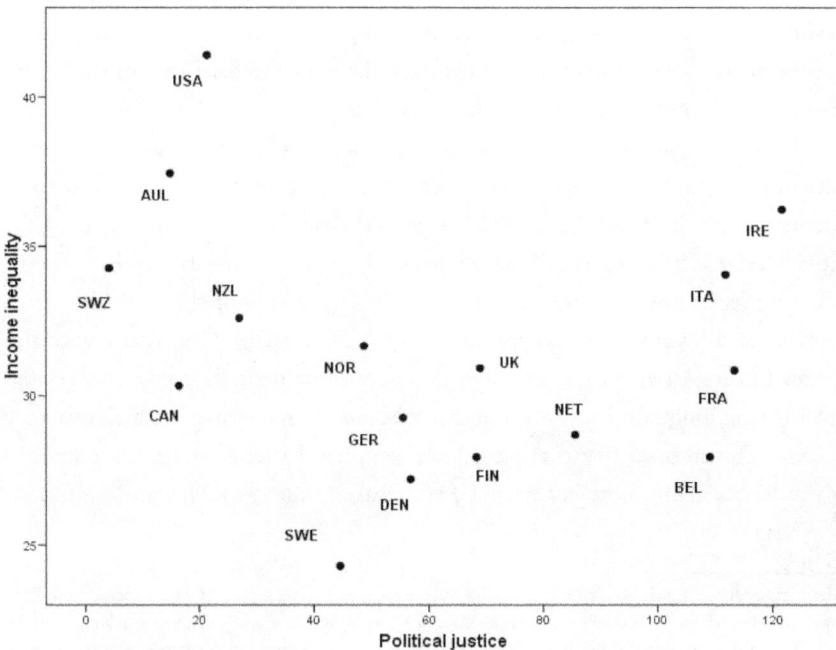

FIG 3 Political Justice and Income Inequality

13. Voter turnout may also have an impact on income inequality (Stack 1979). It is reasonable to infer that the more actively diverse groups—particularly those from lower socioeconomic groups—participate in the political process, the greater the likelihood that one of the benefits will be a more egalitarian distribution of income. Consistent with the inclusive idea of consensus

Because the political institutional measure I am using is such an encompassing one that essentially includes many other political variables, the only remaining factor that is not represented but, for a variety of reasons, should be is the ideological and partisan control of the government. In conjunction with other studies (Boix 1998; Bradley et al. 2003; Bollen and Grandjean 1981; Jackman 1975; Muller 1989), I expect that partisan control of the government is an important factor influencing income distribution. Generally speaking, socialist or social democratic parties tend to pursue policies that "reassign income in order to equalize disparities between the rich and the poor assumed to result from unbridled capitalist 'free-market' competition" (Muller 1989, 369). In contrast, conservative parties are more likely to believe incomes should be determined by market forces not state policy. It is therefore assumed that there will be an inverse relationship between income inequality and governmental control by socialist or social democratic parties. Cumulative left cabinet government is a commonly employed indicator that measures the cumulative proportion of left cabinet seats since 1946 through the final year of each time period examined in my study (Huber et al. 2004).

Two other factors that have been commonly included in other studies are economic growth and openness. Contrary to the claims of many neoclassical economists who hold that economic growth and income inequality are positively related in that more growth involves higher accumulation, which therefore increases the income gap, other studies have shown the opposite effect (Hicks and Swank 1984; Korpi 1985; and Muller 1989). Consistent with the latter findings, I also expect to find that economic growth is inversely related to income inequality. However, it is important to recognize with Kenworthy (2004) that in both the theoretical and empirical literature on the equality-growth trade-off, there has been a great deal of indeterminacy and numerous

democracy (Birchfield and Crepaz 1998) and the correlation between consensus democracy and high turnout, the influence of this variable is considered as subsumed in the key institutional indicator. An alternative way of viewing the role of voter turnout on income distribution is that as voter turnout increases, the income of the median voter decreases and, as economic theory suggests, this would result in a demand for more redistribution of income (Romer 1975; Meltzer and Richard 1981; Austen-Smith 2000). In fact, recent research by Kenworthy and Pontusson (2005) has provided evidence that voter turnout has a measurable impact on distributional outcomes in precisely such terms.

14. GDP and unemployment were also included in previous models but consistently had no effect on income inequality. Given the relatively small sample size and the need to preserve degrees of freedom, I elected to remove them from the final models.

shifts in the debates leading him to conclude that overall there has been "no general tendency for inequality to influence growth in either direction" (68, but see all of Kenworthy's chapter 4). The data I use on economic growth were averaged and recorded for my three time periods (World Bank 2004).

The increasing internationalization of the world's economies has been a popular culprit for politicians as well as some political analysts to explain increasing inequality of incomes. In many ways, the burgeoning globalization literature tends to be largely ahistorical and speculative, and similar to the growth-inequality trade-off debates, it is riddled with contradictory theoretical claims and conflicting empirical evidence as noted by many leading scholars (Kenworthy 2004; Barro 2000; Brandolini and Rossi 1998; Forbes 2000). Comparativists, especially comparative political economists, have long had a tradition of addressing trade openness (Cameron 1978; Gourevitch 1978; Katzenstein 1985; Rogowski 1987), and it is in this vein that a control for economic openness or "globalization" is included here. Some studies argue that globalization has led to increased inequality in many affluent countries as increased trade with labor-abundant countries pushes down demand for unskilled labor in developed countries and the imports from developing countries make production in developed countries uncompetitive. This shifting of assets across borders coupled with heightened competition encourages governments to reduce taxes therefore impinging on their ability to redistribute income. Additionally, firms are in a better position to aggressively oppose union demands for wage increases, and more jobs are shifting to the service sector where there are even higher wage and pay differentials. All of these factors can be potential drivers of growing income inequality. However, scholars such as Cameron (1978), Katzenstein (1985), and more recently Garrett (1998) and Swank (2002), would argue that to mitigate such income inequality, states intervene and provide compensation. Accordingly, globalization creates demand for compensation, and some countries respond with policies to ameliorate the income effects of globalization. Pierson (1996) has shown that in the face of globalization, some states can and do mute the negative effects through transfer payments, progressive taxation, and other social policy programs. Kenworthy and Pontusson (2005) provide recent evidence for this "resilience of welfare states" thesis. Thus, generally when trade openness is found to be linked with increasing income inequality in OECD countries, it occurs in the absence of strong union/corporatist arrangements that would otherwise provide workers with compensation for globalization (Garrett and Lange 1986; Garrett 1998).

Economic openness was also considered in earlier work by Muller (1989) as a potentially influential factor on income distribution. This idea is, again unsurprisingly, drawn from Cameron's (1978) thesis that the more exposed a country is to the international market, the more likely governments are to pursue policies that counteract the negative effects of international economic dependence on their domestic macroeconomic situation. Like Muller, I also expect that the more open the economy, the lower the income inequality. This relationship is also similar to Rogowski's (1987) argument, which effectively extended Cameron's idea, claiming that specific types of institutional arrangements such as parliamentary-PR systems are adopted in response to external trade pressures that require the state to insulate itself from sectoral narrowness and protectionism to secure broader welfare and policy stability. Rogowski's institutional link to Cameron's argument should be considered in this study because the very institutions he includes are also those comprising the consensual system. But we should also keep in mind that the strong correlation between trade openness and consensus institutions may make interpretations of regression results difficult. Despite the potential endogeneity between consensual institutions and higher levels of trade openness, the degree of trade openness is included as a control variable and is measured as the average foreign trade activity (exports plus imports) as a percentage of GDP during each time period (World Bank 2004).

Table 5 presents the bivariate correlations between the key independent and control variables and income inequality. These correlations are generally consistent with the theoretical expectations outlined above. The negative signs for both consensus democracy and political justice are also consistent with the previous scatter diagram, thus confirming that there is a negative relationship between high levels of income inequality and both of the key independent variables. The sign for cumulative left cabinets is likewise negative, indicating that leftist governments have a reductionary impact on income inequality. Stronger economic growth is only moderately correlated with lower income inequality. Though these bivariate correlations are suggestive of the relationships I have posited, it is important now to estimate the effects of values and institutions and their interaction while controlling for political and economic context. The next section presents the results of this more extensive statistical model.

## The Model

The modeling strategy employed here seeks to reflect the causal interaction between values and institutions. As such, the following models incorporate an interactive term capturing both institutions and values, which maintains the assumptions of regression while allowing for a more complex, multiplicative relationship, as opposed to an additive relationship. Therefore, I have constructed a panel design using multivariate cross-sectional/time-series regression (N=16, t=3) with a multiplicative term for values (opinions on justice) and institutions (type of democracy). A key advantage of a pooled design is the increase in sample size; therefore, in the case of the dependent variable under investigation here, examining three time points is important because income distribution is not a static phenomenon, and most experts agree that change must be gauged at approximately ten-year intervals (Slottje and Smeeding 1992). However, it should be noted that even with the time series component, the total number of observations is still just forty-three, which limits the

**Table 5** Bivariate Correlations with Income Inequality

|  | Income Inequality |
| --- | --- |
| Consensus Institutions | −.400 (.004)★ |
| Political Justice | −.200 (.099) |
| Consensus Institutions × Political Justice | −.302 (.025) |
| Cumulative Left Cabinet Score | −.478 (.001) |
| Economic Development (Log GDP per capita) | .057 (.358) |
| Economic Growth | .313 (.021) |
| Trade Openness | −.345 (.012) |
| N (listwise) | 43 |

★ P values, one-tailed significance test in parentheses

statistical analysis due to potential collinearity.[15] In an attempt to mitigate the high collinearity among values, institutions, and the interaction term, these variables have been centered, or recalibrated as differences from the mean, in the multivariate analysis. Although centering these variables helps reduce the effects of collinearity on the standard errors of the centered variables in the model, it does not completely eliminate the problem of underestimating the statistical significance of the collinear variables (in this case values, institutions, and their interaction) nor does it affect the overall fit of the model as measured by standard statistics. The multivariate model allows me to measure the amount of variation in income inequality that can be attributed to the type of democracy (or political institutions) as well as the independent and interactive effect of values (or culture). I predict that although political institutions are strongly related to variations in income inequality, the strength of this relationship varies according to the specific cultural environment within which those institutions operate. More precisely, the impact of consensual political institutions on reducing income inequality is strengthened as the propensity to favor political justice increases and is weakened as market justice becomes the prevailing norm. The specific hypotheses that are subjected to statistical analysis are listed below and illustrated in graphic format in Figure 4.

$H_1$: The more consensually oriented the political system, the lower the degree of income inequality. Conversely, the more majoritarian the political system, the higher the degree of income inequality.

$H_2$: The stronger the preference for political justice over market justice, the smaller the gap between income differentials. The stronger the support for market justice, the larger the gap between incomes of the rich and the poor.

$H_3$: As institutions become more consensual, attitudes toward justice increasingly influence the effect on income inequality.

The scatter diagram and bivariate models generally confirmed the first two hypotheses with slightly weaker results for the second or "values hypothesis," which is nonetheless consistent with the argument that the impact of values may be independent, but contingent on the institutional environment within

---

15. The reason the total number of observations is forty-three rather than an expected $N$ of forty-eight (sixteen cases at three time points) is because of the following missing data: Italy and Switzerland are missing quality 1 data (from UNU-WIDER) prior to 1985.

they operate. Now we examine the results of the full model testing the third hypothesis. Table 6 presents these findings. As expected, both key independent variables continue to have a negative effect on income inequality; this result is consistent across all of the specifications. As model 2 shows, once political factors such as partisan control of government are introduced, the interaction term is in th e expected direction. However, the interaction between values and institutions is highly collinear with other variables in the model according to the estimates of the variance inflation factor (VIF). Multicollinearity does not normally bias the estimates of the coefficients; however, it does bias downward statistical significance (Berry and Feldman 1985). This means we can interpret the size of the coefficients but should not put too much weight on tests of st atistical significance. Even though the interactive term is c ollinear, its effects cannot be interpreted without including estimates of the base variables of which the interaction consists. As Bear Braumoeller (2004) underscores, interactive relationships imply that the impact of $x_1$ on $y$ varies depending on the level of $x_2$; therefore, the idea of the impact of $x_1$ on $y$ in general— as in the case in a str ictly additive model—is in fact meaningless. Brambor, Clark, and Golder (2006) found that out of 156 political science articles published in reputable journals between 1998 and 2002, only 69 percent included the constitutive terms in their interaction models and 38 percent accurately interpreted the terms correctly. These authors' observation reveals that there

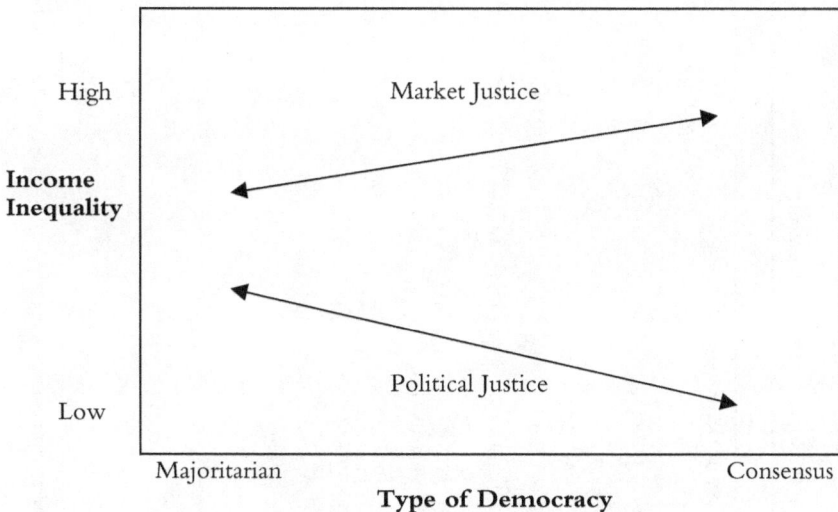

FIG 4 Hypothesized Interactive Effect of Values and Institutions on Income Inequality

**Table 6** Models of Income Inequality

| | 1 | 2 | 3 | 4 | 5 |
|---|---|---|---|---|---|
| Consensus Democracy | -1.688★ (0.678)[a] | -0.859 (0.691) | -0.331 (0.679) | -0.298 (0.670) | 0.294 (0.682) |
| Political Justice | -0.012 (0.018) | -0.026 (0.017) | -0.012 (0.017) | -0.021 (0.018) | -0.007 (0.018) |
| INTERACTION (Values × Institutions) | 0.013 (0.017) | -0.001 (0.017) | -0.002 (0.016) | -0.006 (0.016) | -0.002 (0.015) |
| Cumulative Left Cabinet Government | | -0.180★ (0.065) | -0.152★ (0.061) | -0.162★ (0.061) | -0.156★ (0.058) |
| Social Security Transfers | | | -0.441★ (0.176) | -0.328‡ (0.191) | -0.260‡ (0.183) |
| Economic Growth | | | | 0.673 (0.486) | 1.221† (0.516) |
| Trade Openness | | | | | -0.054† (0.023) |
| (Constant) | 31.724 (0.706) | 34.570 (1.213) | 40.797 (2.725) | 37.358 (3.663) | 38.220 (3.471) |
| Adjusted $R$ Square | 0.121 | 0.256 | 0.352 | 0.368 | 0.439 |
| $N$ | 43 | 43 | 43 | 43 | 43 |

[a] Standard errors in parentheses. ‡p < .1, †p < .05, and ★p < .01, one-tailed test.

are substantial inferential errors being made by those using these models. Whereas the sample size constrains my ability to ameliorate the effects of multicollinearity entirely, the stability of the results across specifications and the consistency of the findings with not only my theoretical argument but also with general understandings of the economic and political determinants of inequality indicate that the specification itself is valid, and the following interpretations do not commit the same errors as much of the previous scholarship.

Whereas the bivariate relationships between values and institutions and income inequality are more straightforward, the functional form of the multiplicative equation is more complicated. In part, this is a result of small sample size and the very close linkages among all of the key variables as well as the control variables. Nonetheless, the results in Table 6 support the general pattern that my theoretical argument predicts and my primary contention that both consensus institutions and political justice values and their interaction tend to reduce income inequality. Models 2–4, which contain a number of important control variables, all support this core thesis. All of the models are somewhat affected by a certain degree of multicollinearity, and this is especially the case for the two independent variables. Interaction models inherently increase multicollinearity, which in turn increases the size of the standard errors, thereby making it less likely that the coefficient on the interaction term will attain significance. Friedrich (1982) has argued that this problem has been overstated and warns that the presence of multicollinearity in multiplicative interaction models should not result in the omission of either the interactive or the constitutive terms. Brambor, Clark, and Golder (2006) warn that the dangers of inferential errors (resulting from omitting constitutive terms) are much greater than merely accepting the consequences of multicollinearity and remind us that high multicollinearity implies that there is insufficient information in the data to estimate the parameters correctly. The authors also claim that significance is not the main concern of those employing interaction terms, but rather what is of most interest is the marginal effect of $x$ on $y$. Interestingly, once trade openness is included in the model, the effects of both economic growth and consensus institutions change, which is indicative of the tight relationships among trade, consensus political institutions, and growth. This finding is also of significance for the globalization debates because it adds further support for the argument mounted by Garrett's (1998) *Partisan Politics in the Global Economy*. Garrett provides solid empirical evidence that domestic political variables, particularly "left-labor" power, have tremendous influence in buffering the purported vicissitudes of the increasingly globalized economy. Such findings have the effect of vitiating the globalization-induced convergence claims and they reinforce the importance of maintaining a primacy on the political, as I have done throughout this study.

Considering the ongoing debates in the literature that address the impact of globalization on welfare state institutions and redistributive policies (Bradley et al. 2003; Swank 2002; Pontusson 2005) these relationships warrant closer attention in light of my own argument. Furthermore, given the insights of the scholars cited above, the lack of statistical significance may be attributed to some salient missing data. Consistent with the recent findings produced by welfare state scholars, the missing information in the model may very well be the actual transfer policies that have the final and concrete reductive influence on income inequality. I argued in earlier chapters that I see the welfare state arguments not as alternative explanations to my thesis but rather the variables used in those quantitative analyses as intervening effects in the context of the larger political-institutional level of analysis that I p ursue here. I am not as concerned as most of these scholars are with pinning down the specific determinants of income inequality but instead want to elucidate the broader value and institutional milieus within which such causal agents operate to explain variance in income distribution across capitalist democracies. However, even when one is not interested in single-variable explanations, it is still undeniably difficult to nail down this broader level of causation with statistical precision and accuracy—as my quantitative analysis illustrates. Furthermore, as Kenworthy and Pontusson's (2005) work demonstrates, there is a great deal of diversity among the welfare states and their varying levels of disposable household income as well as different degrees of generosity; therefore, it is considerable challenge to produce meaningful generalizations. In fact, the most recent debates revolve around complex measurement issues and the relationship between earnings or market inequality and redistributive effort as well as employment. For example, these authors show that individual earnings data fail to capture the impact of unemployment, underemployment, and labor force exit. They argue:

> The analytical problem goes deeper because job losses during economic downturns are not distributed equally across the wage distribution. Evidence indicates that employers are more likely to fire unskilled (low-paid) than skilled (high-paid) workers during cyclical

downturns. Employers are reluctant to fire skilled workers because it is difficult and costly for them to reacquire the skills that such workers embody when demand picks up again. Since low-wage workers disproportionately drop out of the employed labor force, increased unemployment tends to reduce earnings inequality among employed workers during economic downturns. Surely we ought not interpret this to mean that unemployment promotes equality. (Kenworthy and Pontusson 2005, 452)

This argument combined with other discussions of data and measurement problems along with complicating factors of social spending and transfer reinforce the need to more carefully distinguish income inequality from government redistribution. What I explore in this next model is how the welfare state thesis affects the more general argument I have made so far by introducing the actual transfer policies, which are, after all, what constitutes the real

**Table 7** Model of Social Security Transfers

|  | Social Security Transfers |
| --- | --- |
| Consensus Institutions | 0.571 |
|  | (0.626)[a] |
| Political Justice Values | 0.042* |
|  | (0.017) |
| Interaction (Values × Institutions) | 0.000 |
|  | (0.014) |
| Cumulative Left Cabinet | 0.050 |
|  | (0.053) |
| Trade Openness | 0.023 |
|  | (0.021) |
| Economic Growth | −1.419* |
|  | (0.443) |
| GDP/capita (thousands) | 3.756[†] |
|  | (2.726) |
| Intercept | −20.332 |
|  | 26.642 |
| Adjusted $R$ Square | 0.356 |
| $N$ | 43 |

[a] Standard errors in parentheses. [†]$p < .1$, [‡]$p < .05$, and *$p < .01$, one-tailed test.

redistributive impact alongside other factors, such as unemployment and various other labor market institutional factors.

To test for this missing information and to better understand the causal patterns suggested by the models described thus far, I estimated a small model of social security transfers, a widely used measure of redistributive welfare. The transfers are measured as a percentage of GDP and consist of benefits for sickness, old age, and family allowances as well as various forms of social assistance grants and welfare.[16] The results of this additional model are presented in Table 7. The findings of this model suggest that social security transfers may indeed serve as one mechanism by which political institutions and values lead to government policy to reduce market inequalities. Indeed, political institutions, values, and their interaction serve as better predictors of transfer expenditures than the more common political indicator in this literature, cumulative left government. Thus, welfare transfers should be conceived as an intervening factor or one that illustrates the final channel through which institutions and values operate to produce different income inequality. The model suggests that both key independent variables, in addition to government partisanship, all play important roles in the size of redistributive transfers. The relative importance of values, institutions, partisanship, and trade can be evaluated by comparing the standardized coefficients for models of social security transfers and income inequality. The path coefficients of each of these variables are provided in Table 8.[17]

It seems that values and institutions play a larger role in social security transfers than either partisanship or trade. To a large extent, this also underscores the tight linkages (manifested as collinearity in my previous models) among consensus democracy and these two variables. This finding is also perfectly congruent with past scholarship. For the most part, consensus democracies are all heavily trade dependent, and as recent data indicate, there is a very strong correlation between consensual electoral institutions and center-left governments. This connection sheds further light on the causal mechanisms at play when we relate consensus institutions to macroeconomic outcomes.

16. These data were taken from the OECD, Historical Statistics, various years (2001), Table 6.3. Note the following cases for various missing data points: United States: missing 1998–2000, used only 1995–97 for third time period; Switzerland: missing 2000, used only 1995–99 for third time period; New Zealand: missing 1983–2000, used only 1975–82 for first time period; and Canada: missing 1999–2000, used only 1995–98 for third time period.

17. For the record, none of these effects changed when GDP per capita or unemployment were included.

Proportional representation is on e of th e overarching political features of consensual systems, and PR electoral rules are historically and systematically linked to left-leaning governments, which tend to engage in greater redistribution. Using a new data set assembled by Cusack and Engelhardt, Iversen confirms the strong empirical relationship between electoral system and government partisanship. From the period of 1945 to 1998 and measuring the total number of years with right- and left-leaning governments and type of electoral system in s eventeen advanced democracies, 75 percent of go vernments in majoritarian systems were center-right, whereas in proportional representation systems, 70 percent were center-left (2005, 24–25). Iversen (2005) and Iversen and Soskice (2006) show how electoral rules shape coalition behavior producing different partisan compositions of government that in turn will lead to different distributive outcomes. Although this clearly lays out the institutional logic, it is also important to underline the specific role that welfare policies play in reducing income inequality. The findings in Table 8 indeed demonstrate the significant influence of welfare transfers, which is consistent with the recent welfare state literature and is in fact quite intuitive. What my study intends to sh ow is n ot so m uch that th ese types of p olicies actually change inegalitarian market outcomes through redistribution, because this has been amply demonstrated already (Wilensky 1975; Hicks 1999; Bradley et al. 2003; Korpi 1985; Huber and Stephens 2001; Swank 2002; Pontusson 2005; Kenworthy and Pontusson 2005). Instead, I wish to uncover more fundamental forces—albeit difficult ones to capture through statistical manipulations—that provide the ideational impetus and the institutional capacity to effect such changes. This additional statistical analysis do es in f act indicate that v alues and institutions play a larger role in social security than either partisanship or

**Table 8** Path Coefficients

|                                      | Social Security Transfers | Income Inequality |
|--------------------------------------|:-------------------------:|:-----------------:|
| Consensus Institutions               | .147                      | .065              |
| Political Justice Values             | *.418*                    | −.060             |
| Interaction (Values × Institutions)  | −.004                     | −.014             |
| Cumulative Left Cabinet              | .143                      | *−.384*           |
| Social Security Transfers            |                           | *−.225*           |
| Economic Growth                      | *−.487*                   | *.363*            |
| Trade Openness                       | .193                      | *−.383*           |
| GDP/capita (thousands)               | *.206*                    |                   |

NOTE: Standardized regression coefficients. Italic signifies p < .1, one-tailed test.

trade do, and that welfare transfers play the ultimately larger role in reducing income inequality. The paths illustrated in Figure 5 show that values and institutions operate through welfare policies, whereas left cabinet governments appear to have a direct effect on income inequality. On one hand, this finding suggests that the left cabinet variable is somehow endogenous to distributional outcomes or, on the other hand, it suggests that they use mechanisms other than transfers to reduce inequality, which would reinforce the arguments made by Kenworthy and Pontusson about the impact of employment. Nonetheless, as these scholars concluded: "The bottom line is that there are two different paths to increased redistribution. One path involves new policy initiatives or policy changes aimed at redistributing income, such as easing eligibility restrictions or increasing replacement rates. The second path involves a more or less automatic response compensatory response by existing welfare sates to rising market inequality. In the 1980s and 1990s, most affluent OECD countries seem to have been on the second path" (2005, 456).

The extent to which welfare state scholars are finding these extremely complex patterns of inequality and redistribution reaffirms that no single variable approach will answer definitively why some countries are more egalitarian than others. The attention they are beginning to pay to public preferences—highlighting along the way, the inadequacy of models such as Meltzer-Richard, whose assumptions depart from our knowledge of the very real and messy world of politics—is encouraging for the argument I am putting forth here.

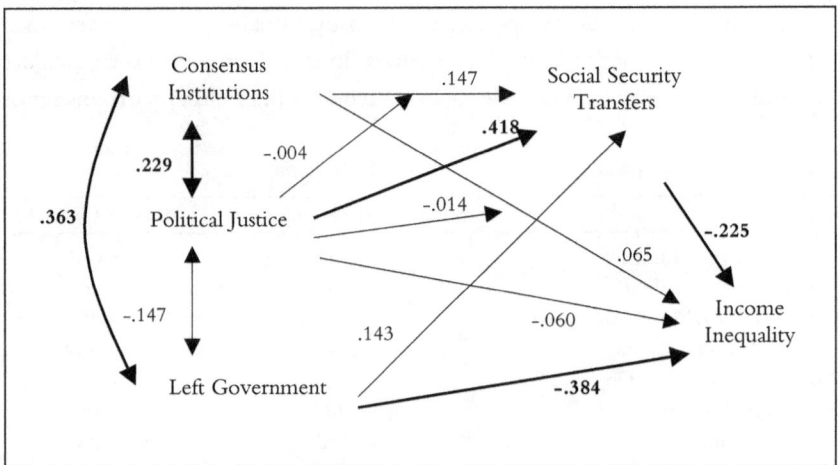

FIG 5  Path Model of Income Inequality

Furthermore, if values themselves are endogenous to inequality because those in more equal societies would not necessarily "agree" that the government should do more to reduce inequality, then the measures of political justice may underestimate the true preference for political justice. Such endogeneity of values would depress the relationship between values and inequality, and were it possible to account for the effects of existing inequality on the values measure, the negative correlation between preference for political justice and inequality would be even more extreme.

As the path diagram shows, political justice values work through consensual institutions to produce concrete policy programs that actively reduce the amount of income inequality in society. Once a variable representing the nature of governments in power was introduced into the model, this causal chain became even clearer. The welfare state literature and the class analytic and power resources models have all provided strong evidence of these relationships (Korpi 1983; Stephens 1979; Huber and Stephens 2001; Bradley et al. 2003), but what my study has introduced is the deeper element of popular democratic support for egalitarian policies in the first place and how different institutional contexts shape whether those values become reflected in material realities. Consistent with democratic theory, we should be concerned to include this factor in the causal chain explaining how government and society may choose to transform (or not) market outcomes into varying levels of egalitarian or inegalitarian distributions. However, as acknowledged in Chapter 2, there may be problems associated with such a broad measure of justice norms that are even further complicated because these existing surveys fail to take into consideration a respondent's sense (accurate or not) of the actual degree of inequality in his or her society. Perhaps in future replications of my model, additional survey questions concerning awareness and attitudes related to legitimate wage differentials could be used as an alternative or a corollary to the survey instruments employed here. Constructing more adequate measures for empirically gauging what is a crucially important, if not the most salient, political cultural trait of a given society vis-à-vis political-economic issues could considerably strengthen and extend the theoretical framework I have devised and initially tested here. What I hope to achieve in this quantitative analysis, albeit less satisfactorily than is the norm for most econometricians, is to move debates in comparative political economy beyond the contending and unnecessarily limiting "culture versus institutions" approaches.

Although these findings are somewhat attenuated due to the relatively small sample and the overall complexity of the model, the general stability of results across the various models suggests that institutions, values, and their interaction have effects consistent with my theoretical expectations; therefore, the relationships themselves should be further evaluated with other methods and different types of data. For instance, when we recall the richness of the data beyond what the quantitative analysis reveals here, it is significant that we found Switzerland to be outranked only by the United States as a society most inclined to favor market justice whereas the prevailing norm of political justice proved stronger in the United Kingdom—the classical exemplar of the Westminster model—than in, for example, the consensus systems of Belgium and Finland. These are very interesting and paradoxical associations and as such will be explored in a more qualitative and historical fashion in Chapter 5. These observations are of critical import for the theory being tested here. While the theoretical affinity between political justice, consensus democracy, and lower income inequality can generally be sustained by the data and, in a weaker fashion, through the statistical analyses presented here, the exceptions are what provide nuance to the broader thesis that institutions and values interact to shape outcomes. If all of the consensus democracies were perfectly congruent with indicators for political justice, then a test for the independent or interactive effects of values and institutions would be meaningless. Fortunately, the richness of these cases and the variation in the ideational or values indicator facilitates further empirical investigation of the relationships between income inequality, political institutions, and values.

Switzerland is the most consensual system according to Lijphart's typology yet it is much more inclined toward market justice and it has very high income inequality make it a prime candidate for further qualitative investigation. The next chapter is devoted to a more in-depth examination of the institutional and cultural roots of income inequality in Switzerland and a critical comparison with the United Kingdom, which in many ways is a mirror opposite except with regard to similarly high income inequality. Comparative case study analysis may reveal more of the nuance and complexity that is difficult to capture in such a highly aggregated quantitative analysis. Although the statistical analyses did not produce conclusive evidence, the findings do confirm the theoretical intuition that there is a conditional effect between institutions and values, and this in turn sheds light on the complex causal patterns that produce such variation in income inequality across these sixteen countries.

# — 5 —

THE EXCEPTIONS PROVE THE RULE: CASE STUDIES IN INCOME
INEQUALITY IN SWITZERLAND AND THE UNITED KINGDOM

Having shown preliminary quantitative evidence of the complex interplay of values and institutions and explained what this tells us about cross-national variation in income inequality, I will now draw out the implications of these findings through comparative-historical analysis and a pair of structured case studies. Chapter 4 confirmed that neither institutions nor values alone fully explain the patterns of income inequality among this set of capitalist democracies, but once their interaction is brought into the equation, we see a fairly systematic relationship between values, institutions, and income inequality. Although it is difficult to capture with statistical precision, it is nonetheless the case that all of the countries that combine a values orientation of political justice and consensual political institutions have the lowest levels of income inequality, and countries that are both market justice in value orientation and majoritarian in their institutional design tend to produce the highest levels of income inequality. While these patterns bear out the core thesis of this book, it is also clear that income inequality is determined by a multitude of societal forces and that these dichotomous ways of characterizing political institutions and societal values are themselves products of history and bound up with other dimensions of national culture and structural conditions.

The quantitative analysis demonstrated, for instance, that institutions and values as broadly conceived here are closely intertwined with other factors, such as government partisanship and welfare transfer schemes, which play significant roles in explaining income differential among countries. Thus, the interplay of institutions and values might be seen as the primary causal context within which more specific processes determine whether governments intervene (or not) to implement policies that reshape distributive outcomes. This

chapter is devoted to tracing out such processes in two of the sixteen countries of my original sample by exploring their historical backgrounds, institutional contexts, and value orientations in greater depth than was possible in
the more highly aggregated quantitative analysis.

In part, the following qualitative exploration anticipates and addresses
potential questions about the measures I used to capture the values dimension
of my thesis and the adequacy of a single survey instrument to capture the
broader argument about the influence of societal values and ideas on actual
distributional outcomes. Hence, one task is to examine critically the extent
to which the survey indicators I used can indeed stand up to more careful historical and analytical scrutiny. Although the institutional indicators I used are
relatively unproblematic, particularly in light of their widespread and continued use by some of the most noted political economists in the field (e.g.,
Iversen 2005; Gourevitch and Shin 2005; Swank 2002), my operationalization
of the values variable is original and perhaps more likely to be subjected to
questions of appropriateness and validity. Therefore, what I seek to show here
is that Switzerland and the United Kingdom are, in fact, truly representative
of the values orientations we found through the limited survey data used. As
shown in Chapter 2, the survey data generally conformed to the abstract theorization of the congruence between types of democratic institutions and
cultural values that I have defined here as beliefs about the proper roles of
states and markets, but I have also identified these two striking exceptions. The
critical test of the relationship between—and the relative explanatory power
of—values and institutions now appears to fall squarely upon cases such as
Switzerland, which has market justice as the prevailing cultural norm yet it
serves as one of Lijphart's chief examples of consensus democracy, and the
United Kingdom, the majoritarian model par excellence, which the survey
data examined here reveal to be a society more oriented toward political justice. It is an interesting paradox that the key exemplars of Lijphart's models of
democracy reflect political cultural orientations that are somewhat out of
character in comparison to the other polities in each typology. Yet it is precisely this exception that may prove the rule in that it allows for a stricter test
of the relative power of political institutions and political culture qua values
or, put differently, their reciprocal causal influence. The following case studies of Switzerland and the United Kingdom seek to elucidate the historical
and political roots of their respective values orientations to more adequately

understand their relationship to, and influence upon, the political institutional environments within which they operate, and to clarify what effect this might have on explaining income differentials.

The Swiss case is an important theoretical exception to Lijphart's framework in that it has all of the requisite institutional features shown previously to produce the types of policies and macroeconomic outcomes typically associated with consensus systems (Lijphart 1994; Crepaz 1996a), but with regard to income inequality, it is much more similar to the other majoritarian systems. Contrary to conventional institutional approaches, I have argued that bringing political culture via specific values into the picture can actually strengthen rather than refute our general institutional explanations. If institutions alone explained such outcomes, this would be a serious challenge to Lijphart's framework and other research employing his institutional typology as a key explanatory variable. However, as my analysis has shown, it is not culture versus institutions but rather culture and institutions working interactively that may best explain broadscale sociopolitical and macroeconomic phenomena such as income distribution. Rather than interpreting the Swiss case as a contradiction to the theoretical model of consensus democracy, I will show more substantial evidence confirming that Switzerland is indeed a market justice society and this is not simply a contrivance or an artifact of random survey data. Therefore, it can be maintained that the interaction between institutions and values does in fact play a critical and determinative role. In this case, the logic derives from the argument and secondary evidence presented in Chapter 3 that consensual systems exhibit stronger congruence between citizen preferences and policy outcomes than do majoritarian systems. Thus, with respect to explaining the high level of income inequality in Switzerland, the confluence of consensus institutions and a predominance of market justice values mean that the translation of preferences into collective outcomes in this specific case actually deters political action (or governmental interference in the economy) and leaves the original market distribution of income intact. Conversely, I will supply similar and more definitive evidence that political justice is a firmly rooted cultural value and that it accurately conveys the British public's views regarding state-market relationships with regard to redistributive policies. This will strengthen the claim that majoritarian institutions are more likely to produce outcomes contrary to societal preferences or at least more aloof to public values and attitudes than we find in the case of consensus democracies.

The structured comparison is crucial, and if either case fails to exhibit deeper historical patterns of attitudes consistent with those justice values found specifically as they relate to questions of income redistribution, then of course the theory I am building will hold considerably less weight. If however historical analysis confirms that both societies are best characterized as market justice (Switzerland) and political justice (the United Kingdom) societies, then rather than challenging Lijphart, "bringing culture in" actually strengthens the typology as these exceptions in fact prove the rule. The rule I refer to has three interconnected elements and essentially expresses the thesis I have articulated throughout this book: (1) institutional logic alone cannot adequately explain variation in outcomes in capitalist democratic societies; (2) the ideational or values context in which institutions function is also crucial to our causal stories; and (3) the link between values and outcomes is stronger in consensual institutional settings than in majoritarian ones. But rather than positing values and cultural theory as a rival to institutional analysis or one requiring a alternative explanatory strategy, I have shown that societal values may be seen as playing a pivotal causal role when we first clearly define and empirically specify which values matter—as opposed to relying on assumptions—and then we analyze their relationship to political institutions as the vehicle through which they have an impact on outcomes. Taking both factors into consideration provides a fuller understanding of differences and similarities among these democracies. It is important to underscore again that the specific content or normative proclivities of a society are not to be theoretically deduced or surmised but should be ascertained empirically. Through such an exercise, I found the Swiss and the United Kingdom cases to have cultural or societal value orientations that departed from the norms of the other constituents of their respective typologies. In other words, out of this philosophical irony, a critical methodological strategy emerges that will supply greater richness of data and a fuller understanding of the variation in income inequality among capitalist democracies. In addition to the main case studies, I will also offer some brief comments on the cases of Sweden and Canada—both of which, like Switzerland and the United Kingdom, represent somewhat surprising but less stark contrasts between their various prevailing values, political institutions, and expected distributive outcomes. Juxtaposing these cases with the inferences drawn from the main case studies will help to further flesh out the nuances of my argument.

## The Case of Swiss Exceptionalism?

Levels of income inequality in Switzerland make the country look much more like the liberal market economy of the VOC typology than either its real classification as a coordinated market economy or its political institutional status as a consensus democracy would predict. Not only is income inequality exceptionally high in Switzerland, but it also ranks with the United States as the country in which the government redistributes the least (Pontusson 2005, 39, 155). Does Switzerland represent a case of exceptionalism to our broader theories of political economy and political institutions? Paradoxical to most cultural approaches, I argue that this seeming case of exceptionalism dissipates once we bring values into our explanatory framework. The objective of this case study is to probe the deeper historical factors and causal processes at work in explaining high levels of income inequality in Switzerland. A brief sketch of Swiss cultural values will demonstrate that, in addition to the survey evidence I presented in Chapter 2, there are other plausible historical factors suggesting that there is indeed a norm or value orientation in Switzerland that discourages direct state intervention in the economy and that it is therefore truly representative of a market justice society. Hence, despite the sheer institutional capacity (i.e., a more direct and inclusionary form of political participation) to redistribute income more equitably, there is a strong propensity toward market justice that disinclines the mobilization of those institutions toward that end. The caricature of the Swiss as conservative, individualistic, and extremely traditionalist but pragmatic people with a strong work ethic emanating from their Calvinist roots may be a useful springboard for a discussion of how cultural traits contribute to the relatively high degree of economic inequality in this society.

Most of the published political science research on Switzerland is concerned with explaining the impressive political stability of this country (Rokkan 1970; Steiner 1974; Linder 1998) despite its substantial linguistic and religious cleavages.[1] With a population of only 6.9 million, there are four official languages, two main religions—Catholic and Protestant—whose conflict

---

1. As Wolf Linder, a native of Switzerland, notes in the preface to his book *Swiss Democracy* (1994), there are very few English publications on Swiss politics. There are a number of German publications and even fewer in French—one of which, *Les Valeurs des Suisses* (Melich 1991), served as the central source of survey data used here. Unfortunately, the body of literature dealing with government and politics of Switzerland is like the country itself—very small.

provoked a civil war at the beginning of Swiss political federation, and different regional cultures, all of which represent the likely causal factors behind "intersubcultural hostility" (Steiner 1974). The important question is whether these various religious, ethnic, and linguistic cleavages also encompass or reflect significant socioeconomic differences. The answer to such a question may shed light on the roots of the Swiss value system and the apparent preference for market justice.

A large body of research on the historical development of the modern welfare state and its ideological underpinnings draws on the insights of T. H. Marshall (1964) who articulated the notion of "social citizenship," or the extension of rights to include an acceptable level of economic security. As the literature suggests, attitudes about the scope of government in the domain of social welfare are related to the degree of acceptance or rejection of such a conception of rights. Whether or not social rights are legitimated through broad public support stems largely from the relative influence of the two dominant (and in many ways competing) social ideologies of economic individualism on the one hand and social equality and collective responsibility on the other (Hasenfeld and Rafferty 1989; McClosky and Zaller 1984; Mishra 1984; Wilensky 1975; Lipset 1960). Based on the most definitive survey research to date, the former ideology predominates in Switzerland.

*Les Valeurs des Suisses* (Melich 1991), documents attitudinal data which show that the work ethic, a culture of self-reliance, and support for free enterprise are meaningful attributes rather than merely caricatures of Swiss culture. In nationwide surveys conducted in 1988–89 nearly 90 percent of respondents declared that work was the most important thing in life after family and friends. Interestingly, in the same survey, only 39 percent declared politics to be of importance (Melich 1991, 19). One Swiss scholar pointed out that "unlike the mass of workers in many other industrialized nations, the workers of Switzerland are still imbued with a belief in the Protestant ethic, which values hard work, sobriety, avoidance of ostentation, honesty, and conscientiousness" (Segalman 1986, 58). As evidence of such values, this scholar refers to the fact that a popular initiative in 1976 proposing cutting the workweek from 44 to 40 hours was "resoundingly rejected" and points to various economic reports showing the high levels of personal savings and capital investments among the Swiss.

Flavio Cotti, Swiss president at the time of the publication of *Les Valeurs des Suisses*, wrote the preface to the study and chose the following words to capture the main emphasis of the Swiss value system: "'C'est aller contre la nature que de travailler dans le seul but de travailler.' Est-ce un hasard si cette sentence n'est pa s d'un Suisse, mais d'un Anglais—en l'occurrence John Locke? Poser la question, c'est y répondre. On sait la valeur que les Suisses traditionnellement attachent au travail. La presente étude, qui n'est d'une pièce d'un ensemble qui e mbrasse plusieurs pays, pourrait bien donner raison à Locke" (Melich 1991, i).

President Cotti asserts that Swiss values essentially embody John Locke's philosophy of labor and claims that th e surveys presented by Melich's study provide confirmation that such is the case. As for his assessment of the overall findings contained in *Les Valeurs des Suisses*, Cotti adds: "Mais le travail, loin d'être la s eule valeur des Suisses, n'est que l'un des aspects d'une mentalité qui en comporte bien d'autres; je pense au sens pratique, au pragmatisme politique, à l'esprit civique, à un sens naturel de la pédagogie, au respect des traditions" (i). Hence, it appears that the survey data confirmed more than the general stereotypical image of the hard-working Swiss; there was also verification of their practical mindedness, the high value attached to education and the respect for tradition.

More than half th e Swiss respondents surveyed (55 percent) declared that religion played a very important role in their lives (256). And, consistent with the traditionalist culture, none of th e newer religious movements have had much influence on the Swiss population (254). Furthermore, with the exception of the environmental movement, virtually none of the social movements—elsewhere gaining strength in Europe—have had much force. In fact, the pacifist and antinuclear movements have generally faced broad opposition in Switzerland (254). The "political pragmatism" that President Cotti referred to may be indicative of the preponderance of m arket values as opposed to political activism in the name of social ju stice or economic equality among the Swiss. A central component of that pragmatism may in fact be the extent to which economic issues are seen as private matters or issues of more concern at the level of the cantons and local governmental structures and not the federal bureaucracy.

Segalman reports that the "general lack of social-class distinctions among the Swiss leads to more frequent communication among the local residents" (1986, 62). In his study of the "Swiss way of welfare," Segalman cites decentralization as the unique feature of th e Swiss approach to iss ues of social welfare. Indeed Swiss public assistance at the local level functions similarly to public welfare programs at the national level in many industrialized nations. Poverty is simply not seen as concern or responsibility of the federal government and there is not even a federal data collecting service related to public assistance. The rather long passage excerpted from his study is worth quoting in full because it quite felicitously illustrates the important historical connection between the emphasis on local responsibility and the cultivation of a culture of market justice.

> Before the days of the Industrial Revolution, people lived in small, close-knit communities where relationships were primary, personal, and affective. Inhabitants never went hungry as long as anyone had food, and no one was homeless as long as anyone had shelter. Public welfare was informal and was provided in the form of aid from one's nuclear family, one's extended family, and one's neighbors. This was the "gemeinschaft" community described by Tönnies (1963, chap. 1).... Residents of the community held mutual obligations. All were more or less in a symbiotic relationship on economic, social, and political levels in that all were responsible to one another. If anyone was in need, the community organized itself to provide help in finding work or in seeking out some other way to help them help themselves. When the marketplace community began to develop, a new form of community relations took place. Tönnies called this the "gesellschaft." In this type of community, the person's status no longer depended upon traditional membership in the community but upon salable skills, or available savings for the entrepreneurship, or on skill in trading and organizing economic production. A person's value to the community was no longer based on past relationships with others and on community membership but, instead, was based alone on marketable qualities. The community emphasis was no longer on sentiment—it now rested entirely on economic values and on the business contract. Thus, the focus of the "gesellschaft" was on profit (and loss) and on salable productivity. Anything that interfered with productivity and profitability was viewed as antagonistic to the free market and the functioning gesellschaft. It was through the expansion of the free-enterprise system that productivity rose to such a level as to provide common people with goods of such quality and quantity as would have made kings and queens jealous in

their time. This level of productivity was achieved primarily by the gesellschaft community patterns and the Protestant ethic, which were adopted by the entire populations. . . . The social-insurance systems, which functions best on a quid pro quo, a reciprocal exchange, mechanical, contractual basis, was placed at a ges ellschaft level of relationships. Although other nations moved to place both welfare and social insurance on a gesellschaft basis, the Swiss elected to keep their services at the level of relationships where they were each best able to s erve. The social-insurance relationship is p rimarily businesslike and is served best on a gesellschaft basis. (Segalman 1986, 188–90)

Now it is important to reconsider the linkage between the foundations of Swiss political institutions and the strong market culture that has been discussed. I believe that the logic of the institutional design and the emergence of market ideology were arguably distinct and unrelated phenomena. First, the industrialization process occurred earlier in Switzerland than in most of Europe, and rather than concentrating in urban areas, the important industries of watch making and textiles were located p rimarily in r ural areas. Such decentralized industrialization prevented the concentration of a mass proletariat in urban areas. Furthermore, William Rappard, one of the most distinguished Swiss historians writing at the beginning of the 1900s, went so far as to claim that the economic necessity of creating a common market was more decisive than the political ideas of Swiss national identity.

The creation of a c ommon market was one manner of p reventing the various regions in S witzerland from being absorbed into the surrounding countries with which linguistic ties were shared. We might infer from this observation, then, that although the adoption of consensual and inclusionary political institutions was critically important for diffusing religious, linguistic, ethical, and even regional divisions and thus facilitating the nation-building process, these same political institutions were not seen as directly strategic or even relevant mechanisms in consolidating the Swiss economy or achieving socioeconomic or class compromise.

Such an interpretation seems even more plausible in light of what Linder observed as "the absence of clear-cut socio-economic, religious and linguistic geographical boundaries" (1998, 25). Thus, he explains the effect of cross-cutting cleavages in the following passage:

Among French-speakers, for example, there are both Catholic and Protestant cantons. Among socio-economically poor cantons, there are both German- and French-speaking states. Thus religious, linguistic, and socio-economic cleavages do not c oincide with geographical boundaries of the cantons, rather they cross-cut each other. The cumulation of d ifferent issues into o ne two-sided political conflict—for instance with poor Catholic French-speakers on one side and rich Protestant German-speakers on the other—could never develop. In practice, Protestant and linguistic majorities differ and vary from issue to issue. Most of the cultural groups have at the same time experienced being part of a m inority, and this has been very important for the development of a culture of tolerance and pluralism. (25)

I would argue that it is precisely these crosscutting cleavages as well as the hard-to-dispute historical origins of the power-sharing arrangements established—not to empower the economically weak but rather to diffuse volatile religious and linguistic differences—that allowed an ethos of market ideology to take root. It is worth highlighting that the presence of these crosscutting cleavages proves the case of Swiss exceptionalism on another count because most consociational or c onsensual institutional settings tend to b e linked instead with the presence of reinforcing cleavages. There is a certain amount of discrepancy in the literature on this point with respect to the nature of the various subcultures in S witzerland. It is b eyond the scope of th is analysis to delve into th is problem here; instead, I will s ummarize the gist of th is conflict by citing Jurg Steiner's reflections, which coincidentally include an important reference to Lijphart: "The Swiss example shows that it is not only possible to have a unidimensional segmentation, which by definition excludes major cross-cuttings, but also a multidimensional segmentation. In summary, I agree with Arend Lijphart, who has described the relations among the Swiss subcultures in terms of a 'multiple balance of power'" (1974, 256).

Robert Dahl noted anoth er dimension of S wiss exceptionalism in h is edited volume, *Political Oppositions in Western Democracies* (1966), in which he finds both the United States and Switzerland to be in sharp distinction to the classical model of government and opposition. Dahl observes that in the United States it is "never easy to distinguish 'opposition' from 'government'; and it is exc eedingly difficult, if not impo ssible to id entify the opposition.

In Switzerland the opposition is perhaps even less distinctive" (341). Although the United States and Switzerland have very different institutional environments, it appears that there is more than the culture of market justice in common. Such interpretations lend credence to the notion that there is much more than the institutional influences that drive particular outcomes.

Even though the institutional infrastructure is available in Switzerland, there is simply no cultural or ideological support for employing the means of participatory democracy to the end of equalizing income differentials. Further supporting evidence can be derived from a brief examination of the two principle institutions conventionally associated with matters of social and economic equality, the Social Democratic party and the type of interest intermediation, particularly corporatist arrangements. These two forces, although extant in Swiss society, are also exceptional in that their historical and structural roots are much different than elsewhere in continental Europe and their goals—among which presumably would include reducing income inequality—are quite distinctive. Although social democratic parties come in a variety of forms depending on the national and historical context in which they emerge, the one common denominator among most social democratic parties is a commitment to using political institutions to foster the values of solidarity and equality. These values in turn shape the formation and promotion of "public policies that would afford basic material security as a citizenship right and that would reduce the inequalities in income produced by the market" (Huber and Stephens 2001, 356). Hence, it is important to ascertain what the character and influence of the Social Democratic party is in Switzerland.[2]

Industrialization took place earlier in Switzerland, but workers were slow to react and the Social Democratic Party, although electorally successful, never

2. Similar goals and ideologies are also linked with the Catholic and Christian Democratic parties. There is also an entire line of research that examines the relationship between the development of the welfare state and contemporary social policy and the relative influence of these types of parties compared to the more conventional labor and social democratic parties. The seminal reference for such research is Wilensky 1975. See also "The Programmatic Emergence of the Social Security State" (Hicks, Misra, and Nah Ng 1995) for a theoretical and empirical examination of the distinct paths and combinations of political institutions and these various forces in the consolidation of social insurance programs at the turn of the century. In the case of Switzerland, the current Christian Democratic Party was formed in the last century during the struggle between the clerical and anticlerical forces and it replaced the Catholic Conservative Party. Because there is substantial crosscutting between religious groups and political parties (Steiner 1974, especially 59–63), I do not attempt to analyze here the extent to which competition between the Social Democratic and the Christian Democratic parties may bear on the problem of income inequality. Such an analysis might yield pertinent insights, but it is beyond the scope of the present study.

achieved great in-roads into securing the organizational and political strength of the working classes. Several factors contributed to the unique character of the Swiss Social Democratic Party when compared to similar parties in Europe. On this point, it is worth quoting the highlights of the historical narrative of Swiss scholar Wolf Linder:

> In the race for the organizational build-up of economic interests, the workers were late starters and did not enter until the end of the nineteenth century. Workers had a common interest to defend: the betterment of their economic conditions, which was promised by emerging socialism in other European countries at that time. But this common interest proved difficult to organise in Switzerland. Workers were spread all over the country and were to a large degree isolated in smaller towns and villages, where the ties of traditional society and patterns of paternalism may have dampened the effects of economic inequality but also hampered collective identity and the organization of the new working class. When the Social Democratic party eventually became organised it achieved rapid electoral success. Social democrats and unions were among the first to use the instrument of the popular initiative as an instrument at the federal level. In 1894 they demanded the right to work and a programme of public industrial policy—40 years before Keynes. But the hope that direct democracy would be the lever of social reform was dashed. In a popular vote the proposed constitutional amendment was rejected by a ratio of four to one. (1998, 29)

Thus, it appears that despite the establishment of the Social Democratic party with the ostensible goals of equality and wealth redistribution, there were a number of obstacles, including the resistance of an overarching paternalistic culture evidenced in part by the rejection of the initiative of 1894 as well as the lack of centralization of the working classes. Furthermore, consistent with what I argued above, religious and cultural differences seemed to outweigh socioeconomic divisions. Linder adds that "cultural ties often proved stronger than economic cleavages" (29) and refers specifically to the fact that the Catholic Conservative Party was able to absorb and unite some of the workers and thus divide the working class. While this did not preclude the social democrats from attaining a large electoral base, their strength did not challenge the stronger bourgeois forces in Swiss society. Steiner's research confirms that "crosscutting between occupational groups and party lines is weakest among the working classes" (1974, 54). Furthermore, he argues that the Swiss Social Democratic Party, unlike similar parties in other European democracies, is not strictly or even primarily a working class party but is rather a very reformist, pragmatic, and inclusive party that makes no "allusion to Marxism" nor does its program refer to the principle of class struggle (55).

In addition to the decentralization of industry and the virtual absence of a "real proletariat," Steiner suggests that three characteristics of the Swiss political system help explain why there is no clear-cut class based party. First, the extensive political rights of workers diminished the sense of alienation and the feeling of being outside the system, thus reducing the need for revolutionary activities. Secondly, federalism prevented workers from the realization of the collective interests and needs. Furthermore, federalism allowed the divisiveness and the rivalry among linguistic groups to thrive and therefore pose an obstacle to the working-class movement at the federal level. And third, Steiner suggests the collegial executive compels collaboration and compromise that has tended to undermine the more socialist aspects of the Social Democratic platforms of the past (1974, 56). Steiner's argument about the impact of federalism on the ideological cohesion (or lack thereof) of the Swiss Social Democratic party is indirectly related but theoretically consistent with the effect that federalism has been shown to have on income inequality—that federalism tends to increase inequality (Birchfield and Crepaz 1998). Although statistical evidence was supplied to support this claim, the logic has yet to be thoroughly articulated and clarified. Crepaz (1996b; Birchfield and Crepaz 1998) has developed a nuanced argument based on what he refers to as the distinction between collective and competitive veto points. Observing a contradiction between the assertions of the veto point literature and Lijphart's conventional classification of majoritarianism with unitary or non-federal systems and consensus democracy with federalism—that is, greater depression power—Crepaz attempts to resolve this impasse by showing that competitive veto points operationalized by symmetry of legislatures and degree of federalism are distinguished by their effects on outcomes in that they involve different political actors operating through separate institutions with mutual veto power. Conversely, collective veto points, measured as multiple party parliamentarism, entail greater face-to-face interaction of political actors, thus enabling rather than constraining policy coordination. This distinction allowed for a d isaggregated or d ifferentiated examination of th e separate institutional effects on an outcome such as income inequality and confirmed that competitive veto points tend to preserve the status quo and collective veto points allow for more active government. Nevertheless, several problems remain.

Although the clarification of different types of veto points is valuable, there remains a tension with Lijphart's framework that links majoritarianism with a concentration of power and consensus democracy as better institutionally characterized by federalism. Lijphart writes: "Majoritarian government is therefore both unitary (non-federal) and centralized. The consensus model is inspired by the opposite aim. Its methods are federalism and decentralization" (1999, 186). Despite the fact that federalism can be captured as a competitive veto point, does that alone extricate it from the theoretical and institutional logic intrinsic to Lijp hart's typology? If w e begin to m ake exceptions or modifications for each separate institutional element according to the desired or expected effect we believe it should have on a given outcome, then we are substantially eroding the logic of Lijphart's framework. Crepaz has begun to draw attention to the incompatible or even contradictory nature of Lijphart's two dimensions, but more systematic treatment is in order.

This is precisely why I argue that the cultural dimensions of institutions must be brought to the fore to salvage what, in encompassing frameworks such as Lijphart's, mechanically risks falling apart at the seams. Another issue involves the variable impact an institutional element such as federalism exerts on outcomes. If we argue that c ompetitive veto points such as federalism make it more difficult to change the status quo, in the case of explaining variation in income inequality, we are then obliged to explain why Germany and Belgium have managed to r educe income differentials whereas the other federalist countries—Austria, Canada, Switzerland, and the United States (based on Lijphart 1999, 189, Table 10.1)—have all experienced an increase in income inequality. To avoid such thorny issues, I chose to employ the aggregate measure, which excluded this dimensions of Lijphart's typology. A further justification for this decision is that, as Steiner points out, the influence of federalism may be indirect at best—that is, shaping overall strength of political parties. Given the powerful role that partisan coloration seems to play in affecting income inequality, the linkage between federalism and political parties should be explored further before a more precise casual argument about the impact of either on income inequality can be more effectively crafted.

Drawing on these previous studies then, we can conclude that the Social Democratic Party, although one of the four major parties in Switzerland, does not derive its ideological mandate from a high degree of class consciousness and working-class solidarity and has consequently not played a very significant a role in inhibiting the preponderance of market justice. This phenomenon is also reflected in the type of interest intermediation that arose in Switzerland. In general, corporatist arrangements have been associated with class compromise and industrial peace agreements (Schmitter 1974, 1981). However, there are important variants of corporatism that largely reflect the balance of power between the participating firms and unions. From what we have learned about the weakness of the working class in Switzerland and the prevalence of market justice, it is not surprising that the former has the upper hand in the Swiss style of corporatism.

Peter Katzenstein (1985) distinguishes between two types of corporatism. Social corporatism is characterized by a strong predominance of labor unions, whereas business associations play a more influential role in liberal corporatism. Katzenstein found Switzerland to typify the model of liberal corporatism. Not only is labor not a partner of equal strength under Swiss corporatism, but as Lehmbruch (1993) pointed out, the cohesion of the interest associations is "superior to that of Swiss political parties" (52). Such cohesion is stronger among the business associations than the trade unions. Hicks and Kenworthy confirm that the "share of companies they represent and their authority vis-à-vis member firms" is much greater among national business confederations in Switzerland (and Japan) than in countries such as the United States and Australia (1998, 6).

When placed in a broader context, the tendencies identified here with the Social Democratic Party, the nature of the corporatist arrangement as well as the weakness of the working classes in general seem to correspond well with the claim that Switzerland exhibits market justice as a predominant cultural ethos.[3] Wolf Linder very aptly sums it up:

> This minority position of labor in politics and industrial relations is a Swiss characteristic. It differs from other small European countries, such as the Netherlands, Austria, Norway, and Sweden, where more of equilibrium between labour and capital, and between the political

3. As Steiner has noted, many workers are of the "worker-farmer" type, and surveys indicate that most do not self-identify as part of a working class (for specific survey responses, see Steiner 1974, 59).

left and right, can be observed. Cultural segmentation was a greater obstacle to the organisation of the political left in Switzerland, and labour forces were never able to make up the organisational lead of business. (1998, 29)

As is quite indisputable, the diverse ethnic and linguistic communities encouraged the establishment of the power-sharing arrangements in Switzerland, or what Lehmbruch and Steiner call the operation of "amicable agreement versus majority rule," as the key pattern of decision making.[4] In reference to Switzerland, Inglehart notes that ethnic diversity gave rise to such institutions to prevent the appearance of one group having political dominance. He remarks: "To anyone familiar with these societies, the claim that the institutions gave rise to the culture would seem preposterous" (1997, 58). The fact that such institutions did permit business groups to dominate the process of industrial development suggests an interesting puzzle, although one that is certainly congruent with my characterization of Switzerland as a market justice society. Further study would be required to determine precisely how this situation transpired. Although it is beyond the purview of the present study, archival research and historical analysis of the various referenda attempting to constrain the influence of business or capital would allow a more definitive assessment of the ideological underpinnings of the Swiss political economy and the complex interplay of culture and institutions.

What is most pertinent is that the institutionalization of various forms of direct democracy did not coincide with a widespread belief that political institutions should be employed to alter or in any way distort the workings of the market. As I have tried to show, this cultural element (the predominance of market justice) is a central part of the causal story about income inequality in Switzerland. From this discussion, then, we might consider Switzerland as an exceptional case on a number of points. First, it is unlike other consensual systems because it has high degree of income inequality. But unlike most of the consensus democracies under examination here, it has a cultural orientation of market justice. This very broad-stroke tableau of the

4. Although Steiner employed Lehmbruch's concept of amicable agreement, he associates his understanding of this pattern of decision making as roughly the same as Lijphart's concept of consociationalism and accommodation. Steiner notes, "Lijphart uses slightly different terms when he writes that political stability can be maintained in culturally fragmented systems if the leaders of the subcultures can engage cooperative efforts to counteract the centrifugal tendencies of cultural fragmentation" (1974, 4).

structural and historical context in which a culture of market justice has
evolved reveals the significance of bringing cultural explanations into consideration when we evaluate the performance and the explanatory power of
institutions. It is important to emphasize that the case of Switzerland here
does not mean culture is the better explanation of why income inequality
is relatively high. The predominant political culture of market justice alone
simply cannot provide a necessary and sufficient explanation. As the Swiss
case elucidates, a more accurate causal explanation is derived from a differen-
tiated view of the role of values and its relationship to political institutions.
As we have argued, in the case of consensus democracy, values are more accurately translated into outcomes or policies, so it is not that values alone do the
explanatory job here but the type of values (market justice) combined with
the type of political institutions (consensus) would predict, and indeed we
confirm, an outcome of greater income inequality.

A more in-depth comparative case study of the United Kingdom will
allow for greater analytical leverage on the question of how values are mediated through political institutions to shape outcomes. It is highly suggestive
that the United Kingdom has a strong propensity toward political justice and
yet still has a high degree of income inequality. Could we surmise then that
majoritarian institutions operate less effectively in translating such norms into
preferred societal outcomes such as reducing income inequality? The objective of the following case study is to determine whether we can substantiate
that the United Kingdom is indeed a political justice society or whether
its association as such is a mere artifact of the specificity of the survey data
employed in this study. If we can show that, in terms of both its historical evolution as well as its contemporary sociocultural ethos, British society is intrinsically and broadly oriented toward political justice when it comes to the issue
of the proper role of government in matters of distributive and redistributive
policy, then my argument and the newly conceptualized understanding of the
consensus-majoritarian typology can be reasonably corroborated.


## Must Winner-Take-All Politics Mean Winner-Take-All Economics? The U.K. Case

Whereas Switzerland was the exceptional case of a consensus democracy
with a strong tendency of favoring market justice, the United Kingdom, a

majoritarian country, displayed a high proportion of its survey respondents who appear to be generally oriented toward political justice, and yet it is nevertheless characterized by a relatively high degree of income inequality. How can we understand the similarities in income inequality in the cases of Switzerland and the United Kingdom when we also have opposing variation in the two independent variables? The key lies in the nature of how certain institutions aggregate preferences into outcomes. On the justice index, the United Kingdom ranked sixth from the bottom, with only the Netherlands, Belgium, Italy, Ireland, and France proving to be more strongly oriented toward political justice. If values matter, why does this strong propensity not lead to lower levels of income inequality? In tackling this question, the central objective of this comparative case is to determine whether we can more fully substantiate the claim that the United Kingdom is indeed a political justice society. Thus, the main thrust of the following analysis is to inquire into the nature and historical evolution of British values about the proper roles of states versus markets in matters of distributive justice. If we can sustain the characterization of the United Kingdom as a political justice society, we may then infer that regardless of the values orientation, winner-take-all political institutions have a proclivity toward producing winner-take-all economics or higher levels of income inequality. Such a claim does not mean that values do not matter at all to outcomes, but that they carry less weight than in consensus systems.

It may seem odd that the country that gave the world the philosophical doctrine of classical liberalism and a model of laissez-faire capitalism could be convincingly portrayed as a society in favor of political over market justice. Yet one of my main concerns about the way in which we use culture or ideas as modes of analysis and factors in causal explanations is that we need to move beyond stereotypical notions of political culture and work toward defining very specific ideas and values that may have empirical salience as well as provide meaning and deeper understanding of societies. I also hope by now to have shown the difference that measuring values at the mass level makes versus elite representations or relying on theoretically deduced or assumed preferences. What I attempt to elucidate in this brief case study of British values as they relate to questions of distributive justice is that despite both the historical association of Britain with free market liberalism and its present image and characterization (along with the United States) as a champion of neoliberalism, public opinion is in fact much less decidedly promarket. If the following narrative indeed substantiates this, then the onus falls even more on the institutionalist, particularly strong proponents of majoritarianism, to explain the incongruence. I shall return to this point in the conclusion.

The one idea most undergraduate students tend to retain from their comparative politics textbooks and the study of the United Kingdom is that it is the democratic society most associated with class politics. This standard characterization already suggests that market ideology may not have achieved the hegemonic status that is widely presumed. Class identity as the most significant of social divisions in British society is typically traced back to the experience of the industrial revolution and the fact that the process of state formation had been completed during the sixteenth and seventeenth centuries resolving many other cultural, linguistic, and regional power struggles. By the end of the seventeenth century, major religious divisions that continued to plague other countries had been settled in Britain, and the power of the Parliament vis-à-vis the monarchy was firmly established. As the first country to industrialize and with many of these other deep-seated societal conflicts more or less resolved, the political and economic terrain represented the canvas upon which class identity would play itself out. The economic and industrial change that transformed British society and created a massive new urban working class would propel a very gradual expansion of the franchise to include male, and eventually female, non-property-holding citizens. Gradualism is the operative word here as each reform resulted in only the most minor extensions of the franchise. For example, the Reform Act of 1832 increased the adult voting population from 5 percent to only 7 percent. Even with the agitation of the Chartist movement and widespread demands for reform and greater democratization, by 1867 the electorate had increased to just over 16 percent. The Franchise Act of 1884 would double this size, but it was not until the Representation of the People Act of 1918 that universal suffrage of all males and females over the age of thirty was achieved, and not until 1969 was the eligible voting age lowered to eighteen. A major class dimension of British politics has its roots in the founding of the Labour Party (circa 1900), and, interestingly, it is one of the few European political parties that did not have its origins in electoral politics. The party itself grew out of trade unions and various socialist societies such as the Fabians, who sought to advance working-class rights. Only later would they mobilize for greater political representation. Ultimately, the enfranchisement of urban and rural workers allowed for a truer realization of parliamentary democracy and began to challenge the narrow interest and influence of property.

What the nonviolent but relatively slow expansion of the franchise tells us is that the British populace may have had radical impulses, but they also exhibited pragmatism and patience in the attainment of political rights. In their classic comparative study of the ideals and beliefs that shape political behavior in democratic societies, Almond and Verba (1963) classified British political culture as one marked by pragmatism, trust, and tolerance, with a clear deference to authority and acceptance of the basic rules of the game but also a competence and proclivity to contest specific issues. If we traced British political culture back through the momentous events of the industrial revolution, debates and reform surrounding the Poor Laws, the Chartist movement, and up through the politics of Victorian era, we would observe a persistent struggle between elite and mass values over the fundamental question of individualism versus collectivism. However, late-Victorian politics would see a break or shift in this pattern as the growing awareness of crushing and persistent poverty challenged prevailing attitudes about the virtues of "self-help" and the efficacy of philanthropy and charity. Concern had also been galvanized during the first half of the century by the writings of novelists such as Dickens and Disraeli, but ultimately the proliferation of charities revealed a fear of social revolution more than a conviction that the economic system itself was fundamentally unjust. The abject poverty amidst growing national wealth would eventually prove too great a contradiction, however, and as one noted historian observed, "In a sense the efficacy of private charity was the main Victorian bulwark against a totally collectivist approach. Once charity was found to be ultimately inadequate to meet the pressures placed upon it, then the floodgates opened and the collectivist tide flowed in" (Fraser 1973, 114).

Before the turn of the century, poverty was known to have encompassed about a third of the population (134). As Fraser's (1973) magisterial study of the evolution of the British welfare state documents, from the late nineteenth century onward, the persistence of poverty and inequality fostered a growing awareness of the need for a more comprehensive and extensive social welfare policy. Certainly the experience of two world wars marked a turning point in British political culture when a consensus emerged across all classes and partisan stripes around the recognition of the need for and the moral rightness of a comprehensive welfare state. I would argue that such values would prevail until the aberration of the Thatcher years, yet as the survey data presented in the following shall reveal, even this episode did not fundamentally shake the bedrock conviction of what is essentially a preference for the norm of political justice vis-à-vis that of market justice. Fraser writes:

> The Welfare State represented the social consensus of the British people in the middle of the twentieth century. It owed much to the past, was indeed rooted in the historical process of change, which had produced an urban industrial society, yet at the same time was distinctively characterised by the universalism of its own day. The British Welfare State was both an end and a beginning. In guaranteeing all its citizens against Beveridge's five giants, British society drew on the best of the past for the benefit of the future. The Welfare State was not the product of a spontaneous act of creation in 1948, but the latest stage on a dynamic process of adjustment between individual and society. The British Welfare State was not born—it had evolved. (1973, 222)

The experience of war had a radicalizing effect on attitudes that meshed well with the expanding role of an interventionist state in pursuit of national defense. Indeed, much of the prewar social policy that had been pushed through by the Liberal government of Lloyd George was based in Bismarkian logic that implemented an insurance scheme to protect citizens but, almost as importantly, provided a blow against socialism, which is once again reflective of the individualism versus collectivism strand of conflict in British political culture. By way of contrast, in the United States, this particular antagonism is virtually absent, and instead most social historians note an early triumph of individualistic values and culture. Although in general I reject the thrust of the American exceptionalism thesis, this particular ideological element is rather difficult to refute. In the British case and moving the pendulum slightly more in the direction of collectivism, Lloyd George saw the steps taken toward better welfare as only a beginning, and characteristic of so many of his speeches and policy goals, social justice was a predominant theme. In one of his most famous speeches defending his "People's Budget," Lloyd George proclaimed it to be a war budget to "wage implacable warfare against poverty and squalidness" that incidentally he thought could be eradicated within a generation (Fraser 1973, 145). For the first time, the national budget was seen as a tool of social policy. However, the overarching suspicion of socialism, the tenacity of individualism among elites, and the strength of the conservative—political as well as commercial/industrial—opposition meant that most of Lloyd George's policies amounted to selective and limited insurance schemes. Nonetheless, his vision and programs would lay the foundation of the British welfare state. Later, the practical needs and pressures of war mobilized state action even more and to such a degree that the *Manchester Guardian* called it "War Socialism" (Fraser 1973, 165). One published survey showed that by the beginning of World War II, only one in three British conscripts was fit enough to join the forces. Widespread recognition of these poor conditions resulted in public opinion that was clamoring for improvement and greater access to health and welfare services than had been attained in the interwar period. Fraser comments that "the war years thus transformed social attitudes and pricked the social conscience" (1973, 166). The immediate postwar condition greatly accelerated the move to universalism and crystallized what is widely known as the "collectivist consensus." The period from 1945 to 1979 was characterized by a broad culture of reconciliation and determination to improve conditions of life for all Britons, and welfare was construed as a fundamental right as opposed to a need or other stigmatizing notions that had prevailed in earlier periods of British history. This notion of collective consensus is certainly closer to an orientation of political justice than market justice, but we must ask what transpired in the Thatcher years as well as what has followed in the form of New Labour and "Third Way" approaches to managing the economy and reforming the welfare state. Can we still conclude that this political justice orientation is deeply enmeshed in British political culture today?

In their examination of public perceptions about growing poverty and inequality, Danzinger and Haveman (2001) found the British case to be quite different from that of American attitudes. For example, they report the results of the British Social Attitudes Survey and one particular survey question that asked whether the government should spend more money on welfare benefits for the poor, even if such spending might require higher taxes; 43 percent of the public agreed, only 26 percent disagreed, and 68 percent said they would favor even more support and spending for working parents with very low incomes. Furthermore, the British public also showed more concern about inequality than did the American public. Approximately 80 percent of Britons believe that the gap between those with high incomes and those with low incomes is too wide compared to only about 50 percent of the Americans saying the same. Even more important for the argument I am making, 75 percent of the British public thinks that the government should do something about inequality, with more than 50 percent agreeing that taxes on the better-off should be raised to spend more on the poor (2001, 470).

Nonetheless, even in the face of massive public opposition, a steady erosion of the welfare state took place, and for at least the past twenty years—even under the current Labour government—reform has fuelled a steady drift away from universalism and insurance-based programs toward more means-testing and leaner welfare provisions, thus increasing inequality. Analyzing the partisan economic strategies in Britain and the radical break with the postwar period of heavy economic management that Thatcher engineered, Carles Boix argues:

> Conservatives went into office with the conviction that theirs was a program for the moral and political renewal of Britain. Accordingly, the Tory cabinet was particularly determined to use its economic policies to mold public opinion in favor of its program of social and political change. The transformation of the British citizenry implied, above all, a general change in its attitudes toward the role of the state in running the economy. Economic change could not come solely from specific policy changes or even from a thorough deregulatory strategy. It depended as well on the transformation of the basic social values among all private agents. For the Conservative economic strategy to be successful and lead to rapid economic growth, a renewed entrepreneurial ethos had to replace the excessive economic interventionism practiced by the British government since 1945. (1998, 181–82)

Whereas the Thatcher government clearly attempted to orchestrate a general shift in public attitudes toward laissez-faire economic policies, Boix and others have clearly documented that this shift did not occur in the realm of social spending and the commitment to the maintenance of the welfare state. Instead there has been a strong and unchallenged consensus toward a prominent role and responsibility of the state to provide welfare. Boix presents more supporting data showing that close to 90 percent of British public opinion consistently supported public expenditure to end poverty and that the proportion of respondents believing that welfare benefits should be maintained or increased went up from 66 percent in 1974 to 76 percent in 1987. Furthermore, 4 out of 5 respondents say it is the government's responsibility to secure health and retirement benefits (1998, 192–93).

As George and Wilding's (1999) study of British society and social welfare illustrates, values are perhaps the key element in securing a sustainable and equitable society. While their analysis of contemporary British society showed that "poverty and gross inequality remain striking characteristics of British society" (202), and although they believe this is in par t a fu nction of an aggressively individualistic culture that was inculcated during the Thatcher years, they detect a reemerging consensus that sees different forms and degrees of private and public provisions as necessary in contemporary society and a consensus that the state is being restored to favor vis-à-vis the market. More significantly they report:

> There is evidence, however, showing that the public is beginning to accept the importance of the common good. Every year, the UK Henley Centre asks people whether they think society does best when people look after their own interests or when society acts collectively. The proportions of people supporting each option did not change much from the mid 1980s until the mid 1990s, but the 1996 figures tell a very different story. Those believing in collective action now number 70 percent, and the individualists have shrunk to 30 percent (1999, 205).

While an extensive consideration of the impact of Thatcherism is beyond the scope of this analysis, it should be noted that there is a great deal of contentious debate about the extent of the popularity of Thatcherite reforms. In a very provocative account of the rise of free market politics in Britain and a comparison with the United States, Germany, and France, Prasad acknowledges such debates but concludes, "It is tr ue that there was no full-blown conversion to Thatc herism in the public, and indeed the government was unpopular for most of its time in office (except, of course during the elections)" (2006, 142–43). Although certain policies like the Council house sales and the privatization of British Telecom were successful and earned the support of the public, others were fiercely opposed, explaining why core elements of reform of the welfare state were not attempted until Thatcher's third term. While the public opinion data do not show a clear embrace of free market principles at any point throughout Thatcher's ten years in power, reforms nevertheless moved the British economy and society much further along the neoliberal path even in the face of public rejection of her radical ideas such as the infamous denial of the existence of society. In part, this is made possible because of the way in which majoritarian institutions concentrate power in the hands of the prime minister, which is the opposite tendency of the institutional logic in consensus systems where power sharing is more the norm. Reaching similar conclusions, Iversen's study finds that in majoritarian systems, strong leaders can exercise power in ways that outweigh long-term investment in social protection and also that "parties deviate more from preferences of the median voter" (2005, 123). These findings serve to reinforce my argument that we need to take both the institutional and the ideational logics into consideration to gain greater insight into why some capitalist democracies are generating greater income inequality even when their sociocultural ethos would appear to militate against it.

Conventional wisdom suggests that the British have greater ideological affinity with citizens of the United States than with her fellow Europeans when it comes to attitudes and beliefs about market economies and social justice. Challenging this view are the most recent opinion data revealing a somewhat different story. In a recent Pew Global Attitudes Survey (2002) examining opinions on government's responsibility for the poor, the British out-ranked France, Italy, Germany, and the United States with the highest percentage of their respondents (59 percent) saying that they "completely agree" that government has the responsibility to take care of the poor. Fifty percent of the French respondents agreed (the country that ranked the highest on the political justice index), and only 29 percent of Americans felt it is the government's responsibility. Although this is more current than the time period we are studying, it is indicative of a consistent pattern in British political culture that in many ways seems contrary to the conventional views of a country that has been long characterized by a conservative tradition representing the classic example of a "night watchman state" and a classically liberal economy.

The United Kingdom is neither a leader nor a laggard when it comes to welfare state development, but until the Thatcher revolution, a universal welfare state was largely intact since the post–World War II era. Esping-Andersen (1990) classified it as having characteristics of both the social democratic and liberal regimes and Hicks (1999) confirmed that the United Kingdom took a Lib-Lab (Liberal-Labor) route to the welfare state. These facts are important to recall given the association in the varieties of capitalism (VOC) literature and in the broader comparative political economy scholarship of the United

Kingdom as a liberal market economy and virtually identical to the American neoliberal model. It is perhaps misleading to refer continually to the Anglo-American model as if the two political economies were one in the same. As the public opinion data show, Britain differs vastly from its purported twin political economy, the United States.

The Blair government's antipoverty campaign and strategy to win widespread public support by focusing especially on combating child poverty and ending social exclusion further lends support to the argument that public values matter and that there is a solid and long-standing pattern of a preference for political as opposed to market justice in British society. In his recent essay printed in *The Economist* titled "What I've Learned," Prime Minister Blair whose three-term, ten-year period of governing did as much if not more than the Thatcher government to trim back the welfare state and toughen entitlements to benefits, nonetheless made a special appeal to confront the issue of social exclusion so prevalent in market economies. He writes: "From 1979 to 1997 the incomes of the richest 20 percent in Britain grew faster (2.5 percent) than the incomes of the poorest 20 percent (0.8 percent). That has been reversed. Since 1997 the incomes of the poorest have risen faster (2.2 percent) than the richest (2 percent). However, this masks a tail of under achievers, the socially excluded. The rising tide does not lift their ships" (Blair 2007, 28). There are very intense debates now about whether inequality has increased or decreased under Blair's government, and it is quite clear that the selection of different facts and statistics alters our perception and assessment of income inequality in a given society. In fact, a recent article in the *Financial Times* reported that despite increased public spending and an overall reduction in poverty, the gap between the rich and the poor has gotten wider under the Labour government. This is contrary to what was cited in *The Economist*. Consistent with the statistics Blair refers to, those toward the bottom of the income distribution have done better relative to the middle, but if one examines the top and bottom 10 percent, inequality has in fact worsened. Most interestingly for my argument about the importance of ideational factors, however, is the following point made in the article that now "Conservatives argue with Labour over how to improve social justice, public services and the U.K.'s welfare state—rather than debating, as the Thatcherite wing of their party did throughout the 1980s and 1990s, how to dismantle it" (*Financial Times,* 2 May 2007, 11). The degree to which Blair has changed the tenor of the debate and forced the opposition to formulate their positions in these terms—essentially the language of a modern social democratic party—perhaps illustrates that the extreme free market liberalism of the Thatcher era was indeed an aberration rather than a fundamental shift in popular values and political culture.

Britons are concerned with matters of social justice and are aware—despite the more favorable statistics Blair cited—that the net result of market reforms has been greater inequality. The extent to which both Conservatives and Labour see this as a main agenda item further shows the continued commitment to the welfare state and the necessary political justice values that sustain it. The centrality of social justice in recent public discourse coupled with the latest surveys reported earlier indicate that the British have sent a clear signal rejecting Thatcherite ideas of "society as nothing more than a collection of individuals," thereby implying stronger political support for the role of the state in providing welfare and promoting greater egalitarianism. However, what we may ultimately infer from this analysis is that these values and preferences are not as determinative or influential in a majoritarian system as they would be in a consensual system. Both historically and in the current period, British attitudes and values are quite supportive of government intervention in the economy to redistribute income in a more egalitarian direction. Yet, there is a lack of congruence between the cultural norm of political justice and the persistent trends of increasing income inequality in Great Britain. Thus it appears that winner-take-all institutions are more likely to produce winner-take-all socioeconomic outcomes.

While this holds up a core assertion running through this book, I hasten to add that my emphasis is on broad patterns of the *relative* and *reciprocal* relations between institutions and values and their joint impact on income inequality. These two case studies help to tighten the causal logic by confirming the historical roots of the values orientations in both countries that then allowed us to better substantiate the nature of their political institutions and trace out this impact on distributive outcomes. The winner-take-all nature of majoritarian institutions does not necessarily mean we should discount the role of values all together in these political settings but simply that relative to consensus democracies the power of their impact is more attenuated. Income inequality is in fact slightly lower in the United Kingdom than in other majoritarian systems where market justice is the prevailing norm, for example, the United States and Australia. As the path model of welfare transfers showed in the previous chapter, policies obviously play a direct role in the final distributive outcomes. Furthermore, we know that employment and labor market dynamics (Pontusson 2005) as well as a host of specific redistributive mechanisms including taxation schemes (Steinmo 1998) all play significant roles in explaining cross-national differences in income inequality. However, my main purpose has been to put these causal forces of income inequality in broader political context by producing an original and more nuanced generalization that combines institutionalist and ideational logics in a single explanatory framework. A brief look at two other cases may offer additional insights and better contextualize the broad conclusions of this qualitative analysis.

## Values, Institutions, and Redistribution in Canada and Sweden

Whereas the Swiss and U.K. cases ultimately sustain the argument that institutions and values together make for a more persuasive and generalizable explanation of cross-national variation in income inequality, Canada and Sweden could potentially be seen as challenges to the thesis. In this concluding section, I offer some reflections on how the findings of the two main case studies relate to the mix of values, institutions, and income inequality in two other countries to reassess the logic of my argument. First, it bears repeating that these case studies do not reveal a "values trumps institutions" dynamic (or vice versa), but rather show that both institutions and values shape outcomes and that consensus systems more faithfully translate preferences and values into desired societal outcomes. Thus, because market justice was the norm in the consensus democracy of Switzerland, we conclude that it is the interaction of values and institutions and not an "either/or" or a "one factor is more significant" type of result. Claims about the causal weight of values and ideas even in this contingent fashion, however, are often received with more skepticism than purely institutional arguments, but I believe the approach I have taken succeeds in reconciling the tensions that have characterized the two broad approaches in comparative political analysis and hopefully pushes us beyond the culture versus institutions impasse.

To interpret my foregoing argument and the qualitative analysis as one in which there is a trumping of culture or values in the Swiss case but of institutions in the U.K. case would be missing the point entirely. The real causal logic resides in the way in which specific kinds of cultural values interact with certain types of political institutions to produce varying levels of cross-societal income inequality. However, in addition to acknowledging the inevitable role of redistributive policies and employment factors in shaping d istributional outcomes, it is n ecessary to qual ify further the complex polyvalence and volatility of values as well. Although both the quantitative and the qualitative analyses demonstrate the relationship between our two main independent variables and their varying impact on income inequality, we have not looked at how values and opinions might be interrelated with redistributive policies and the subsequent degree of inequality. In light of the fact that political institutions are the most invariant of all of th ese causal factors, it is worth considering the potential effect that policies and actual outcomes might have on societal values. Juxtaposing the cases of Canada and Sweden with those of the United Kingdom and Switzerland will help draw this point out a bit further.

Whereas the U.K. and Swiss cases were extraordinarily striking in their values predispositions, Sweden and Canada also bring differentiation into the typologies in terms of the values dimension and the comparative distributive outcomes. Sweden, like Switzerland manifested a values orientation that was slightly unexpected given the associations we had found between political justice and consensus democracy. Although it was not classified as a market justice society, it did fall in the middle category along with the United Kingdom, yet it still has the lowest level of income inequality of all the countries.[5] Does this challenge the idea that consensus democracies are better conveyor of values? A closer examination of patterns of income inequality and values in this country provides an additional test of my argument. Similarly, while Canada manifested the expected relationship between market justice values and majoritarianism, it falls in th e moderately high category of in come inequality. What explains the similar level of income inequality to the United Kingdom despite the opposing values orientations in the two countries? A closer look at the values and policy context in both countries in relation to their varying levels of income inequality will further qualify the role of institutions and more clearly expose the contingency of the causal mechanisms at work.

Given Canada's image as a progressive and socially conscious society, her ranking on the values index as the third most strongly oriented market justice society is quite s urprising. Consequently, the finding supplied an e ven

5. It in fact is the weakest political justice society in this middle category, with a score of 44.5 compared with the U.K. score of 68.9. Recall that the higher the number, the more inclined toward political justice. See Figure 1 in Chapter 2.

stronger rationale for choosing the United Kingdom as the main case to pair with Switzerland. Initially I expected that Canada would likely serve as the exception to the other majoritarian systems, but the survey data told a different story; in fact, it was the United Kingdom that had the necessary variance on the values variable because it proved to be the more strongly political justice society. It should be noted that France is a potential candidate as well, but it is a more complicated case in terms of its mixed or ambiguous institutional features as well as its lack of fit with the models of capitalism and welfare state typologies. Both Hall and Soskice (2001) and Pontusson (2005) consider it to be more or less in a category of its own or possibly representing a different category along with Southern European countries such as Spain and Portugal. For the purposes of this study, however, we could in reasonably interpret France—the majoritarian country with the strongest political values orientation and moderately high income inequality—as fairly consistent with the findings for the United Kingdom and Canada. This observation nuances the "winner-take-all politics produces winner-take-all economics" claim somewhat by showing that this is not a categorical association but rather one of degrees. In other words, both the strength of institutions and the intensity of the values matter.

No less a reputable scholar than Seymour Martin Lipset has long maintained the argument that Canada is a much less classically liberal society than the United States with greater popular support for and beliefs in the role of government in the economy. His extensive study of Canadian values and political culture has led him to conclude that Canada, despite past British heritage and present influence of her neighbor to the South, is in many ways ideologically closer to continental Europe. Lipset cites a wide range of survey data that provide evidence of the Canadian propensity to favor a strong role of government especially regarding their commitment to redistributive egalitarianism. Lipset sums up his cultural assessment of Canadian attitudes by invoking the words of Canadian novelist Robertson Davies, who opined "beneath all of this we are a people firmly set in the socialist pattern" (quoted in Lipset 1990, 70). In an article in which Crepaz and Lijphart attempt to explicate the theoretical and empirical linkages between consensus democracy and corporatism, the authors admit that "our measure is unable to recognize Canada's many informal consensual norms which to some extent counteract its formally majoritarian institutions" (1991, 246). So why did Canada exhibit this propensity to favor market justice given the strong underlying egalitarian ethos that Lipset and other scholars have historically attributed to it? Answering this question would take us into territory better left to more extensive research into the sources of attitudes and values, but it provides a dose of relativism about the meaning of values and public opinion and serves to remind us also of the limitations of the culturalism-versus-institutionalism approach to political economic inquiries. On the former point, we must come to terms with the reality of contradictory ideological impulses in national political cultures. Just as the short historical narrative of Britain illustrated with regard to the struggle between individualism and collectivism, so too does Canada have an internally complex and often contradictory pull between a frontier culture that prizes individualism and its more socialist or social democratic impulses. Recognition of this polyvalent nature of culture and public values does not mean that it is futile to treat such forces with as much analytical and empirical rigor as possible; on the contrary, our interest in granting ideas and institutions equal causal weight but perhaps doing so with modesty and caution when it comes to social scientific notions of causal precision and predictability is connected to the latter point.

If we compare Canada simultaneously with the United States and the United Kingdom, how can we claim that the stronger political justice values in the U.K. case may have contributed to its lower level of income inequality than in the United States, but in Canada, which has essentially the same average Gini coefficient as the United Kingdom (30.3 and 30.9, respectively), we find even stronger market justice values than in the United States? Theoretically, we could argue that once again this shows the less-than-congruent relationship between preferences and actual outcomes in majoritarian systems. In light of the tensions between the market justice orientation and Canada's otherwise egalitarian ethos, however, I believe this would be a rather contorted argument. Instead we might find the answer in the attitudes of Canadians that tap into perceptions that they already live in an egalitarian society; therefore, they tend to respond less favorably toward more government intervention. In terms of policy, there is in fact supportive evidence of this in the findings of Kenworthy and Pontusson (2005, 459–61) showing a relatively strong positive association between market inequality and redistribution in most OECD countries with the unsurprising exception of the United States. Canada compares favorably with Sweden and Germany and even exceeds the compensatory and redistributive effort of Finland and Denmark. Thus, despite the persistent and relatively high levels of inequality in Canada, the Canadian state—as its citizens seem well aware—does seek to redress increases in household market inequalities. Along these lines, Kenworthy notes, "Egalitarian shifts are possible even in circumstances in which institutions are relatively inhospitable. . . . [Canada] has managed to construct a set of policies that yield substantially less income inequality than in the United States with little or no sacrifice in terms of employment or living standards" (2004, 172). These policies include more generous social welfare programs, more effective targeting, and higher spending levels including income supplements for the elderly and low income individuals. Additionally, on the employment front, Pontusson's study revealed that over the period of the 1980s through 1997, public-sector employment—which could have a mitigating role on market inequalities—increased in Canada but contracted in the United Kingdom (2005, 84–86). But how then does the United Kingdom reach a similar level of income inequality? When looking at the redistributive effects of taxes and income transfers in both countries, we may find a reasonable explanation that is also in line with the different degrees of market and political justice values in the two societies. Separating the redistributive effects of taxes and transfers, Pontusson reports the percentage change in Gini coefficients as we move from gross to net (posttax) market income in fourteen of the sixteen countries under consideration in my study, omitting information only for the cases of Ireland and New Zealand. In Canada, there is a 6.9 percent change due to taxation and a 17.9 percent change as a result of transfers. In contrast, transfers in the United Kingdom produce a larger change at 23 percent and a much smaller change through taxation at 1.6 percent. According to Pontusson, "the bulk of the redistribution produced by welfare transfers occurs through the provision of benefits rather than through taxation" (2005, 156). That the welfare state is the more direct agent of redistribution and that this is the mechanism by which Britain, a more political justice oriented society, minimizes income inequality as compared to the Canadian approach of public employment and taxation, which are incidentally more in line with its market justice orientation, further corroborates my proposition that not only do values matter, they are also reflected in the different types of policies that are intended to reduce income differentials. The different policy paths by which the two countries obtain similar levels of income inequality is in fact consistent with and reflects the differences in their values orientations and at the same time shows the relative limitations of relying on either values or institutions alone to explain variation.

Drawing on these secondary findings provides both n uance as well as additional analytical support that I b elieve highlights the consistency of my argument—albeit without statistical proof. As Pontusson pointed out, there is so much variation among certain groupings of countries like the continental social market economies (SMEs) versus the liberal market economies (LMEs) that it is d ifficult to ge neralize about the differences between them. This is precisely why, rather than focu sing on redistributive effort of go vernments per se as is standard for welfare state scholars, I have chosen to look at the out-come of income inequality and explain why it varies cross-nationally through a wider political lens. Canada and the United Kingdom are, in fact, the least inegalitarian of all the majoritarian countries. I have tried to show how their differentiation in the values context leads to similar outcomes on the depen-dent variable via the distinctive policy approaches taken by both governments while still maintaining the ideational and institutional logic of my thesis. This interpretation, although limited, is generally consistent with the results pre-sented in the path model in Chapter 4. Furthermore, it is significant to note that all three of these majoritarian democracies, even with the considerable differences between them on the independent variables as well as policy and employment factors, nonetheless have much greater levels of income inequal-ity than the consensus democracies with political justice value orientations. A comparison with Sweden, however, could also be interpreted as another strain on the logic of my argument because it is a strong consensual system that has considerable market justice values but still has the lowest level of in come inequality of all the countries in the study. How does its mix of values, insti-tutions, and income inequality interact with its redistributive policy approach?

It is in deed counterintuitive that S weden, a paragon of eg alitarianism, exhibited the strongest propensity toward market justice of all of the consen-sus democracies except for S witzerland. More careful scrutiny of it s survey values, however, reveals that S wedish attitudes toward redistribution weak-ened and were very volatile in the 1970s and the 1980s, which accounts at least partially for the higher average values in favor of market justice. By the time of the 1999 ISSP survey, which asks whether it is the responsibility of the government to reduce income inequality, 24 percent of Swedish respondents agreed strongly and 36 percent agreed, with only 6 percent strongly disagree-ing. Although 60 percent represents a rath er solid consensus, it still leaves us with a country where nearly 20 percent expressed no real opinion and 20 percent either disagree or strongly disagree, which suggests that while the historically strong egalitarian ethos may remain intact, there is some popular resistance. As in the Canadian case, we could reasonably conjecture that the self-understanding or identity of most Swedes as inhabiting an already extremely egalitarian society (which is true for Sweden as opposed to mere perception in the Canadian case) could explain the higher market justice values than might otherwise be expected. What we really need to show, however, are the policy shifts that might be consistent with the fluctuating political and market justice values even though these changes may not have necessarily produced greater income inequality in the long run.

Interestingly, Sweden did in fact experience a decline in the average annual growth of total social spending per capita during the same period when market values were stronger. Figures drawn from the OECD Social Expenditure Database indicate a 4.2 percentage point reduction in the amount of social spending per capita in Sweden from the 1970–80 period to the 1980–90 period (Pontusson 2005, 184–85). Of course, this was also a general trend across almost all of the OECD countries, but it furnishes at least tentative support for the argument that policy shifted along with attitudes in Sweden. Pontusson also notes that there was some reduction of redistribution in Sweden during 1980s (195). However, it is significant to recall that overall and certainly according to the most recent data for the late 1990s, Sweden stands out as the country that redistributes the most. Although taxation efforts were found to be regressive, the redistributive effects of welfare transfers were stronger than in any of the other countries. Even in relation to the social market economies, Sweden redistributes more with a 38 percent change in Gini coefficient compared to only a 31.9 percent change as the average for all the Nordic SMEs (Pontusson 2005, 154, 155). Not only does the Swedish welfare state significantly alter market distributions of household income, we should also acknowledge the substantial role that labor unions (79 percent unionization rate in Sweden, the highest rate among all other OECD countries) and collective wage bargaining play in reducing inequalities. With one out of every five Swedish citizens working in the public sector and an unemployment rate of only 5 percent as of 2002, it is noteworthy that real GDP per capita also increased by 17 percent between 1995 and 2001 and real median household increased by 14 percent. These facts led Kenworthy (2004) to conclude that Sweden appears to be a model country in its ability to combine active labor market institutions and welfare policies that sustain both growth and equality. With respect to whether we can accurately consider Sweden as a political justice society, this brief analysis leads me to con cur with Kenworthy, who finds that the "commitment to a h igh-equality, high employment society remains largely intact in Sweden" (2004, 136). I would emphasize the necessity of the underlying political will and values that drive and sustain both of these goals. In the case of S weden and its peculiar ranking on the justice index, it is reasonable to conclude that the self-identity of Swedes as already living in a ge nerous and egalitarian society may have influenced the high numbers of respondents who were disinclined to support more government redistribution. It is also striking to note that th e values shifted back toward greater political justice in the 1990s, the time at which Sweden was experiencing a deep economic recession, which implies, perhaps, recognition of the limits of market forces for sustaining the kind of egalitarian society they are accustomed to and quite clearly prefer.

Overall I believe these supplementary stylized facts and brief interpretative remarks about the cases of Cana da and Sweden help to sustain my thesis. Whereas values may be more malleable and are certainly more difficult to measure and interpret definitively than political institutions, we must consider the impact of both of these societal forces simultaneously and in conjunction with one another. Even though the comparative-historical analysis of Switzerland and the United Kingdom provides evidence that supports the generalization, there are some subtle but significant qualifications to be made. In the case of Canada, market justice values and majoritarian institutions obtained virtually the same degree of income inequality as found in the United Kingdom but at considerably lower levels than in the United States and the other majoritarian, market justice societies. The degree to which the winner-take-all institutions did not yield as extreme a winner-take-all outcome with respect to income inequality is due to social ju stice values that were not captured in the single survey question soliciting approval for more government redistribution. This instead can be inferred from support for a d ifferent policy approach in the form of greater public employment and taxation. Sweden has stronger market justice values than any other consensus democracy besides Switzerland, yet it still has the least amount of income inequality. Fluctuating Swedish values toward less support for government redistributive spending as well as some element of taxation or welfare generosity fatigue may explain away part of this anomaly, but labor market institutions, collective bargaining, and public employment all counterbalanced any reduction in social spending that may have taken place. The net result is still greater equality of income distribution than in any of the other countries under study here. Rather than seeing either of the cases as potential holes in the argument, this discussion sheds light again on the contingency but also the analytical necessity of considering both values and institutions as well as highlights the significant role that redistributive policies and labor market institutions play both in relation to values and actual outcomes.

Perhaps the most important points to take away from this chapter's more qualitative look at variation in income inequality across these capitalist democracies are that, although values and policies may shift over time, there are still rather enduring pulls in one direction or the other when it comes to support for government redistribution, and that the specific policy paths taken may also be shaped by this overarching sociocultural ethos in a given society. Finally, the most durable and unchanging of all of these forces is, in fact, the political institutional context, which, in the final analysis, largely shapes the extent to which the rest of it matters. Although not always in a linear and unconditional fashion, each of these factors play a critical role in the complex causal chain that explains varying levels of income inequality among capitalist democracies.

# CONCLUSION

Justice is the end of Government. It is the end of civil society. It ever has
been and ever will be pursued until it be obtained, or until liberty be lost in the
pursuit. In a society under the forms of which the stronger faction can readily
unite and oppress the weaker, anarchy may as truly be said to reign as in a state
of nature, where the weaker individual is not secured against the violence of the
stronger; and as, in the latter state, even the stronger individuals are prompted,
by the uncertainty of their condition, to submit to a government which may
protect the weak as well as themselves; so, in the former state, will the more
powerful factions or parties be gradually induced, by a like motive, to wish
for a government which will protect all parties, the weaker as well as the
more powerful.

—JAMES MADISON, *Federalist Paper # 51*

This book aims to explain why some capitalist democracies have recently experienced a growing divide between the rich and the poor in their societies,
while other countries facing similar global economic pressures maintain more
egalitarian income distributions. The starting point of my argument was that
the normative underpinnings of socioeconomic outcomes such as growing
income inequality has been neglected in previous scholarship and should be
a corollary to our empirical investigations of such problems facing democratic countries. Theoretically and empirically, the study shows that consensual
polities with societal values favoring political justice rather than market justice tend to produce the lowest levels of income disparity, while majoritarian
political systems, regardless of ideational or value preferences, tend to have
the highest levels of income inequality. Although this generalization provided
a fairly robust explanation of differences in levels of income disparity across

the sixteen capitalist democracies under investigation, complex and varying combinations of the two broad institutional and ideational factors permitted a rigorous test of its underlying logic.

For instance, in majoritarian systems where political justice values were strong, we found slightly lower levels of income inequality than in majoritarian systems where market justice values prevailed, confirming that values do indeed matter. Although supporting the "values matter" thesis, the analysis substantiated the proposition that values seems to exert less causal influence in majoritarian as opposed to consensus democracies. In the unusual case where market justice values predominated in a consensus system, income inequality was as high as that of the most inegalitarian of the sixteen countries under investigation here. This finding provides further evidence for a previously established claim (Huber and Powell 1994) that consensus systems generate outcomes that are more congruent with public preferences. Thus, although this study confirms that certain types of institutions are better aggregators of public values than others are, the major innovation of the present study is my demonstration that the ideational factors such as these societal values have causal—though contingent—weight in their own right. In a nutshell, cross-national patterns of income inequality among this set of sixteen capitalist democracies can be systematically explained by examining the intensity and direction of values combined with the degree of strength of consensualism or majoritarianism in the political institutional environment. This finding should spark new debates across the literatures of political science, political economy, and comparative politics because it challenges conventional theories that rely exclusively on institutions or values (and culture) as core explanatory variables.

As the selected passage from Madison earlier is meant to convey, a key motivation of this study was to investigate cross-national variation in income inequality as a matter of social justice. If persistent and growing poverty, obscene disparities between top management and average workers, and expansion of the working poor did not accompany rising levels of income inequalities, perhaps the growing gap between the rich and the poor would not seem so problematic. Unlike the philosopher or political theorist, I did not build a normative edifice upon which I defended or advocated an idealized income distribution that I deemed just. Rather, I interpret social justice to mean the collective political force deriving from competing ideas in society about the legitimacy of states and markets. In other words, I wanted to know what citizens in these democratic societies thought about income inequality as a matter of social justice, which could be inferred from whether government redistribution was seen as legitimate and necessary. Madison claims that justice is the end of government, but he is quick to point out that a potential hazard in the pursuit of justice may be a loss of liberty. This is the classic dilemma we find in both political economy and democratic theory, and my approach to this comparative analysis of income inequality was to bring this dilemma to the surface rather than assume its irrelevance to my empirical investigation.

My study contends that the degree of income inequality in democratic societies should be a matter of public choice, societal deliberation, and autonomous national decision making. Both the tenor of much of the globalization debates and the purported shrinking of the world's varieties of capitalism tend to render this statement rather naive. Interestingly, the bulk of the evidence being supplied by welfare state scholars provides a bulwark against these pessimistic conclusions, but little research has sought to frame income inequality in the democratic theoretical terms that my study has attempted. As my extensive comments on the welfare state literature have made clear, and particularly with respect to the latest work addressing income distribution (e.g., Bradley et al. 2003; Soskice 2006; Kenworthy and Pontusson 2005), the varying ways of measuring and comparing income inequality and the wide variance of institutions, policies, and macrostructural factors enlisted to explain cross-national variation have produced valuable knowledge and intricate, finely detailed insights about the impact of a multitude of influences, but no broad generalizations have yet to be produced. As such, my study sought to provide such a generalization that is compatible with much of the literature I have engaged with throughout this study. The results of my analysis certainly should not be seen as an alternative to these approaches but rather a complementary one in which my purpose was to specify the broader ideational-institutional parameters within which the policies and practices (as so precisely and carefully measured and assessed by these scholars) are carried out and to what effect on cross-national income inequality.

Thus, a primary goal of the book has been to place the problem of income inequality into a broad framework in which comparative analysis, democratic theory, and political economy were integrated in a manner that facilitated an empirical investigation without evading fundamentally important normative questions. All too often our social scientific inquiries treat the empirical and normative dimensions of social problems as if they were mutually exclusive. The perspective of "political economy as applied democratic theory" that I developed at the outset of this book intended to elucidate the ideological as well as the analytical consequences of this tendency and argued that a corrective might be achieved by bridging the institutional and ideational logics of our explanatory strategies. The singular disciplinary confines of political science, sociology, and economics have not produced an adequate understanding of how income gets distributed nor have previous studies isolated the determinative factors associated with cross-national variations in income inequality. Recognizing that practical questions of democratic theory and conceptions of justice can and should play a decisive role in shaping large-scale economic outcomes is the first step in demystifying the law-like assumptions that are often the starting point for most analyses of economic outcomes such as income distribution.

As societies become ever more closely integrated through the forces of technology and the global economy, ways of organizing relations between the polity and the economy as well as the underlying values about the legitimacy of states versus markets need to be constantly reevaluated and articulated in both philosophical and practical terms. The key contribution of this study lies in its reconceptualization and empirical corroboration of the thesis that material and ideational forces work interactively to play a systematic and decisive role in explaining why very similar societies with market economies and democratic polities nevertheless vary significantly with regard to how equally or unequally income is distributed among its citizenry. Although institutional variation, understood through Lijphart's typology, has proven to be a strong and reliable predictor of a wide range of socioeconomic phenomena, my research has uncovered a key weakness of the previous applications of Lijphart's models by demonstrating that it is not institutions alone but also the cultural environment within which those institutions function that actually permits greater analytical precision as well as more valid causal inferences and reliable generalizations about the role they play in shaping outcomes.

My operationalization and extension of Robert Lane's insights about different conceptions of justice added considerable theoretical depth from which I constructed an ideational typology through the specification of key cultural attitudes and values that are most pertinent to shaping macroeconomic outcomes. This ideational typology then allowed us to better discern the potential causal role of ideas as well as their interplay with institutions. However, to validate this claim empirically, it was necessary to demonstrate that the political justice/market justice dichotomy accurately captures the different cultural values with regard to questions of income inequality and then shows how such ideational factors are translated into action or policy outcomes through the filtering mechanism of political institutions. Douglass North has argued that institutions "determine the opportunities in a society" (1990, 7), but the question I have posed was the following: do particular constellations of institutions determine such opportunities in a systematically different manner if those institutions operate in different types of cultural value systems? In other words, the underlying values and norms of a given society may, in fact, be simultaneously shaped by the institutions within which they are formed as well as be independent and even determinative of the capacity of institutions to aggregate public preferences. Retooling Lijphart's institutional typology by bringing culture and values in systematically and empirically allowed for a test of this assertion and proved to substantiate the general thrust of my theory and provided us with a stronger more encompassing generalization capable of explaining cross-national patterns of income inequality.

As a scholar working in the tradition of historical institutionalism has stated, "neither institutions nor values nor economic interests for that matter by themselves provide adequate explanations for significant political outcomes over time; these variables interact with one another and, in so doing, change with time" (Steinmo 1993, 201). More significant than any of the specific findings, what my study clearly shows is the analytical power yielded by the interaction rather than the singular explanatory force of institutional and ideational variables. Too often political scientists engage in methodologically driven studies that pit the two critical explanatory variables against one another. Such sectarian and limited approaches do little to advance knowledge and even less to produce potential solutions to real-world problems such as growing poverty and income inequality. In this sense, my argument should advance the theoretical and methodological debates laid out in the important Lichbach and Zuckerman (1997) volume, *Comparative Politics: Rationality, Culture and Structure*, especially the clarion call for greater cross-fertilization among institutionalists and culturalists. A more careful analysis of how the implications of my critical reassessment and application of Lijphart's typology relates to these broader intellectual discussions as well as to significant policy debates about constitutional and institutional reform may be a worthy diversion before drawing the final conclusions of this book.

In his acceptance speech for the Johan Skytte Prize in Political Science, Arend Lijphart may be seen as taking a turn toward culture as the cultural explanations (or "political science stories") of consensus democracy predominate, despite his intention to show the legitimacy of various competing approaches.[1] Furthermore, both in the speech and in his revised book, the author is very much concerned with demonstrating "the kinder, gentler" qualities of consensus democracy which one would surely associate with the cultural face of this form of governance. Lijphart notes: "Consensus democracy itself and what I have just called its 'consequences' may both be argued to spring from a general cultural inclination toward a strong community orientation and social consciousness" (1999, 105). This is almost identical to what Robert Lane refers to as the "community point of view" or a society in which political justice is not subordinate to or overshadowed by market justice. Influenced by both of these scholars and intrigued by the affinity of their insights, yet perplexed by the undertheorization of this element in the consensus-majoritarian framework, my study has tried to draw the linkage between values and institutions in a more systematic fashion at both the conceptual and empirical levels to shed light on the broad forces that help us to understand varying patterns of income disparity in contemporary capitalist democracies.

Lijphart concluded his classic work *Democracies* (1984) by arguing that his typologies of consensus and majoritarian democracy were "rational, prescriptive, and empirical" models. Well over two decades have passed since that publication, and scholars continue to employ Lijphart's framework not only as a descriptive classification of two distinct patterns of collective decision making but also as an independent variable employed to explain a host of political phenomena. Toward the end of *Patterns of Democracy,* the 1999 revised and extended version of his 1984 book, Lijphart reflects:

> Consensus democracy and majoritarian democracy are alternative sets of political institutions, but more than that: they also represent what John D. Huber and G. Bingham Powell (1994) call the "two visions" of democracy. . . . My final example concerns the connection found in Chapter 16 between consensus democracy and several kinder and gentler public policies. It appears more plausible to

---

1. The speech was delivered in Uppsala on 4 October 1997, and published in 1998 as "Consensus and Consensus Democracy: Cultural, Structural, Functional and Rational-Choice Explanations" in *Scandinavian Political Studies* 21:99–108.

assume that both c onsensus democracy and these kinder, gentler policies stem from an u nderlying consensual and communitarian culture than that th ese policies are the direct result of c onsensus institutions. (1999, 306–7)

My study has supplied evidence that Lijphart's intuitions here are basically correct. Does this mean that a cultural e xplanation trumped an institutional one and therefore weakened Lijphart's original framework? Based on my own investigations of the distinctive and powerful role of consensual political in-stitutions, I would suggest that Lijphart's framework is actually strengthened in the long run by coupling it with an expl icit political cultural typology as I have done in this study. In a recent and quite trenchant critique of Lijphart's research program, Ian Lustick cites ear lier criticism by Barry and others who accused Lijphart of "packing too much unacknowledged theory into his typology" (1997, 104). My criticism of Lijphart is precisely the contrary: there has not been enough theory, especially with regard to the more recent asser-tions Lijphart makes about the "kinder and gentler" policy outcomes associ-ated with consensus democracy. What my empirical analysis has demonstrated is that although such an assertion is borne out as a generalization, the excep-tions also compellingly illustrate the "culture matters" thesis with r egard to the underlying logic of institutional capacity and our arguments about social and economic change.

Lijphart has been reticent on the normative front, yet he has proceeded to discuss matters that are directly relevant to the central questions posed by democratic theory. Furthermore, he has made sweeping claims abo ut the superior "quality of democracy" associated with consensual systems without ever specifying the underlying principles of democracy upon which he might make such a judgment. The consequence of this particular lacuna is increas-ingly transcending the narrow confines of a cademic debate as Lijphart has become a frequent advisor to countries such as South Africa and others who are adopting new constitutions and redesigning entire political systems. Thus, in the very precarious business of making such critical suggestions about the nature of certain institutional arrangements and their likely benefits in a given society, it seems that th e relation between those institutions and prevalent political cultural values should be a salient part of the equation. In this sense, Lijphart's work is indeed "applied democratic theory," and as such, the contri-bution of the present study has been to underscore the importance of making the dialogue between political economy, cultural values, and democratic theory central to our theoretical explorations and causal explanations of institutions and institutional effects on outcomes.

In Ian Shapiro's work *Democracy's Place* there is an extensive review of Lijphart's recommendation that South Africa adopt a consociational form of government and more significantly a critique of this decision, siding with a chief critique of Lijphart and consociationalism, Donald Horowitz (Shapiro, 1996; see especially chap. 4, pp. 79–108). The particulars of this debate are not directly relevant to this study, but it does signify a narrowing—and rightly so, in my estimation—of the chasm between normative and empirical democratic theory. The preceding discussion brings to mind the relevance of Karl Popper's essay "Piecemeal Social Engineering" (1945) and its similarity to the kinds of criticism of Lijphart's theory of consensus democracy or consociationalism raised by scholars such as Shapiro and Lustick and others who make the "institutional engineering" charge. The intent of my study has been to avoid both institutional and cultural determinism by grounding my investigation in both empirical analysis and democratic theory. A brief review of Popper's argument helps put into perspective the important stakes in these debates and crystallizes the need for a more sophisticated and explicit theorization of consensus democracy and its use as both a normative and an empirical model of governance—an objective that I hope to have successfully initiated through this study.

It is quite telling that Popper opens his famous essay by attacking historicism as an approach or a method of understanding the world. Popper associates holism, central planning, and even totalitarianism with the historicist doctrine. It is against the idea that society can be drastically overhauled that Popper proposes instead a practical technological approach of "piecemeal social engineering" and advocates the scientific method of deduction for the social sciences. A piecemeal engineer is described as one who attempts to achieve certain goals in small adjustments and readjustments and who resists redesigning the system as a whole; "he will avoid undertaking reforms of a complexity and scope which make it impossible for him to disentangle causes and effects, and to know what he is really doing" (309). Popper proceeds to contrast his preferred piecemeal approach with that of holistic or Utopian social engineering, which he deems to be antiscientific and incapable of making reforms primarily because of the lack of experimental knowledge needed for their undertaking. Ultimately, Popper seems to be arguing that the holistic approach to problems of politics and society will fail because we can't possibly have the perfect blueprint for planning or reforming society, and furthermore, we could not accurately assess the changes and attribute the results to the any particular measures but rather we could only attribute the whole result to it. It is str ikingly convenient that Popper's starting point was one of dismissing the historicist method as a legitimate tool of inquiry and explanation. If we cannot rely on historical interpretation and experience then we are left with no alter native to th e instrumentalist, scientific method. This logic is not only somewhat tautological but it is al so premised upon a very narrow conception of the value of history for informing social science and an even narrower view of freedom, which consequently has a restrictive or chilling effect on innovative political expression and organization.

In terms of Isaiah Berlin's famous distinction between positive and negative freedom, Popper (1945) is much more committed to securing negative freedom—"freedom from." This position is d eveloped in h is essay "The Paradoxes of Sovereignty" where he suggests that the proper question to the problem of politics is not the traditional one of "who should rule?" but rather how to organize political institutions to prevent bad rulers from doing too much damage. In other words, for Popper the sum of politics is the prevention of tyranny. In his pessimistic view, we do not have the capacity to learn from "really big mistakes." Therefore, there can be little innovation or progressive evolution in the form of our politics; instead, what we see are repeated and limited attempts to check political power. It is not surprising that Popper explicitly states support for majoritarian decision making as the best form of democratic control. This is precisely where his vision of science and politics pose a challenge to the work of Lijphart and other proponents of consociationalism or consensus democracy because it comes closest to the more recent critiques. The most effective way of considering the implications of Popper's work for the concept of consociational democracy might be to ask whether Lijphart's support for consensual decision making is a form of social engineering or mere piecemeal tinkering. A glance at the range of perspectives critical of the consociational model—from the Marxist criticism that it glo sses over class conflict (Kieve 1981), to the traditional view that it is ant idemocratic and elitist and tends to in flate minority interests (Barry 1975)—lends support to the idea that there is more at stake in this debate—and indeed with the adoption of the consociational model—than "slight tinkering." Lijphart himself, perhaps unwittingly, divulges the normative elements of his theory

and the optimistic belief that consensus-based decisions can in his view produce more democratic outcomes.

I would argue that consociationalism entails more than minor adjustments
but something less than what Popper refers to as Utopian engineering. For
instance, in its original form, consociationalism was employed as a descriptive
category for explaining the actual governmental arrangements in some of the
smaller European countries that did not fit Almond's typological breakdown.
This use of the model as an empirical and analytical device in the comparative method can hardly be associated with any form of utopian planning or
redesigning of society. Conversely, its promotion as an effective new constitutional form of decision making in South Africa has significant ramifications
for all aspects of this society in transition, which ultimately means it faces
the risk of blame if stability and peaceful coexistence between segments are
not maintained. Such is the burden of applied political science. And so does
it reveal the irony of the Popperian tradition, which distrusts historical interpretation and discounts the value of inductive methods. The irony is this:
in its vigorous attempt to resist tyranny, it reduces both politics as praxis and
our scientific methods of understanding and explaining political phenomena
to an excessively narrow view and use of science—deductive logic. In essence,
this method is in conflict with the very idea that democracy is a progression,
an idea that can only be expanded through our political imagination and ex-
perimentation. In my view, the imposition of this method has more tyrannical
tendencies than that which it fears.

It is precisely the fact that the model has been attacked from such divergent
schools of thought that its credibility and validity may actually be enhanced—
being attacked from both sides is an indication that the model itself—both
theoretically and practically—has surpassed the ideological strictures of its
opponents. This certainly does not mean that there is no room for refinement
or new criticisms of consociational theory and consensus democracy. On the
contrary, the model, like politics itself, will be ineffective if it remains static
and unresponsive to new constraints and opportunities. As responsible political scientists, it seems that our loyalties should lie not with science as an end
in itself but rather with science as a broad enterprise that helps us to realize
better government and more meaningful democracy.

As with any scientific discipline, political analysis advances by discovering
limitations of earlier theories. Rather than abandoning Lijphart's approach to
institutions and democratic governance, my study reveals that further research

on consensus democracy must avoid the problem of "institutional determin-ism." One way of doing so is to bring culture into our understanding of in-stitutions and their impact on political outcomes. Unlike Lijphart's presump-tive statement about certain policies being more attributable to underlying consensual cultures, I have shown that it is both possible and necessary to empirically examine the impact of values and that this can be done without necessarily jeopardizing methodological rigor.

The obvious weaknesses of the statistical analysis, such as the relatively small number of cases and a high degree of aggregation, did not preclude overall corroboration of the fundamental thesis that culture and institutions work interactively to shape the degree of income inequality among this set of capitalist democracies. Furthermore, the qualitative evidence presented has served to strengthen the overall argument and added depth and nuance to the statistical analysis. The cases of Swiss and British exceptionalisms and the underlying forces that produce income inequality in these societies demon-strates that "culture matters" not to the exclusion of institutions but rather through those institutions. If we accept that consensual institutions provide a more accurate and responsible aggregation of mass preferences (Huber and Powell 1994), then Lijphart's framework can indeed be interpreted as sur-viving the initial challenge that the case of Swiss exceptionalism imposed. The cultural dimension of institutions—or, what I argued at the outset of this study, the theoretical congruence between consensus democracy and political justice— simply does not apply in the case of Lijphart's prototypical consen-sus democracy. However, if we take preferences of citizens seriously and if, as others claim, consensual institutions are more faithful translators of these preferences into outcomes than their majoritarian counterparts, then Swiss political institutions are still a driving force. What I have largely done is to qualify the role of institutions by demonstrating that the types of outcomes they produce are contingent upon underlying cultural values and policy pref-erences of their citizens. Rather than revealing any insurmountable flaw in Lijphart's framework, to the contrary, this study has begun to strengthen his typology by fleshing out this important relationship between institutions and political culture and its consequences for political economic outcomes. In other words, this reformulated consensus-majoritarian typology can actually gain explanatory leverage by taking the cultural embeddedness of institu-tions seriously. Models of political economy and particularly the burgeoning Varieties of Capitalism school stand to benefit from this insight as well, as I believe the attention that scholars such as Iversen (2005), Kenworthy (2004), and Kenworthy and McCall (2008) are now paying to attitudes and preferences clearly indicates.

I raised a concern in Chapter 3 that the excitement over the theoretical power of the Varieties of Capitalism research program and its growing dominance in the field may have an unintended consequence of dislodging the imperative of keeping democratic theoretical problems at the center of comparative political economic analysis. One significant contribution I hope to have made here is to elucidate how unfortunate that would be because, after all, political economy should be seen as applied democratic theory in the first place. Lane Kenworthy's (2004) articulation of an "egalitarian capitalism" reminds us that a vision of a dynamic, productive, and not-too-unequal form of capitalism is realizable. More importantly, what we both have emphasized is that most people throughout the capitalist democratic world prefer to live in this kind of world. Values matter and different types of institutional mechanisms vary in the degree to which they work to incorporate and reflect those values or negate them by producing winner-take-all solutions to complex policy dilemmas. Capitalism and democracy exist in a symbiotic and dialectical relationship, and it is intellectually insufficient to place blame one or the other systems for the numerous social and political ills that face contemporary societies. Libertarians may resent "too much democracy," and socialists may attribute all evils in the world to capitalism, but such thinking does little more than sustain ideologies and often derail pragmatic compromises. Instead, what I proposed in Chapter 1 as the theoretical bedrock and starting premise of my study is that a more fruitful way to conceive of this important relationship is to think of each organizing system as mitigating the excesses of the other.

Ultimately, I believe that the history of democracy and political struggle have more lessons to offer than do the history of market economy and capitalism, broadly speaking, because all too often the latter forces tend to privilege the already strong. The democratic polity has its own device for correcting the excesses of democracy, one example of which is the protection of minority rights, but there are also constitutional mechanisms such as checks and balances and, of ultimate significance, frequent elections. What about the excesses of capitalism? As Polanyi reminded us, there is no self-regulating mechanism. Is it not the polity that must intervene if society deems the capitalist market system to violate certain norms of fairness? The point is that democracy and political action are required, and this is p recisely why a p redominance of market justice values could be threatening to the idea of popular sovereignty and, indeed, the social fabric of democracy. Thus, the normative conclusion to be drawn from this study is that p olitical justice, as a value preference, coupled with inclusive institutional environments offers the best guarantee or line of defense against the growing gap between the rich and the poor.

The impact of the cultural factor that I elu cidated through Lane's conceptualization provides a fresh perspective on the classic comparative debates centered on the vices and virtues of par liamentarism versus presidentialism that also forms the core of Lijphart's typology. In staking his claims for "the centrality of cultur e," Seymour Martin Lipset argues the following: "Cultural factors deriving from varying histories are extraordinarily difficult to manipulate. Political institutions—including electoral systems and constitutional arrangements—are more easily changed. Hence, those concerned with enhancing the possibilities for stable democratic government focus on them" (1990, 79).

Paradoxically, in this age of globalization, it may actually be cultural values or ideology that are more malleable and subject to change than institutions. As many American economists and social critics are documenting (e.g., Frank and Cook's *The Winner-Take-All Society*, 1995; Paul Krugman's "The Spiral of Inequality," 1996; Frank Levy's *The New Dollars and Dreams*, 1998; and Mickey Kaus's *The End of Equality*, 1992), it is p recisely this fundamental shift in values that is permitting the widening of income differentials in the United States. In fact, in a r ecent treatment of r ising economic insecurity in the United States, Jacob Hacker (2006) has powerfully demonstrated how what he labels "The Great Risk Shift" represents as much an ideological change as an economic change because the "personal responsibility crusade" was a deliberate political drive put in motion by the radical right to shift economic risk from the government and the corporate sector to ordinary Americans, all in the name of enhancing individual choice and opportunity. Such views, supported here as public opinion surveys in the United States, indicated the extreme preference for market justice over political justice. I have demonstrated that there is, in fact, a significant relationship between Lijphart's two types of democracies and corresponding political cultural or ideational typology, specified here as justice values, and their impact on large macrosocial outcomes such as income distributions. Like Rothstein, I believe institutional conditions play a strong role in determining whether economic rationality (market justice) or a m ore collectivist logic (political justice) prevails in a given society. To Rothstein's observation I would add that social nor ms and values may in f act represent the overarching feature of a soci ety's general political culture; thus, in the American case, a strict economic rationality may be seen as a manifestation of political institutions that encourage zero-sum or winner-take-all approaches to sociopolitical problems and policymaking. The powerful interaction of cultural forces and institutional mechanisms yields far greater understanding and explanatory leverage than does the traditional view that one factor is more determinative than the other. No longer is it s atis-factory to point out that "institutions matter." Instead, current research must avoid the pitfalls of institutional determinism by properly specifying micro-macro linkages (Allen 1990). In this regard, the "agency versus structure" prob-lem that pervades almost all modes of analysis in pol itical science has been mitigated in this study by taking expressed preferences seriously and figuring such forces into the empirical analysis through an integration of both aggre-gate institutional data and individual level variables. Institutions may serve to constrain human behavior, but they may also represent "social forces in their own right" (Grafstein 1992, 1). If we are to avoid institutional determinism, we must make agency as expressed here—albeit imperfectly, through societal values—endogenous to our analytic and explanatory strategies. I have shown that political institutions may mediate the dictates of structure—the capital-ist market economy and the superstructural realm of culture—the aggrega-tion of individuals' ideas, values, and preferences that sum up to what we refer to broadly as political culture.

The cultural explanation of the origins and nature of Swiss political in-stitutions tells us more than the previous strictly institutional analysis could with regard to explaining how and why consensual institutions produce cer-tain outcomes. The case of Swiss exceptionalism as it relates to the underly-ing forces behind income inequality demonstrates that "culture matters" not to the exclusion of institutions but rather through those institutions. In con-trast, the strength of p olitical justice values in the United Kingdom c ould not completely prevail against the institutional force of majoritarianism and winner-take-all approaches to p olitics, thus allowing policies to cut ag ainst the will of a p reference for greater egalitarianism. If we accept that consen-sual institutions provide a more accurate and responsible aggregation of mass preferences (Huber and Powell 1996), then Lijphart's framework can with-stand the initial challenge that the case of Swiss exceptionalism imposed. The cultural dimension of institutions—or, what I argued at the outset of this study, the theoretical congruence between consensus democracy and political justice—simply does not maintain in the case of Lijphart's prototypical consensus democracy. However, if we take preferences of citizens seriously and if, as others claim, consensual institutions are more faithful translators of these preferences into outcomes than their majoritarian counterparts, then Swiss political institutions are still a driving force. What my qualitative analysis achieved was to qualify the role of institutions by demonstrating that the types of outcomes they produce are contingent upon underlying cultural values and policy preferences of their citizens. Rather than revealing any weakness in Lijphart's framework, to the contrary, this study has begun to strengthen his typology on theoretical grounds by fleshing out this important relationship between institutions and political culture. Ultimately, by deploying multiple methodological approaches in this study of income inequality and seeking to substantiate a larger normative claim about the power of values, I hope to have elevated the status of ideational factors as causal variables.

It is important to recall that Lijphart concluded *Democracies* (1984) by arguing that his models were "rational, prescriptive, and empirical," and, indeed, ensuing scholarship has helped to validate this claim. The implications of this study of cross-national income inequality suggest that there is also an important dimension of political culture that gives Lijphart's framework even greater explanatory power. In this vein it aspires to contribute to a more holistic form of institutional analysis by connecting individuals' underlying attitudes and preferences to the actual political-institutional environments they inhabit thereby enhancing our understanding of the institutional effects on economic outcomes. Within this analytical framework culture can be seen to enter the picture by conceptualizing political economy as applied democratic theory, thus showing that values should and do, in fact, matter. Furthermore, these findings contribute to discussions within the subfield of comparative political economy and specifically to what Pontusson (1995) calls the "comparative study of advanced capitalism" by showing that structural or institutional variables in isolation from underlying ideational forces cannot adequately explain the systemic power of capitalism and market dynamics or one manifestation of how that power varies in different societies—income inequality. If citizens and policymakers in consensual systems continue to eschew the winner-take-all approach to politics, it is very likely that these societies will remain strongly egalitarian because both the weight of cultural power and institutional capacity within these countries individually (and increase collectively) will enable and assure this resistance to the forces of globalization and winner-take-all economics. With regard to the element of change over time, it is important to note that most prior research has assumed that people's views about how much inequality in society is too much remain roughly constant over time (Kenworthy and McCall 2008). This element is nonetheless one that researchers should be more concerned with as new and more sophisticated attitudinal data are generated. Sweden will be a very interesting case to watch over time because their values orientation has been in flux in the past, and, given the partisan coloration of the most recent election, there could be even deeper shifts on the horizon. We know with certainty as a result of this present study that values will matter more in this consensus democracy than they would if those shifts were occurring in a majoritarian context.

From this point of view, then, I hope to have contributed both to the scholarly literature as well as to a larger project articulated by Dryzek, who wrote:

> Karl Marx (1963, 15) noted long ago that "Men make their own history, but they do not make it just as they please; they do not make it under circumstances chosen by themselves, but under circumstances directly encountered, given and transmitted from the past." Both empirical social science and normative political theory are required to locate and give significance to these circumstances, in which political innovators might find and create the means to make their own history. (1992, 538)

Although labor market institutions, centralized wage bargaining, and the welfare state may explain a great deal about the degree of economic egalitarianism in society, my study pursued a broader level of analysis that sought to identify the deeper structures of power—both ideational and institutional—within which such redistributive mechanisms operate. In so doing, I hope to have produced a more meaningful portrait of the determinants of socioeconomic change in democratic capitalist societies. Social science does not have an impressive record when it comes to understanding or predicting change, yet globalization, which may represent an emerging conceptual paradigm, is in fact predicated on the very notion of change. Cross-national patterns of income inequality as analyzed and explained here suggest that in our

theorizations of change we should not leave public values out of the equation even though they are less tractable than other institutional and material
indicators. As recent strikes and massive mobilizations in France and Germany along with the rise of extraparliamentary social movements throughout Europe serve to illustrate, "market justice" is fiercely resisted by citizens
on the continent, and although many fear the neoliberal direction of current
leadership and initiatives of the European Union, the defense of the European
"social model" is alive and well. Lest we content ourselves with the notion
that values alone can produce change, it is significant to recall the critical role
that institutional design plays in shaping how ideas and values are filtered
through various types of political institutions. The more inclusive and proportionate that European polities remain at the national as well as the supra-
national levels, the stronger the influence of values will be. While alarmists and
extremists on both sides of the ideological spectrum oversimplify the external threats from globalization, the most serious threats may actually be internal
in the form of increasing market justice orientations as well as institutional
reforms away from proportional systems toward greater majoritarianism.

Over the course of time, many advanced democracies contemplate piecemeal constitutional change or some type of electoral reform, and many countries recovering from conflicts or emerging from totalitarian political systems
and command economies must choose wholesale such institutions and governing structures as they rebuild and reshape their societies. The innovation
of the institutional analysis carried out here is that values were brought in as
an integral part of the investigation showing that once we take culture and
ideas seriously, the relevance and power of institutional design is even greater.
Political institutions are fairly stable forces in society that establish the rules
of the game and the nature of the political process. My study provides additional support for previous scholarship that has demonstrated that consensual and more proportionate and inclusive political institutions tend to better
transmit values and preferences and shape them into actual policy outcomes.
As such, my study lends support and adds a more qualified and contingent
perspective on the capacity of the consensus-majoritarian typology to explain
cross-national variations in macroeconomic outcomes. Values may be at once
quite enduring in terms of deep-seated political cultural proclivities but also
polyvalent with respect to ideological contestation and debate, and malleable
and volatile in terms of attitudinal shifts revolving around questions of policy
and government responsibility. Consequently, whether seeking to influence

policy direction, implement new electoral rules, or change the system alto-gether—and even if we merely wish to study how the mix of these factors shape the kind of society we live in—the most fundamental conclusion flowing from this cross-national analysis of income inequality is that both institu-tions and values matter. More importantly, they matter in reciprocal, dynamic, and systematic fashion. From this perspective, I hope that my study will open up new avenues for research in which the holistic ideational-institutional framework I have constructed can be applied to other policy areas that increas-ingly lie at the intersection of comparative and global political economy.

# BIBLIOGRAPHY

Albert, Michel. 1993. *Capitalism vs. Capitalism*. New York: Four Walls Eight Windows.

Allen, Christopher S. 1990. "Trade Unions, Worker Participation, and Flexibility: Linking the Micro to the Macro." *Comparative Politics* 22 (3): 253–72.

Almond, Gabriel. 1990. "The International-National Connection." In *A Discipline Divided: Schools and Sects in Political Science,* 263–89. Newbury Park, Calif.: Sage Publications.

Almond, Gabriel, and G. Bingham Powell. 1996. *Comparative Politics: A Theoretical Approach.* New York: HarperCollins.

Almond, Gabriel, and Sidney Verba. 1963. *The Civic Culture: Political Attitudes and Democracy in Five Nations.* Princeton: Princeton University Press.

Althusser, Louis. 1971. *Lenin and Philosophy and Other Essays.* Translated by Ben Brewster. New York: Monthly Review Press.

Amoore, Louise, Richard Dodgson, Barry K. Gills, Paul Langley, Don Marshall, and Iain Watson. 1997. "Overturning 'Globalisation': Resisting the Teleological, Reclaiming the 'Political.'" *New Political Economy* 2 (1): 179–95.

Anderson, Benedict. 1991. *Imagined Communities: Reflections on the Origins and Spread of Nationalism.* Rev. ed. London: Verso.

Anderson, Christopher J., and Christine A. Guillory. 1997. "Political Institutions and Satisfaction with Democracy: A Cross-National Analysis of Consensus and Majoritarian Democracy." *American Political Science Review* 91:66–81.

Anderson, Liam. 2001. "The Implications of Institutional Design for Macroeconomic Performance: Reassessing the Claims of Consensus Democracy." *Comparative Political Studies* 34 (4): 429–52.

Anderson, Perry. 1974. *Lineages of the Absolutist State.* London: New Left Books.

———. 1977. "The Antinomies of Antonio Gramsci." *New Left Review* 100 (1): 5–81.

Arrow, Kenneth J. 1951. *Social Choice and Individual Values.* New Haven: Yale University Press.

Atkinson, A. B., L. Rainwater, and T. M. Smeeding. 1995. *Income Distribution in OECD Countries: Evidence from the Luxembourg Income Study.* Paris: OECD.

Atkinson, Robert D. 2005. "Inequality in the New Knowledge Economy." In *The New Egalitarianism,* ed. Anthony Giddens and Patrick Diamond, 52–68. Cambridge: Polity Press.

Augelli, Enrico, and Craig Murphy. 1988. *America's Quest for Supremacy and the Third World.* London: Pinter Publishers.

Austen-Smith, David. 2000. "Redistributing Income Under Proportional Representation." *The Journal of Political Economy* 108 (6): 1235–69.

Axelrod, R. 1984. *The Evolution of Cooperation*. New York: Basic Books.

Barro, Robert. 2000. "Inequality and Growth in a Panel of Countries." *Journal of Economic Growth* 5 (1): 5–32.

Barry, Brian. 1975. "Review Article: Political Accommodation and Consociational Democracy." *British Journal of Political Science* 5 (4): 477–505.

Baylis, Thomas. 1989. *Governing by Committee: Collegial Leadership in Advanced Studies*. Albany: State University of New York Press.

Berger, Suzanne, and Ronald Dore, eds. 1996. *National Diversity and Global Capitalism*. Ithaca: Cornell University Press.

Berry, William D., and Stanley Feldman. 1985. *Multiple Regression in Practice*. Thousand Oaks, Calif.: Sage Publications.

Birchfield, Vicki. 1996. "The Impact of Political Institutions on Income Inequality: An Analysis of Eighteen Industrialized Democracies, 1970–1990." Paper presented at the Annual Meeting of the Southern Political Science Association, Atlanta, Georgia, November.

Birchfield, Vicki, and Markus M. L. Crepaz. 1998. "The Impact of Constitutional Structures and Collective and Competitive Veto Points on Income Inequality in Industrialized Democracies." *European Journal of Political Research* 34 (October): 175–200.

Blackburn, McKinley L., and David E. Bloom. 1987. "Earnings and Income Inequality in the United States." *Population and Development Review* 13 (4): 575–609.

Blair, Tony. 2007. "What I've Learned." *The Economist*, 2 June, 28.

Block, Fred. 1977. "The Ruling Class Does Not Rule." *Socialist Revolution* 33 (1):6–28.

———. 1990. *Postindustrial Possibilities: A Critique of Economic Discourse*. Los Angeles and Berkeley: University of California Press.

Boix, Carles. 1998. *Political Parties Growth and Equality*. New York: Cambridge University Press.

Bollen, Kenneth A., and Burke D. Grandjean. 1981. "The Dimensions(s) of Democracy: Further Issues in the Measurements and Effects of Political Democracy." *American Sociological Review* 46 (5): 651–59.

Booth, William James. 1994. "On the Idea of the Moral Economy." *American Political Science Review* 88 (3): 653–67.

Borg, S., and F. G. Castles. 1982. "The Influence of the Political Right on Public Income Maintenance Expenditure and Equality." *Political Studies* 24:604–21.

Bowles, Samuel, and Herbert Gintis. 1986. *Democracy and Capitalism: Property, Community, and the Contradictions of Modern Social Thought*. New York: Basic Books.

Boyer, Robert. 1990. *The Search for Labor Market Flexibility: The European Economies in Transition*. Oxford: Oxford University Press.

Boyer, Robert, and Daniel Drache, eds. 1996. *States Against Markets: The Limits of Globalization*. London: Routledge.

Boyer, Robert, and J. Rogers Hollingsworth. 1997. "The Variety of Institutional Arrangements and Their Complementarity in Modern Economics." In *Contemporary Capitalism: The Embeddedness of Institutions,* ed. Robert Boyer and J. Rogers Hollingsworth, 49–54. Cambridge: Cambridge University Press.

Bradley, David, Evelyne Huber, Stephanie Moller, François Nielsen, and John D. Stephens. 2003. "Distribution and Redistribution in Postindustrial Democracies." *World Politics* 55:193–228.

Brady, Henry E., and David Collier. 2004. *Rethinking Social Inquiry: Diverse Tools, Shared Standards*. Lanham, Md.: Rowman & Littlefield Publishers, Inc.

Brambor, Thomas, William Roberts Clark, and Matt Golder. 2006. *Political Analysis* 14 (1): 63–82.

Brandolini, Andrea, and Nicola Rossi. 1998. "Income Distribution and Growth in Industrial Countries." In *Income Distribution and High-Quality Growth*, ed. Vito Tanzi and Ke-young Chu, 69–106. Cambridge, Mass.: MIT Press.

Braumoeller, Bear F. 2004. "Hypothesis Testing and Multiplicative Interaction Terms." *International Organization* 58:807–20.

Brenner, Robert, and M. Glick. 1991. "The Regulation Approach: Theory and History." *New Left Review* 188 (July–August): 45–120.

Brenner, Y. S. 1966. *Theories of Economic Development and Growth*. Westport, Conn.: Praeger.

Brenner, Y. S., Hartmut Kaelble, and Mark Thomas. 1991. *Income Distribution in Historical Perspective*. New York: Cambridge University Press.

Cable, Vincent. 1995. "The Diminished Nation State: A Study in the Loss of Economic Power." *Daedalus* 124 (1): 23–54.

Cameron, David. 1978. "The Expansion of the Public Economy: A Comparative Analysis." *American Political Science Review* 72:1243–61.

———. 1988. "Politics, Public Policy, and Distributional Inequality: A Comparative Analysis." In *Power, Inequality, and Democratic Politics: Essays in Honor of Robert Dahl*, ed. Ian Shapiro and Grant Reeher, 219–62. Boulder, Colo.: Westview Press.

Caporaso, James, and David Levine. 1992. *Theories of Political Economy*. Cambridge: Cambridge University Press.

Castles, Francis G., and S. Dorwick. 1990. "The Impact of Government Spending Levels on Medium Term Economic Growth in the OECD, 1960–85." *Journal of Theoretical Politics* 2 (2): 173–204.

Chilcote, R. H. 1994. *Theories of Comparative Politics*. Boulder, Colo.: Westview.

Coates, D. 2000. *Models of Capitalism: Growth and Stagnation in the Modern Era*. New York: Polity Press.

Cohen, G. A. 1981. "Freedom, Justice, and Capitalism." *New Left Review* 126:3–16.

———. 2000. *Rescuing Justice from Constructivism*. Oxford: Oxford University Press.

Collini, Stafan, Ed. 1989. *J. S. Mill: On Liberty and Other Writings*. Cambridge: Cambridge University Press.

Cox, Robert. 1996. "A Perspective on Globalization." In *Globalization: Critical Reflections*, ed. J. H. Mittleman. Boulder, Colo.: Lynee Rienner.

Crepaz, Markus M. L. 1996a. "Consensus Versus Majoritarian Democracy: Political Institutions and Their Impact in Macroeconomic Performance and Industrial Dispute." *Comparative Political Studies* 29 (1): 4–26.

———. 1996b. "Constitutional Structures and Regime Performance in 18 Industrialized Countries—A Test of Olson's Hypothesis." *European Journal of Political Research* 29:87–104.

———. 1998. "Inclusion vs. Exclusion: Political Institutions and the Welfare State." *Comparative Politics* 31 (1): 61–80.

———. 2002. "Global, Constitutional, and Partisan Determinants of Redistribution in 15 OECD Countries." *Comparative Politics* 34 (2): 169–88.

Crepaz, Markus M. L., Thomas Koelbe, and David Wilsford. 2000. *Democracy and Institutions: The Lifework of Arend Lijphart*. Ann Arbor: University of Michigan Press.

Crepaz, Markus, M. L., and Arend Lijphart. 1991. "Corporatism and Consensus Democracy in Eighteen Countries: Conceptual and Empirical Linkages." *British Journal of Political Science* 21 (2): 235–46.

Crouch, Colin, and Wolfgang Streeck, eds. 1997. *Political Economy of Modern Capitalism*. London: Sage Publications.

Dahl, Robert, ed. 1966. *Political Oppositions in Western Democracies*. New Haven, Conn.: Yale University Press.

———. 1985. *A Preface to Economic Democracy*. Cambridge: Cambridge University Press.

Danziger, Sheldon H., and Robert H. Haveman, eds. 2001. *Understanding Poverty*. New York: Russell Sage Foundation.

Dryzek, John. 1992. "The Good Society Versus the State: Freedom and Necessity in Political Innovation." *The Journal of Politics* 54: 518–40.

———. 1996. "Political Inclusion and the Dynamics of Democratization." *The American Political Science Review* 90 (3): 475–88.

Dworkin, Ronald. 1981. "What is Equality? Part 2: Equality of Resources." *Philosophy and Public Affairs* 10 (4): 283–345.

Elster, Jon. 1989. *Nuts and Bolts for the Social Sciences: More Nuts and Bolts for the Social Sciences*. Cambridge: Cambridge University Press.

Esping-Andersen, Gosta. 1985. *Politics Against Markets*. Princeton: Princeton University Press.

———. 1990. *The Three Worlds of Welfare Capitalism*. London: Polity Press.

———. 2005. "Inequality of Incomes and Opportunities." In *The New Egalitarianism*, ed. Anthony Giddens and Patrick Diamond, 8–38. Cambridge: Polity Press.

Evans, P. B., D. Rueschmeyer, and T. Skocpol. 1985. *Bringing the State Back In*. Cambridge: Cambridge University Press.

Flora, Peter, and Arnold J. Heidenheimer, eds. 1981. *The Development of Welfare States in Europe and America*. New Brunswick, N.J.: Transaction Publishers.

Forbes, Kristin J. 2000. "A Reassessment of the Relationship Between Inequality and Growth." *American Economic Review* 90 (4): 869–87.

Frank, Robert H., and Philip J. Cook. 1995. *The Winner-Take-All Society*. New York: Penguin Books.

Fraser, Derek. 1973. *The Evolution of the British Welfare State: A History of Social Policy Since the Industrial Revolution*. London: Macmillan.

Freeman, Robert B. 1989. *Labor Markets in Action: Essays in Empirical Economics*. Cambridge, Mass.: Harvard University Press.

Friedland, Roger, and Jimy Sanders. 1985. "The Public Economy and Economic Growth in Western Market Economies." *American Sociological Review* 50 (4): 421–37.

Friedman, Milton. 1962. *Capitalism and Freedom*. Chicago: University of Chicago Press.

Friedman, Milton, and Rose Friedman. 1980. *Freedom to Choose*. New York: Harcourt Brace and Jovanovitch.

Friedrich, Robert J. 1982. "In Defense of Multiplicative Terms in Multiple Regression Equations." *American Journal of Political Science* 26:797–825.

Fukuyama, Francis. 1989. "The End of History?" *The National Interest* 16 (Summer): 3–18.

Gagnier, Regenia. 1997. "Neoliberalism and the Political Theory of the Market." *Political Theory* 25 (3): 434–54.

Garrett, Geoffrey. 1997. "The Nation-State in the Global Economy: Obstinate or Obsolete?" Paper presented at the APSA annual meeting, Washington, D.C., August. Subsequently published in the 50th anniversary volume of *International Organization*, 1997.

———. 1998. *Partisan Politics in the Global Economy.* New York: Cambridge University Press.

Garrett, Geoffrey, and Peter Lange. 1986. "Performance in a Hostile World." *World Politics* 38:517–45.

Geertz, Clifford. 1973. *The Interpretation of Cultures.* New York: Basic Books.

George, Vic, and Paul Wilding. 1999. *British Society and Social Welfare: Towards a Sustainable Society.* New York: Macmillan.

Giddens, Anthony. 1971. *Capitalism and Modern Social Theory.* Cambridge: Cambridge University Press.

———. 1990. *The Consequences of Modernity.* Cambridge: Polity Press.

Gill, Stephen. 1990. *American Hegemony and the Trilateral Commission.* Cambridge: Cambridge University Press.

———. 1995. "Globalisation, Market Civilisation, and Disciplinary Neoliberalism." *Millennium* 24 (3): 399–423.

Gill, Stephen, and James H. Mittelman, eds. 1997. *Innovation and Transformation in International Studies.* Cambridge: Cambridge University Press.

Glazer, Nathan. 2000. "Disaggregating Culture." In *Culture Matters: How Values Shape Human Progress,* ed. Lawrence E. Harrison and Samuel P. Huntington, 219–31. New York: Basic Books.

Goldstein, J., and R. O. Keohane. 1993. "Ideas and Foreign Policy: An Analytical Framework." In *Ideas and Foreign Policy: Beliefs, Institutions, and Political Change,* ed. J. Goldstein and R. O. Keohane, 3–31. Ithaca: Cornell University Press.

Goodin, Robert E. 2003. "Choose Your Capitalism?" *Comparative European Politics* 1 (2): 203–13.

Goodin, Robert E., Bruce Headey, Ruud Muffels, and Henk-Jan Dirven, eds. 1999. *The Real Worlds of Welfare Capitalism.* Cambridge: Cambridge University Press.

Gottschalk, P., and T. M. Smeeding. 1997. "Cross-National Comparisons of Earnings and Income Inequality." *Journal of Economic Literature* 35 (2): 633–87.

Gourevitch, Peter A. 1978. "The Second Image Reversed: The International Sources of Domestic Politics." *International Organization* 32:881–912.

Gourevitch, Peter A., and James Shin. 2005. *Political Power and Corporate Control: The New Global Politics of Corporate Governance.* Princeton: Princeton University Press.

Grafstein, Robert. 1988. "The Problem of Institutional Constraint." *Journal of Politics* 50:577–99.

———. 1992. *Institutional Realism: Social and Political Constraints on Rational Actors.* New Haven, Conn.: Yale University Press.

Gramsci, Antonio. 1971. *Selections from the Prison Notebooks.* Quintin Hoare and Geoffrey Nowell Smith, ed. New York: International Publishers.

Green, Daniel M., ed. 2002. *Constructivism and Comparative Politics.* Armonk, N.Y.: M. E. Sharpe.

Green, Donald P., and Ian Shapir o. 1994. *Pathologies of Rational Choice Theory*. New Haven, Conn.: Yale University Press.

Grofman, Bernard. 2000. "Arend Lijphart and the New Institutionalism." In *Democracy and Institutions: The Lifework of Arend Lijphart,* ed. Marcus Crepaz, Thomas Koelbe, and David Wilsford, 43–73. Ann Arbor: University of Michigan Press.

Habermas, Jürgen. 1973. *The Legitimation Crisis*. Boston: Beacon Press.

Hacker, Jacob S. 2006. *The Great Risk Shift*. Oxford University Press.

Hall, Peter A. 1986. *Governing the Economy: The Politics of State Intervention in Britain and France*. New York: Oxford University Press.

———, ed. 1989. *The Political Power of Economic Ideas: Keynesianism Across Nations*. Princeton: Princeton University Press.

———. 1997. "The Role of Interests, Institutions, and Ideas in the Comparative Political Economy of the Industrialized Nations." In *Comparative Politics,* ed. M. Lichbach and A. Zuckerman, 174–207. Cambridge: Cambridge University Press.

Hall, Peter A., and Daniel W. Gingerich. 2004. "Varieties of Capitalism and Institutional Complementarities in the Macroeconomy: An Empirical Analysis." *Max Planck Institute for the Study of Societies Discussion Paper*. Cologne, Germany.

Hall, Peter A., and David Soskice, eds. 2001. *Varieties of Capitalism: The Institutional Foundations of Comparative Advantage*. Oxford: Oxford University Press.

Hall, Peter A., and Rosemary C. R. Taylor. 1996. "Political Science and the Three New Institutionalisms." *Political Studies* 44:952–73.

Harrison, Lawrence E., and Samuel P. Huntington, eds. 2000. *Culture Matters: How Values Shape Human Progress*. New York: Basic Books.

Harvey, David. 1989. *The Condition of Postmodernity*. Oxford: Basil Blackwell.

Hasenfeld, Yeheskel, and Jane Rafferty. 1989. "The Determinants of Pub lic Attitudes Toward the Welfare States." *Social Forces* 67:1027–48.

Hattam, Victoria C. 1993. *Labor Visions and State Power: The Origins of Business Unionism in the United State*s. Princeton: Princeton University Press

Hayek, F. A. 1944. *The Road to Serfdom*. Chicago: University of Chicago Press.

———. 1960. *The Constitution of Liberty*. London: Routledge and Kegan Paul.

———. 1976. *The Mirage of Social Justice*. Chicago: University of Chicago Press.

Held, David. 1995a. *Cosmopolitan Democracy: An Agenda for a New World Order*. London: Polity Press.

———. 1995b. *Democracy and the Global Order*. Stanford: Stanford University Press.

Hicks, Alexander. 1988. "Social Democratic Corporatism and Economic Growth." *The Journal of Politics* 50 (3): 677–704.

———. 1999. *Social Democracy and Welfare Capitalism*. Ithaca: Cornell University Press.

Hicks, Alexander, and Lane Kenworthy. 1998. "Cooperation and Political Economic Performance in A ffluent Democratic Capitalism." *American Journal of Sociology* 103 (6): 1631–72.

Hicks, Alexander, Joya Misra, and Tang Nah Ng. 1995. "The Programmatic Emergence of the Social Security State." *American Sociological Review* 60 (4): 329–49.

Hicks, Alexander, and Duane Swank. 1984. "Governmental Redistribution in Rich Capitalist Democracies." *Policy Studies Journal* 13:265–86.

Hirst, Paul, and Grahame Thompson. 1996. *Globalization in Question: The International Economy and the Possibilities of Governance*. Cambridge: Polity Press.

Hochschild, Jennifer, L. 1981. *What's Fair? American Beliefs About Distributive Justice.* Cambridge: Harvard University Press.

Howell, Chris. 2003. "Varieties of Capitalism: And Then There Was One?" *Comparative Politics* 36 (1): 103–24.

Huber, Evelyne, and Michelle Dion. 2002. "Revolution or C ontribution? Rational Choice Approaches in the Study of Latin American Politics." *Latin American Politics and Society* 44 (3): 1–28.

Huber, Evelyne, Charles Ragin, John D. Stephens, David Brady, and Jason Beckfield. 2004. *Comparative Welfare States Data Set.* Northwestern University, University of North Carolina, Duke University, and Indian University.

Huber, Evelyne, and John D. Stephens. 2001. *Development and Crisis of the Welfare State: Parties and Policies in Global Markets.* Chicago: Chicago University Press.

Huber, John, and Bingham Powell. 1994. "Congruence Between Citizens and Policymakers in Two Visions of Liberal Democracy." *World Politics* 46:291–326.

Immergut, E. M. 1992. *Health Politics: Interests and Institutions in Western Europe.* New York: Cambridge University Press.

Inglehart, Ronald. 1977. *The Silent Revolution: Changing Values and Political Styles.* Princeton: Princeton University Press.

———. 1988. "The Renaissance of Political Culture." *American Political Science Review* 82 (4): 1203–30.

———. 1990. *Culture Shift in Advanced Industrial Society.* Princeton: Princeton University Press.

———. 1997. *Modernization and Postmodernization.* Princeton: Princeton University Press.

Iversen, Torben. 2005. *Capitalism, Democracy, and Welfare.* New York: Cambridge University Press.

Iversen, Torben, and David Soskice. 2006. "Electoral Institutions and the Politics of Coalitions: Why Some Democracies Redistribute More Than Others." *American Political Science Review* 100:165–81.

Jackman, Robert. 1975. "Socialist Parties and Income Inequality in Western Industrial Societies." *The Journal of Politics* 42:135–49.

Jessop, Bob. 1990. "Regulation Theories in Retrospect and Prospect." *Economy and Society.* 19 (2): 153–216.

Juhn, Chinhui, Kevin M. Murphy, and Brooks Pierce. 1993. "Wage Inequality and the Rise in Returns to Skill." *The Journal of Political Economy* 101 (3): 410–42.

Katz, C. J., V. Mahler, and M. G. Franz. 1983. "The Impact of Taxes on Growth and Distribution in Developed Capitalist Countries: A Cross-national Study." *American Political Science Review* 77:871–86.

Katz, Lawrence F., and Kevin M. Murphy. 1992. "Changes in Relative Wages, 1963–1987: Supply and Demand Factors." *The Quarterly Journal of Economics* 107 (1): 35–78.

Katzenstein, Peter. 1978. *Between Power and Plenty: Foreign Economic Policies of Advanced Industrial States.* Madison: University of Wisconsin Press.

———. 1985. *Small States in World Markets.* Ithaca: Cornell University Press.

———, ed. 1996. *The Culture of National Security: Norms and Identity in World Politics.* Cambridge: Cambridge University Press.

Kaus, Mickey. 1992. *The End of Equality.* New York: Basic Books.

Keesing, Robert. 1974. "Theories of Culture." *Annual Review of Anthropology* 3:73–97.

Kenworthy, Lane. 1995. "Equality and Efficiency: The Illusory Tradeoff." *European Journal of Political Research* 27:225–54.

———. 2004. *Egalitarian Capitalism: Jobs, Incomes, and Growth in Affluent Countries.* New York: Russell.

Kenworthy, Lane, and Leslie McCall. 2008. "Inequality, Public Opinion, and Redistribution." *Socio-Economic Review* 6:35–68.

Kenworthy, Lane, and Jonas Pontusson. 2005. "Rising Inequality and the Politics of Redistribution in Affluent Countries." *Perspectives on Politics: American Political Science Association* 3 (3): 449–72.

Keynes, John Maynard. 1936. *The General Theory of Employment, Interest, and Money.* London: Macmillan.

Kieve, Ronald A. 1981. "Pillars of Sand: A Marxist Critique of Consociational Democracy in the Netherlands" *Comparative Politics* 13 (3): 313–37.

King, Gary, Robert O. Keohane, and Sidney Verba. 1994. *Designing Social Inquiry.* Princeton: Princeton University Press.

Kitschelt, Herbert, Peter Lange, Gary Marks, and John D. Stephens. 1999. *Continuity and Change in Contemporary Capitalism.* New York: Cambridge University Press.

Knight, Jack. 1992. *Institutions and Social Conflict.* New York: Cambridge University Press.

Koelbe, Thomas A. 1995. "The New Institutionalism in Political Science and Sociology." *Comparative Politics* 27 (2): 231–43.

Korpi, Walter. 1983. *The Democratic Class Struggle.* London: Routledge and Kegan Paul.

———. 1985. "Economic Growth and the Welfare State: Leaky Bucket or Irrigation System." *European Sociological Review* 1 (2): 97–118.

———. 1989. "Power, Politics, and Sate Autonomy in the Development of Social Citizenship: Social Rights During Sickness in Eighteen OECD Countries Since 1930." *American Sociological Review* 54 (3): 309–28.

Korpi, Walter, and Joakim Palme. 1998. "The Paradox of Redistribution and Strategy of Equality: Welfare State Institutions, Inequality and Poverty in the Western Countries." *American Sociological Review* 3 (5): 661–87.

Kregel, J. A. 1979. *A Keynesian Approach to Inflation Theory and Policy.* Upper Saddle River, N.J.: Prentice Hall Publishers.

Krugman, Paul. 1995. *Peddling Prosperity: Economic Sense and Nonsense in the Age of Diminished Expectations.* New York: W. W. Norton.

———. 1996. "The Spiral of Inequality." *Mother Jones Magazine* 21 (6): 44–49.

Kuttner, Robert. 1984. *The Economic Illusion.* Boston: Houghton Mifflin.

Kuznets, Simon. 1955. "Economic Growth and Income Inequality." *American Economic Review* 45 (1):1–218.

Laitin, David D. 1986. *Hegemony and Culture.* Chicago: Chicago University Press.

———. 1995. "The Civic Culture at 30." *American Political Science Review* 89:168–73.

———. 2002. "Comparative Politics: The State of the Subdiscipline." In *Political Science: The State of the Discipline*, ed. Ira Katznelson and Helen V. Milner, 630–59. Cambridge: Harvard University Press.

Lane, Robert. 1986. "Market Justice, Political Justice." *American Political Science Review* 80:383–402.

Lasswell, Harold. 1936. *Politics: Who Gets What, When, How.* New York: Whittlesey House.

Lehmbruch, Gerhard. 1993. "Consociational Democracy and Corporatism in Switzerland." *Publius* 23:43–60.

Levi, Margaret, 1988. *Of Rule and Revenue*. Los Angeles and Berkeley: University of California Press.

———. 1996. "Social and Unsocial Capital: A Review Essay of Robert Putnam's *Making Democracy Work*." *Politics and Society* 24 (1): 45–56.

———. 1997. "A Model, a Method, and a Map: Rational Choice in Comparative and Historical Analysis." In *Comparative Politics: Rationality, Culture, and Structure*, ed. Mark Irving Lichbach and Alan S. Zuckerman, 19–41. Cambridge: Cambridge University Press.

Levy, Frank. 1998. *The New Dollar and Dreams: American Incomes and Economic Change*. New York: Russell Sage Foundation.

Levy, Frank, and R. Murnane. 1992. "U.S. Earnings Levels and Earnings Inequality: A Review of Recent Trends and Proposed Explanations." *Journal of Economic Literature* 30 (3): 1333–82.

Lichbach, Mark Irving, and Alan S. Zuckerman, eds. 1997. *Comparative Politics: Rationality, Culture, and Structure*. Cambridge: Cambridge University Press.

Lie, John. 1993. "Visualizing the Invisible Hand: The Social Origins of 'Market Society' in England, 1550–1750." *Politics and Society* 21: 275–305.

Lijphart, Arend. 1968. *The Politics of Accommodation: Pluralism and Democracy in the Netherlands*. Berkeley and Los Angeles: University of California Press.

———. 1971. "Comparative Politics and the Comparative Method." *The American Political Science Review* 65 (3): 682–93.

———. 1977. *Democracy in Plural Societies: A Comparative Exploration*. New Haven: Yale University Press.

———. 1984. *Democracies: Patterns of Majoritarian and Consensus Government in Twenty-One Countries*. New Haven: Yale University Press.

———. 1992. *Parliamentary Versus Presidential Government*. Oxford: Oxford University Press.

———. 1994. "Democracies: Forms, Performance, and Constitutional Engineering." *European Journal of Political Research* 25:1–17.

———. 1999. *Patterns of Democracy: Government Forms and Performance in Thirty-Six Countries*. New Haven: Yale University Press.

Lindblom, Charles, and Robert Dahl. 1977. *Politics and Markets*. New York: Basic Books.

Linder, Wolf. 1998. *Swiss Democracy*. New York: St. Martin's Press.

Linz, Juan. 1990. "The Perils of Presidentialism." *Journal of Democracy* 1 (1): 51.

———. 1993. "The Virtues of Parliamentarism." In *The Global Resurgence of Democracy*, ed. Larry Diamond and Marc Plattner, 133–37. Baltimore: Johns Hopkins University Press.

Lipset, Seymour M. 1960. *Political Man*. Garden City, N.Y.: Anchor.

———. 1990. *Continental Divide: The Values and Institutions of the United States and Canada*. New York: Routledge.

Lockhart, Charles. 1989. *Gaining Ground*. Los Angeles and Berkeley: University of California Press.

———. 2001. *Protecting the Elderly: How Culture Shapes Social Policy*. University Park: The Pennsylvania State University Press.

Lustick, Ian S. 1993. *Unsettled States, Disputed Lands: Britain and Ireland, France and Algeria, Israel and the West Bank.* Ithaca, N.Y.: Cornell University Press.

———. 1997. "Lijphart, Lakatos, and Consociationalism." *World Politics* 50:88–117.

Macpherson, C. B. 1973. *Democratic Theory: Essays in Retrieval.* Oxford: Clarendon Press.

Mahler, Vincent, A.1989. "Income Distribution Within Nations: Problems of Cross-National Comparison." *Comparative Political Studies* 22 (1): 3–32.

———. 2004. "Economic Globalization, Domestic Politics, and Income Distribution in the Developed Countries: A Cross-National Study." *Comparative Political Studies* 37 (9): 1025–53.

March, J. G., and J. P. Olsen. 1984. "The New Institutionalism: Organizational Factors in Political Life." *The American Political Science Review* 78 (3): 734.

Marshall, T. H. 1964. *Class, Citizenship, and Social Development.* New York: Doubleday.

Marx, Karl. 1968. *A Critique of the Gotha Programme.* In *Karl Marx and Frederick Engels: Selected Works.* New York: International Publishers.

———. 1973. *Grundrisse.* London: Penguin Books. Original ed. 1941.

McClosky, Herbert, and John Zaller. 1984. *The American Ethos: Public Attitudes Toward Capitalism and Democracy.* Cambridge, Mass.: Harvard University Press.

Melich. Anna. 1981. "A Rational Theory of the Size of Government." *Journal of Public Economics* 8:913–27.

———. 1991. *Les Valeurs des Suisses.* Berne, Switzerland: Peter Lang.

Mendell, Marguerite, and Daniel Salée, eds. 1991. *The Legacy of Karl Polanyi: Market, State, and Society at the End of the Twentieth Century.* New York: St. Martin's Press.

Midlarsky, Manus ed. 1997. *Inequality, Democracy, and Economic Development.* New York: Cambridge University Press.

Miliband, Ralph. 1969. *The State in Capitalist Society.* New York: Basic Books.

Mill, John Stuart. 1904. *Principles of Political Economy.* London: Longmans, Green, and Co. Original ed., 1848.

Miller, Gary J. 1997. "The Impact of Economics on Contemporary Political Science." *Journal of Economic Literature* 35 (3): 1173–1204.

Mishra, R. 1984. *The Welfare State in Crisis.* New York: St. Martin's Press.

Moene, Karl Ove, and Michael Wallerstein. 1989. "Distribution of Income in Advanced Capitalist States: Political Parties, Labor Unions, and the International Economy." *European Journal of Political Research* 17:367–400.

———. 2001. "Inequality, Social Insurance and Redistribution." *American Political Science Review* 95 (4): 859–74.

———. 2003. "Earnings Inequality and Welfare Spending: A Disaggregated Analysis." *World Politics* 55 (4): 485–516.

Noel, Alain. 1987. "Accumulation, Regulation, and Social Change: An Essay on French Political Economy." *International Organization* 41 (2): 303–33.

North, Douglass C. 1990. *Institutions, Institutional Change, and Economic Performance.* New York: Cambridge University Press.

Nozick, Robert. 1974. *Anarchy, State and Utopia.* Oxford: Basil Blackwell.

OECD. *Economic Outlook* (various editions from 1970 to 1996). Available at http://www.oecd.org/findDocument/0,3354,en_2649_201185_1_119660_1_1_1,00.html.

Offe, Claus. 1984. *Contradictions of the Welfare State.* London: Hutchinson.

Okun, Arthur. 1975. *Equality and Efficiency: The Big Tradeoff.* Washington, D.C.: Brookings Institute Press.

Ostrom, Elinor. 1990. *Governing the Commons: The Evolution of Institutions for Collective Action.* New York: Cambridge University Press.

———. 1995. "The Horizons in Institutional Analysis." *American Political Science Review* 89:174–78.

Patterson, Orlando. 2000. "Taking Culture Seriously: A Framework and an Afro-American Illustration." In *Culture Matters: How Values Shape Human Progress,* ed. Lawrence E. Harrison and Samuel P. Huntington, 202–18. New York: Basic Books.

Peters, B. Guy. 1998. "Political Institutions, Old and New." In *A New Handbook of Political Science,* ed. Robert E. Goodin and Hans-Dieter Klingemann, 205–21. Oxford: Oxford University Press.

———. 1999. *Institutional Theory in Political Science: The "New Institutionalism."* London: Continuum.

Pierson, Paul. 1996. "New Politics of the Welfare State." *World Politics* 48 (2): 143–79.

Pierson, Paul, and Theda Skocpol. 2002. "Historical Institutionalism in Contemporary Political Science." In *Political Science: The State of the Discipline,* ed. Ira Katzelson and Helen Milner, 693–721. New York: W. W. Norton.

Polanyi, Karl. 1944. *The Great Transformation: Political and Economic Origins of Our Time.* Boston: Beacon Press. Reprint 1957.

Pontusson, Jonas. 1995. "From Comparative Public Policy to Political Economy." *Comparative Political Studies* 28:117–47.

———. 2005. *Inequality and Prosperity: Social Europe vs. Liberal America.* Ithaca: Cornell University Press.

Pontusson, Jonas, David Rueda, and Christopher R. Way. 2002. "Comparative Political Economy of Wage Distribution: The Role of Partisanship and Labor Market." *British Journal of Political Science* 32:281–308.

Popper, Karl. 1945. *The Open Society and Its Enemies.* Vol. 2, *Hegel and Marx.* London: Routledge.

Poulantzas, N. 1969. "The Problem of the Capitalist State." *New Left Review* 58 (1): 67–78.

Powell, Bingham. 1982. *Contemporary Democracies: Participation, Stability, and Violence.* Cambridge, Mass.: Harvard University Press.

Prasad, Monica. 2006. *The Politics of Free Markets: The Rise of Neoliberal Economic Policies in Britain, France, Germany and the United States.* Chicago: University of Chicago Press.

Przeworski, Adam. 1991. *The State and the Economy Under Capitalism.* New York: Harwood Academic Publishers.

Przeworski, Adam, and Henry Teune. 1970. *The Logic of Comparative Social Inquiry.* Malabar, Fla.: Kreiger Publishing Company.

Putnam, Robert. 1993. *Making Democracy Work.* Princeton: Princeton University Press.

Rawls, John. 1971. *Theory of Justice.* Cambridge, Mass.: Harvard University Press.

Ricardo, David. 1903. *On the Principles of Political Economy and Taxation.* London: Georgia Bell and Sons. Original ed., 1817.

Riggs, F. W. 1988. "The Survival of Presidentialism in America: Para-Constitutional Practice." *International Political Science Review* 9 (4): 247–78.

Rodrik, Dani. 1997. *Has Globalization Gone Too Far?* Washington, D.C.: Institute for International Economics.

Roemer, John E. 1980. "A General Equilibrium Approach to M arxian Economics." *Econometrica* 48 (2): 505–31.

———. 1996. *Theories of Distributive Justice.* Cambridge, Mass.: Harvard University Press.

Rogowski, Ronald. 1987. "Trade and Variety of D emocratic Institutions." *International Organization* 41:203–23.

Rogowski, Ronald, and Mark Andreas Kayser. 2002. "Majoritarian Electoral Systems and Consumer Power: Price-Level Evidence from the OECD Countries." *American Journal of Political Science* 46 (3): 526–40.

Rokkan, Stein. 1970. *Citizens, Elections, Parties: Approaches to the Comparative Study of the Processes of Development.* Oslo: Universitetsforlaget.

Romer, Thomas. 1975. "Individual Welfare, Majority Voting, and the Properties of a Linear Income Tax." *Journal of Public Economics* 4:163–85.

Ross, Marc Howard. 1997. "The Relevance of C ulture for the Study of Political Psychology and Ethnic Conflict." *Political Psychology* 18 (2): 299.

Rothstein Bo. 1996. "Political Institutions: An Overview." In *A New Handbook of Political Science,* ed. R. E. Goodin, and H.-D. Klingemann, 133–66. Oxford: Oxford University Press.

———. 1998. *Just Institutions Matter.* Theories of Institutional Design series, ed. Robert E. Goodin. Cambridge: Cambridge University Press.

Rupert, Mark. 1995. *Producing Hegemony: The Politics of Mass Production and American Global Power.* Cambridge: Cambridge University Press.

Ryu, Hang K., and Daniel J. Slottje. 1994. *Measuring Trends in the U.S. Income Inequality: Theory and Applications.* New York: Springer Verlag Berlin Heidelberg.

Scharpf, Fritz W., and Vivien A. Schmidt. 2000. *Welfare and Work in the Open Economy.* Vol. 1, *From Vulnerability to Competitiveness.* Oxford: Oxford University Press.

Schattschneider, E. E. 1965. *The Semisovereign People: A Realist's View of Democracy in America.* New York: Holt, Reinhart, and Winston.

Schiller, Herbert. 1969. *Mass Communications and the American Empire.* New York: Augustus Kelly.

Schmidt, Vivien A. 1996. *From State to Market? The Transformation of French Business and Government.* Cambridge: Cambridge University Press.

———. 2000. "Values and Discourse in the Politics of Adjustment." In *Welfare and Work in the Open Economy.* Vol. 1, *From Vulnerability to Competitiveness,* ed. Fritz W. Scharpf and Vivien A. Schmidt, 229–309. Oxford: Oxford University Press.

———. 2002. *The Futures of European Capitalism.* Oxford: Oxford University Press.

Schmitter, Philippe C. 1974. "Still the Century of Corporatism?" *The Review of Politics* 36 (1): 85–131.

———. 1982. "Reflections on Where the Theory of Neo-Corporatism Has Gone and Where the Praxis of N eo-Corporatism May Be Going." In *Patterns of Corporatist Policy-Making,* ed. Gerhard Lehmbruch and Philippe C. Schmitter, 259–79. London: Sage Publications.

Schumpeter, Joseph A. 1942. *Capitalism, Socialism, and Democracy.* New York: Harper and Row Publishers, Inc.

Schwartz, Herman. 1994. "Small States in Big Trouble: State Reorganization in Australia, Denmark, New Zealand, and Sweden in the 1980s." *World Politics* 46 (4): 527–55.

Segalman, Ralph. 1986. *The Swiss Way of Welfare.* New York: Praeger Publishers.

Sen, Amartya K. 1980. "Equality of What?" In *The Tanner Lectures on Human Values,* ed. Sterling McMurrin, 195–220. Cambridge: Cambridge University Press.

———. 1992. *Inequality Re-examined.* New York: Russell Sage Foundation.

———. 1993. "Capability and Well-Being." In *The Quality of Life,* ed. Martha C. Nussbaum and Amartya Sen, 30–53. New York: Oxford University Press.

Shapiro, Ian. 1996. *Democracy's Place.* Ithaca, N.Y.: Cornell University Press.

———. 1998. "Can the Rational Choice Framework Cope with Culture?" *PS, Political Science and Politics* 31 (1): 40–43.

Shepsle, K. A. 1989. "Studying Institutions: Some Lessons from the Rational Choice Approach." *Journal of Theoretical Politics* 1 (2): 131–47.

Shonfield, Andrew. 1965. *Modern Capitalism.* Oxford: Oxford University Press.

Shorris, Earl. 1994. *A Nation of Salesmen: The Tyranny of the Market and the Subversion of Culture.* New York: W. W. Norton.

Sikkink, K. 1991. *Ideas and Institutions: Developmentalism in Brazil and Argentina.* Ithaca: Cornell University Press.

Slottje, Daniel, and Timothy Smeeding. 1992. *Research on Economic Equality.* London: JAI Press.

Smeeding, Timothy, and Michael Higgins. 2000. "Empirical Evidence on Income Inequality in Industrialized Countries." In *Handbook of Income Distribution,* ed. A. B. Atkinson and F. Bourguignon, 261–308. Amsterdam-North Holland: Cody Books LTD.

Smith, Adam. 1937. *An Inquiry into the Nature and Causes of the Wealth of Nations.* New York: Random House. Original ed., 1776.

Stack, Steven. 1979. "The Effect of Political Participation and Socialist Party Strength on the Degree of Income Inequality." *American Sociological Review* 44: 168–71.

Steiner, Jurg. 1974. *Amicable Agreement Versus Majority Rule.* Chapel Hill: University of North Carolina Press.

Steinmo, Sven. 1993. *Taxation and Democracy: Swedish, British, and American Approaches to Financing the Modern State.* New Haven: Yale University Press.

———, ed. 1998. *Tax Policy.* London: Edward Elgar Publisher.

Steinmo, Sven, Kathleen Thelen, and Frank Longstreth. 1992. *Structuring Politics: Historical Institutionalism in Comparative Analysis.* New York: Cambridge University Press.

Stephens, John. D. 1979. *The Transition from Capitalism to Socialism.* London: Macmillan.

Streeck, Wolfgang. 1996. "Public Power Beyond The Nation-State." In *States Against Markets,* ed. Robert Boyer and Daniel Drache, 307–8. London: Routledge.

Swank, Duane. 1998. Review of "Modernization and Postmodernization" *Comparative Political Studies* 31(3): 247–58.

———. 2001. "Mobile Capital, Democratic Institutions, and the Public Economy in Advanced Industrial Studies." *Journal of Comparative Policy Analysis* 3 (2): 133.

———. 2002. *Global Capital, Political Institutions, and Policy Change in Developed Welfare States.* Cambridge: Cambridge University Press.

———. 2003. "Withering Welfare? Globalisation, Political Economic Institutions, and Contemporary Welfare States." In *States in the Global Economy: Bringing Domestic*

*Institutions Back In,* ed. Linda Weiss, 58–82. Cambridge: Cambridge University Press.

Swank, Duane, and A. Hicks. 1985. "The Determinants and Redistributive Impacts of State Welfare Spending in the Advanced Capitalist Democracies, 1960–1980." In *Political Economy in Western Democracies,* ed. N. J. Vig and S. E. Schier, 115–39. New York: Holmes & Meier.

Swenson, P. 1992. "Union Politics, the Welfare State, and Interclass Conflict in Sweden and Germany." In *Bargaining for Change: Union Politics in North America and Europe,* ed. M. Golden and J. Pontusson, 45–76. Ithaca: Cornell University Press.

Tarrow, Sidney. 1995. "Review: Bridging the Quantitative-Qualitative Divide in Political Science." *American Political Science Review* 89 (2): 471–74.

———. 1996. "Making Social Science Work Across Space and Time: A Critical Reflection of Robert Putnam's *Making Democracy Work." American Political Science Review* 90:389–97.

———. 2004. "Bridging the Quantitative-Qualitative Divide." In *Rethinking Social Inquiry,* ed. Henry E. Brady and David Collier, 171–80. Lanham, Md. Rowman & Littlefield Publishers, Inc.

Thelen, Kathleen. 1999. "Historical Institutionalism in Comparative Politics." *Annual Review of Political Science* 2 (1): 369–404.

Thompson, Michael, Richard Ellis, and Aaron Wildavsky. 1990. *Cultural Theory.* Boulder, Colo.: Westview Press.

Thurow, Lester C. 1980. *The Zero-Sum Society: Distribution and the Possibilities for Economic Change.* New York: Basic Books.

Tönnies, Ferdinand. 1963. *Community and Society.* New York: Harper & Row.

Tsebelis, George. 1995. "Decision Making in Political Systems: Veto Players in Presidentialism, Parliamentarism, Multicameralism, and Multipartyism." *British Journal of Political Science* 25 (3): 289–325.

Tucker, Robert C, ed. 1978. *The Max-Engels Reader,* 2nd ed. New York: W. W. Norton & Company.

UNU-WIDER, United Nations University—World Institute for Development Economics Research. 2005. World Income Inequality Database. Available online at http://www.wider.unu.edu/wiid/wiid.htm.

van der Pijl, Kees. 1997. "Transnational Class Formation and State Forms." In *Innovation and Transformation in International Studies,* ed. Stephen Gills and James H. Mittelman, 118–33. Cambridge: Cambridge University Press.

Wade, Robert. 1996. "Globalization and Its Limits: Reports of the Death of the National Economy Are Greatly Exaggerated." In *National Diversity and Global Capitalism,* ed. Suzanne Berger and Ronald Dore, 60–88. Ithaca: Cornell University Press.

Weaver, R. Kent, and Bert A Rockman. 1993. *Do Institutions Matter? Government Capabilities in the U.S. and Abroad.* Washington, D.C.: Brookings Institute Press.

Weede, Erich. 1986. "Income Inequality and Political Violence." *American Sociological Review* 51 (3): 438–41.

Weingast, Barry R. 2002. "Rational-Choice Institutionalism." In *Political Science: The State of the Discipline,* ed. Ira Katznelson and Helen V. Milner, 660–92. New York: W. W. Norton.

Weiss, Linda, ed. 2003. *States in the Global Economy: Bringing Domestic Institutions Back In.* Cambridge: Cambridge University Press.

Wilensky, H. L. 1975. *The Welfare State and Equality: Structural and Ideological Roots of Public Expenditures.* Los Angeles and Berkeley: University of California Press.

World Bank. 2004. *World Development Indicators.* CD-ROM. Washington: World Bank Publications.

Young, Iris Marion. 1998. "Political Theory: An Overview." In *A New Handbook of Political Science,* ed. Robert E. Goodin and Hans-Dieter Klingemann, 479–502. Oxford: Oxford University Press.

Ziegler, Nicholas J. 1997. *Governing Ideas: Strategies for Innovation in France and Germany.* Ithaca: Cornell University Press.

Zucker, Ross. 2001. *Democratic Distributive Justice.* Cambridge: Cambridge University Press.

# INDEX

www.ingramcontent.com/pod-product-compliance
Lightning Source LLC
Chambersburg PA
CBHW021858020426
42334CB00013B/387

9 780271 034416